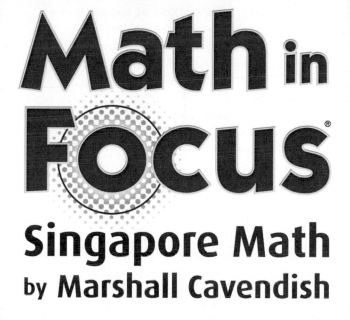

Math in Focus®
Singapore Math
by Marshall Cavendish

Authors
Yap Shin Tze
Yow How Kian

U.S. Consultants
Dr. Richard Bisk
Andy Clark

Marshall Cavendish
Education

US Distributor

COMMON
CORE

HOUGHTON MIFFLIN HARCOURT

© 2013 Marshall Cavendish International (Singapore) Private Limited

Published by Marshall Cavendish Education
An imprint of Marshall Cavendish International (Singapore) Private Limited
Times Centre, 1 New Industrial Road, Singapore 536196
Customer Service Hotline: (65) 6411 0820
E-mail: tmesales@sg.marshallcavendish.com
Website: www.marshallcavendish.com/education

Distributed by
Houghton Mifflin Harcourt
222 Berkeley Street
Boston, MA 02116
Tel: 617-351-5000
Website: www.hmheducation.com/mathinfocus

First published 2013

Math in Focus® Course 3 Student Book B
ISBN 978-0-547-56009-0

Printed in United States of America

2 3 4 5 6 7 8   1401   18 17 16 15 14 13 12
4500355403   A B C D E

Course 3B Contents

CHAPTER 7

The Pythagorean Theorem

Chapter Opener How far can you throw a baseball across the field?. 2

Big Idea The Pythagorean Theorem describes the relationship among the three sides of a right triangle.

Recall Prior Knowledge • Understanding squares and square roots
• Understanding cubes and cube roots • Finding lengths of horizontal and vertical line segments • Finding the volume of a solid. 3

7.1 Understanding the Pythagorean Theorem and Plane Figures 6
• Discover the Pythagorean Theorem • The Converse of the Pythagorean Theorem • Solve Real-World Problems Involving the Pythagorean Theorem

Hands-On Actvities • Use Rearrangement to Prove the Pythagorean Theorem
• Explore Pythagorean Triples

In Student Book A and Student Book B, look for

Practice and Problem Solving	Assessment Opportunities
• **Practice** in every lesson • Real-world and mathematical problems in every chapter • Brain @ Work in every chapter • *Math Journal* exercises	• **Quick Check** at the beginning of every chapter to assess chapter readiness • **Guided Practice** after every Example to assess readiness to continue lesson • **Chapter Review/Test** in every chapter to review or test chapter material • **Cumulative Reviews** five times during the year

7.2   **Understanding the Distance Formula** **20**
      • Use the Pythagorean Theorem to Find the Distance Between Two Points on a
      Coordinate Plane • Understand the Distance Formula

7.3   **Understanding the Pythagorean Theorem and Solids** **31**
      • Use the Pythagorean Theorem to Solve Problems Involving Solids

7.4   **Identifying Volumes of Composite Solids** **36**
      • Use the Pythagorean Theorem to Find Volumes of Composite Solids

Brain @ Work **43**

Chapter Wrap Up • Concept Map • Key Concepts **44**

Chapter Review/Test **45**

Geometric Transformations

Chapter Opener How do animators make characters move?. **48**

Big Idea Geometric transformations move figures about on a plane. Each type of transformation changes some properties of a figure, but leaves other properties unchanged.

Recall Prior Knowledge • Recognizing a symmetric point on the coordinate plane
• Identifying directly proportional quantities • Recognizing perpendicular bisectors. . . **49**

8.1   Translations **51**
• Understand the Concept of a Translation • Draw Images After Translations
• Find the Coordinates of Points After Translations

Technology Activity Explore the Properties of Translations with Geometry Software

8.2   Reflections **61**
• Understand the Concept of a Reflection • Draw Images After Reflections
• Find the Coordinates of Points After Reflections

Technology Activity Explore the Properties of Reflections with Geometry Software

8.3 **Rotations** **73**

▬▬▬ • Understand the Concept of a Rotation • Draw Images After Rotations • Find the Coordinates of Points After Rotations

Technology Activity Explore the Properties of Rotations with Geometry Software

8.4 **Dilations** **86**

▬▬▬ • Understand the Concept of a Dilation • Find the Dimensions of Figures After Dilations • Draw Images After Dilations • Find the Center of a Dilation

Technology Activity Explore the Properties of Dilations with Geometry Software

8.5 **Comparing Transformations** **98**
• Compare Translations, Reflections, Rotations, and Dilations

Technology Activity Compare Transformations with Geometry Software

Brain @ Work **106**

Chapter Wrap Up • Concept Map • Key Concepts **107**

Chapter Review/Test **109**

CHAPTER 9
Congruence and Similarity

Chapter Opener How tall is a water tower? **112**

Big Idea Congruent figures have the same shape and size. Similar figures have the same shape but need not be the same size. Two congruent figures or two similar figures are related by a series of geometric transformations.

Recall Prior Knowledge • Identifying the scale factor in diagrams • Solving problems involving scale drawings or models • Finding the measures of the interior and exterior angles of a triangle • Finding measures of angles formed by parallel lines and a transversal **113**

9.1   Understanding and Applying Congruent Figures **116**
  • Understand the Concept of Congruence • Apply the Concept of Congruence
  • Use Tests for Congruent Triangles

  Technology Activity Observe the Congruence in Triangles

9.2   Understanding and Applying Similar Figures **129**
  • Understand the Concept of Similarity • Apply the Concept of Similarity
  • Use Tests for Similar Triangles

  Hands-On Activities • Explore Angle Measures in Similar Triangles • Explore a Minimum Condition for Two Similar Triangles

9.3 Relating Congruent and Similar Figures to Geometric Transformations **144**

• Relate Congruent Figures Using Geometric Transformations • Relate Similar Figures Using Geometric Transformations • Describe a Sequence of Transformations • Relate Congruent and Similar Figures Using a Sequence of Transformations

Technology Activity Explore Sequences of Transformations

Brain @ Work **158**

Chapter Wrap Up • Concept Map • Key Concepts **159**

Chapter Review/Test **160**

Cumulative Review for Chapters 7 – 9 . . . . **166**

CHAPTER 10 Statistics

Chapter Opener Have you ever been in a bike race? **172**

Big Idea A line of best fit can be used to model the linear association of bivariate quantitative data. A two-way table displays the relative frequencies of categorical data.

Recall Prior Knowledge • Finding relative frequencies **173**

10.1 Scatter Plots **174**
• Construct a Scatter Plot Given Two Sets of Quantitative Data • Identify Patterns of Association Between Two Sets of Quantitative Data • Identify Outliers in a Scatter Plot

10.2 Modeling Linear Associations **186**
• Understand Line of Best Fit • Write a Linear Equation for a Line of Best Fit
• Use an Equation for a Line of Best Fit

Hands-On Activity Construct and Interpret Scatter Plots

Technology Activity Use a Graphing Calculator to Graph a Line of Best Fit for a Scatter Plot

10.3 Two-Way Tables **198**
• Read Data from a Two-Way Table • Construct and Interpret a Two-Way Table
• Convert Data to Relative Frequencies in a Two-Way Table

Brain @ Work **209**

Chapter Wrap Up • Concept Map • Key Concepts **210**

Chapter Review/Test **211**

CHAPTER 11 Probability

Chapter Opener Have you ever gone fishing? **216**

Big Idea Compound events consist of simple events that can be dependent or independent. You can use probability of simple events to compute the probability of compound events.

Recall Prior Knowledge • Finding the probability of a simple event **217**

11.1 Compound Events **219**
• Understand Compound Events • Represent Compound Events • Represent Compound Events Using Tree Diagrams

11.2 Probability of Compound Events **229**
• Use Possibility Diagrams to Find Probability of Compound Events

11.3 Independent Events **236**
• Understand Independent Events • Use the Multiplication Rule of Probability to Solve Problems with Independent Events • Use the Addition Rule of Probability to Solve Problems with Independent Events

Technology Activity Simulate Randomness

11.4 Dependent Events 252

▬▬▬ • Understand Dependent Events • Use the Multiplication Rule of Probability to Solve Problems with Dependent Events

Brain @ Work 263

Chapter Wrap Up • Concept Map • Key Concepts 264

Chapter Review/Test 265

Cumulative Review for Chapters 10 – 11 268

Selected Answers 274

Glossary 292

Table of Measures, Formulas, and Symbols 297

Graphing Calculator Guide 302

Credits 306

Index 307

Welcome to

Math in Focus®

Singapore Math
by Marshall Cavendish

What makes
Math in Focus® different?

This world-class math program comes to you from the country of Singapore. We are sure that you will enjoy learning math with the interesting lessons you will find in these books.

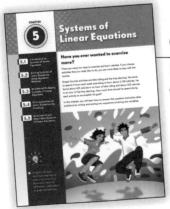

▶ **Two books** The textbook is divided into 2 semesters. Chapters 1–6 are in Book A. Chapters 7–11 are in Book B.

▶ **Longer lessons** More concepts are presented in a lesson. Some lessons may last more than a day to give you time to understand the math.

▶ **Multiple representations** will help you make sense of new concepts and solve real-world and mathematical problems with ease.

About the book   Here are the main features in this book.

Chapter Opener

Introduces chapter concepts and big ideas through a story or example. There is also a chapter table of contents.

Recall Prior Knowledge

Assesses previously learned concepts, definitions, vocabulary, and models relevant to the chapter.

Quick Check assesses readiness for the chapter.

Look for these features in each lesson.

Instructions make use of multiple representations to help you become familiar with new ideas.

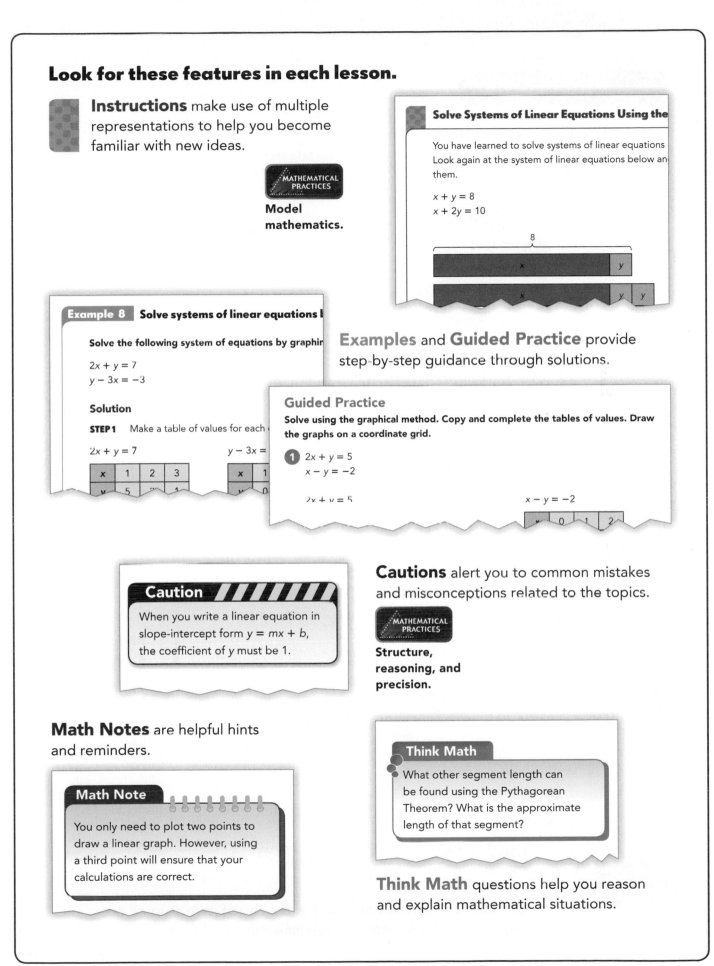

MATHEMATICAL PRACTICES

Model mathematics.

Solve Systems of Linear Equations Using the

You have learned to solve systems of linear equations Look again at the system of linear equations below and them.

$x + y = 8$
$x + 2y = 10$

Example 8 **Solve systems of linear equations**

Solve the following system of equations by graphin

$2x + y = 7$
$y - 3x = -3$

Solution

STEP 1 Make a table of values for each

$2x + y = 7$ $y - 3x =$

x	1	2	3
y	5		1

Examples and **Guided Practice** provide step-by-step guidance through solutions.

Guided Practice

Solve using the graphical method. Copy and complete the tables of values. Draw the graphs on a coordinate grid.

1 $2x + y = 5$
$x - y = -2$

$2x + y = 5$ $x - y = -2$

x	0	1	2

Caution ///////

When you write a linear equation in slope-intercept form $y = mx + b$, the coefficient of y must be 1.

Cautions alert you to common mistakes and misconceptions related to the topics.

MATHEMATICAL PRACTICES

Structure, reasoning, and precision.

Math Notes are helpful hints and reminders.

Math Note

You only need to plot two points to draw a linear graph. However, using a third point will ensure that your calculations are correct.

Think Math

What other segment length can be found using the Pythagorean Theorem? What is the approximate length of that segment?

Think Math questions help you reason and explain mathematical situations.

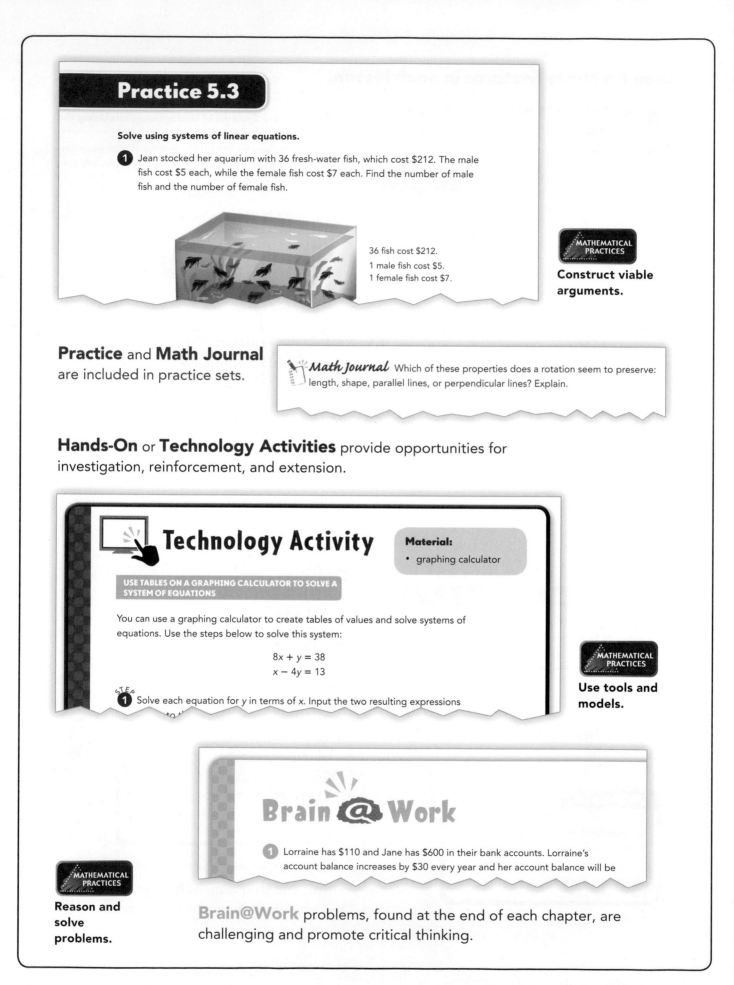

Practice 5.3

Solve using systems of linear equations.

1 Jean stocked her aquarium with 36 fresh-water fish, which cost $212. The male fish cost $5 each, while the female fish cost $7 each. Find the number of male fish and the number of female fish.

36 fish cost $212.
1 male fish cost $5.
1 female fish cost $7.

MATHEMATICAL PRACTICES

Construct viable arguments.

Practice and **Math Journal** are included in practice sets.

Math Journal Which of these properties does a rotation seem to preserve: length, shape, parallel lines, or perpendicular lines? Explain.

Hands-On or **Technology Activities** provide opportunities for investigation, reinforcement, and extension.

Technology Activity

Material:
• graphing calculator

USE TABLES ON A GRAPHING CALCULATOR TO SOLVE A SYSTEM OF EQUATIONS

You can use a graphing calculator to create tables of values and solve systems of equations. Use the steps below to solve this system:

$$8x + y = 38$$
$$x - 4y = 13$$

STEP 1 Solve each equation for y in terms of x. Input the two resulting expressions

MATHEMATICAL PRACTICES

Use tools and models.

Brain @ Work

1 Lorraine has $110 and Jane has $600 in their bank accounts. Lorraine's account balance increases by $30 every year and her account balance will be

MATHEMATICAL PRACTICES

Reason and solve problems.

Brain@Work problems, found at the end of each chapter, are challenging and promote critical thinking.

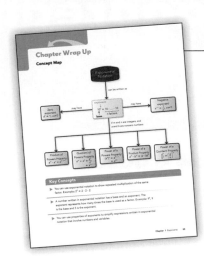

Chapter Wrap Up

Key concepts, definitions, and formulas are summarized for easy review.

The Chapter Wrap Up summaries contain concept maps like the one shown below.

The lines and arrows show how all the concepts in the chapter are related to one another and to the big ideas.

There may be more than one way to draw a concept map. With practice, you should be able to draw your own.

The red center boxes contain the big idea.

Other boxes represent key concepts of the chapter.

Structure, reasoning, and precision

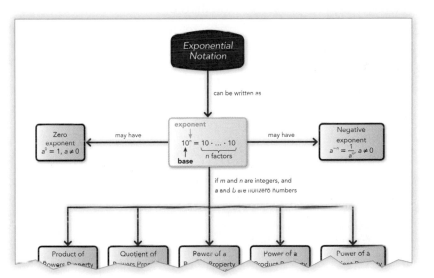

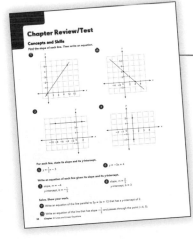

Chapter Review/Test

A practice test is found at the end of each chapter.

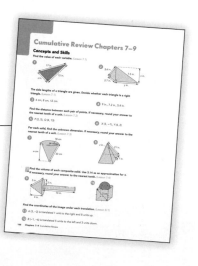

Cumulative Review

Cumulative review exercises can be found after Chapters 2, 4, 6, 9, and 11.

CHAPTER

7

The Pythagorean Theorem

7.1 Understanding the Pythagorean Theorem and Plane Figures

7.2 Understanding the Distance Formula

7.3 Understanding the Pythagorean Theorem and Solids

7.4 Identifying Volumes of Composite Solids

How far can you throw a baseball across the field?

You are playing third base in a baseball game. There are runners on first and second base. The batter hits a ground ball right to you. You step on third base. One runner out! You then hurl the ball to first base just in time to get the batter out. Double play!

It all happened so fast and you wonder just how far you had to throw the ball to get it from third base to first base. You can use the Pythagorean Theorem to find the answer.

BIG IDEA

▶ The Pythagorean Theorem describes the relationship among the three sides of a right triangle.

Recall Prior Knowledge

Understanding squares and square roots

To square a number, you multiply the number by itself.

$5^2 = 5 \cdot 5$

$\quad = 25$

The square root of a number is a value that can be multiplied by itself to produce the number. Numbers that have square roots always have two roots, a positive one and a negative one. For example, 5 and −5 are the square roots of 25.

The square root symbol is $\sqrt{}$.

5 squared

| 5 | 25 |

square root of 25

−5 squared

| −5 | 25 |

square root of 25

✔ Quick Check

Find the square of each number.

1 3

2 $\frac{1}{4}$

3 −7

Find the square roots of each number.

4 16

5 64

6 400

Understanding cubes and cube roots

The cube of a number is the value of the number raised to an exponent of 3.

$6^3 = 6 \cdot 6 \cdot 6$

$\quad = 216$

The cube root of a number is a value that, when cubed, equals the number. The cube root of 216 is 6.

The cube root symbol is $\sqrt[3]{}$.

6 cubed

| 6 | 216 |

cube root of 216

✔ Quick Check

Find the cube of each number.

7 $\frac{1}{2}$

8 7

9 11

Find the cube root of each number.

10 8

11 27

12 125

Finding lengths of horizontal and vertical line segments

You can find the lengths of horizontal and vertical line segments on the coordinate plane by counting the number of units between the endpoints of the segments. The length of $\overline{AB}$ is 5 units because there are 5 units between the points A and B. The length of $\overline{CD}$ is 3 units because there are 3 units between the points C and D.

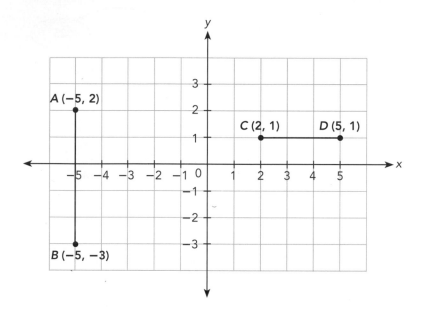

Another way to find the distance between points with either the same x-coordinates or y-coordinates is to find the absolute value of the difference of those coordinates.
For example, length of $\overline{AB} = |\,2 - (-3)\,|$
$$= |\,2 + 3\,|$$
$$= 5 \text{ units}$$
$$\text{length of } \overline{CD} = |\,5 - 2\,|$$
$$= 3 \text{ units}$$

 Quick Check

Use graph paper. Plot each pair of points on a coordinate plane. Connect the points to form a line segment and find its length.

13 (3, 5) and (3, 9)

14 (3, −6) and (3, −9)

15 (−4, 9) and (−8, 9)

16 (−2, 5) and (8, 5)

Finding the volume of a solid

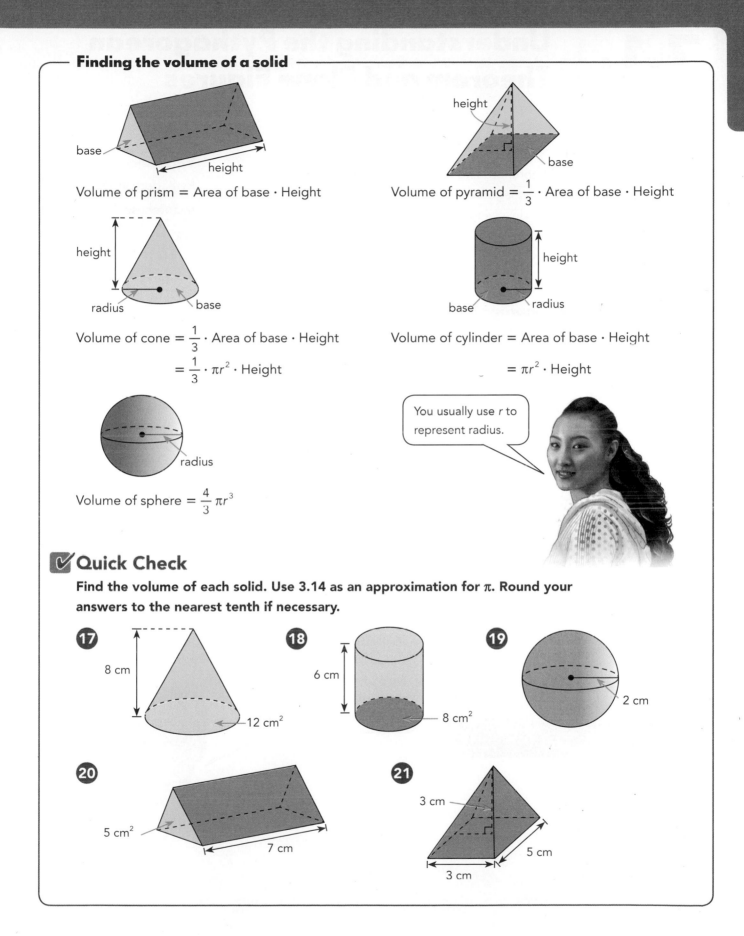

Volume of prism = Area of base · Height

Volume of pyramid = $\frac{1}{3}$ · Area of base · Height

Volume of cone = $\frac{1}{3}$ · Area of base · Height

$= \frac{1}{3} \cdot \pi r^2$ · Height

Volume of cylinder = Area of base · Height

$= \pi r^2$ · Height

You usually use r to represent radius.

Volume of sphere $= \frac{4}{3} \pi r^3$

✓ Quick Check

Find the volume of each solid. Use 3.14 as an approximation for π. Round your answers to the nearest tenth if necessary.

17 8 cm — 12 cm²

18 6 cm — 8 cm²

19 2 cm

20 5 cm² — 7 cm

21 3 cm, 5 cm, 3 cm

7.1 Understanding the Pythagorean Theorem and Plane Figures

Lesson Objectives

- Use the Pythagorean Theorem to find unknown side lengths.
- Use the converse of the Pythagorean Theorem.
- Solve real-world problems involving the Pythagorean Theorem.

Discover the Pythagorean Theorem.

A cable-stayed bridge uses cables to connect the roadway to vertical towers. Notice that the towers, roadway, and cables form many right triangles. You can find the length of each cable if you know how the sides of a right triangle are related to one another.

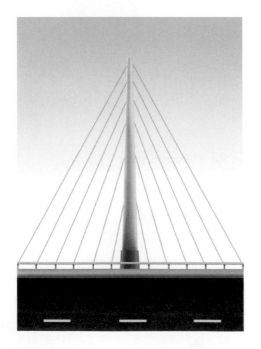

There are 12 right triangles in the illustration of a bridge. You should be able to see that there are 6 triangles on one side of the tower and 6 identical right triangles on the other side.

Hands-On Activity

Materials:
- scissors

In a right triangle, the longest side is known as the **hypotenuse**. The two shorter sides are called **legs**.

STEP 1 Draw four identical right triangles, with side lengths a, b, and c, on a piece of paper and cut them out. Make one leg shorter than the other.

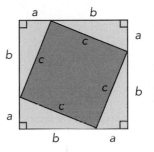

STEP 2 Arrange the triangles to form a square with side length c.

STEP 3 What is the area of the square whose sides are c units long?

Label the large square with its area.

STEP 4 Draw two squares on a different piece of paper. One square should have side lengths of b units, and the other should have side lengths of a units. You can use one of the triangles as a guide to mark off a units and b units. Cut out these square and arrange the four triangles and the two new squares to form a large square like the one shown.

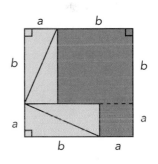

STEP 5 Write an algebraic expression in terms of a and b for the combined area of the two small squares.

 Math Journal Compare the areas of the squares found in **STEP 3** and **STEP 5**. Write an equation that relates the area of one square to the sum of the areas of the other two squares.

In the activity, you explored the relationship among the sides of a right triangle. This relationship is true for all right triangles and is described by the Pythagorean Theorem.

Continue on next page

In the activity, you observed the following:

> **Pythagorean Theorem**
> The square of the length of the hypotenuse of a right triangle is equal to the sum of the squares of the two legs. For the triangle shown, you can write this equation: $a^2 + b^2 = c^2$.
>
>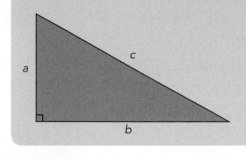

Example 1   **Find the length of a hypotenuse.**

Alan can ride his bike on two highways to get from his house to his friend Carl's house. He can also ride his bike on an unpaved road between the two houses. How far does he bike if he takes the unpaved road?

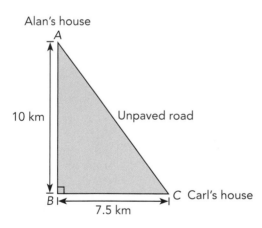

> The unpaved road forms the hypotenuse of a right triangle. The two highways form the legs of the right triangle.

Solution

$AC^2 = AB^2 + BC^2$	Use the Pythagorean Theorem.
$AC^2 = 10^2 + 7.5^2$	Substitute values for AB and BC.
$AC^2 = 100 + 56.25$	Multiply.
$AC^2 = 156.25$	Add.
$AC = \sqrt{156.25}$	Find the positive square root.
$AC = 12.5$ km	Simplify.

He bikes 12.5 kilometers if he takes the unpaved road.

Guided Practice

Complete.

1 Merlin wants to put a fence around a right triangular garden. He measures two sides. Find the length of the unknown side.

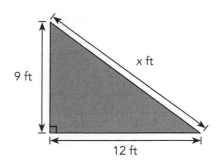

$x^2 = 9^2 + \underline{\ \ ?\ \ }$ Use the Pythagorean Theorem.

$x^2 = \underline{\ \ ?\ \ } + \underline{\ \ ?\ \ }$ Multiply.

$x^2 = \underline{\ \ ?\ \ }$ Add.

$x = \underline{\ \ ?\ \ }$ Find the positive square root.

$x = \underline{\ \ ?\ \ }$ Simplify.

The length of the unknown side is $\underline{\ \ ?\ \ }$ feet.

Example 2   **Find the length of a leg of a right triangle.**

Find the length of $\overline{YZ}$. Round your answer to the nearest tenth.

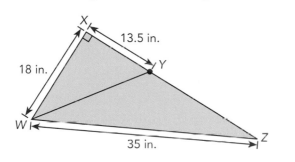

Notice that triangle *WXZ* is a right triangle. The hypotenuse is *WZ*, and the other two sides are *XW* and *XZ*. So, you can use the Pythagorean Theorem to find the answer.

Solution

First find the length of $\overline{XZ}$.

$WZ^2 = WX^2 + XZ^2$ Use the Pythagorean Theorem.

$35^2 = 18^2 + XZ^2$ Substitute values for *WZ* and *WX*.

$1{,}225 = 324 + XZ^2$ Multiply.

$1{,}225 - \mathbf{324} = 324 + XZ^2 - \mathbf{324}$ Subtract 324 from both sides.

$901 = XZ^2$ Simplify.

$XZ = \sqrt{901}$ Find the positive square root.

$XZ \approx 30.0$ in.   Round to the nearest tenth.

Then find the length of $\overline{YZ}$.

$YZ = XZ - XY$ Subtract.

$YZ = \sqrt{901} - 13.5$ Substitute values for *XZ* and *XY*.

$YZ \approx 16.5$ in.   Simplify.

The length of $\overline{YZ}$ is approximately 16.5 inches.

Think Math

What other segment length can be found using the Pythagorean Theorem? What is the length of that segment?

Guided Practice

Complete.

2 Find the values of x and y. Round your answer to the nearest tenth.

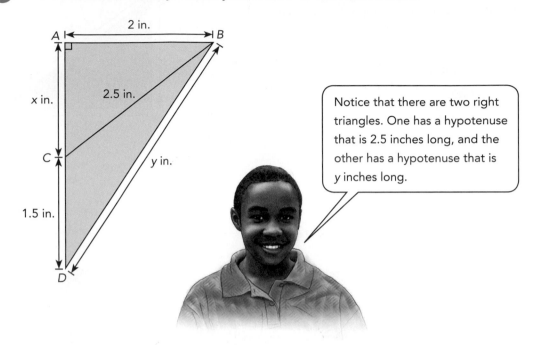

Notice that there are two right triangles. One has a hypotenuse that is 2.5 inches long, and the other has a hypotenuse that is y inches long.

First find the value of x.

$BC^2 = AB^2 + AC^2$	Use the Pythagorean Theorem.
$2.5^2 = \underline{\ ?\ } + x^2$	Substitute values for BC and AB, and use x for AC.
$6.25 = \underline{\ ?\ } + x^2$	Multiply.
$6.25 - \underline{\ ?\ } = \underline{\ ?\ } + x^2 - \underline{\ ?\ }$	Subtract $\underline{\ ?\ }$ from both sides.
$\underline{\ ?\ } = x^2$	Simplify.
$x = \underline{\ ?\ }$	Find the positive square root.
$x = \underline{\ ?\ }$	Round to the nearest tenth.

The value of x is $\underline{\ ?\ }$.

Then find the value of y.

$BD^2 = AB^2 + AD^2$	Use the Pythagorean Theorem.
$y^2 = \underline{\ ?\ } + (\underline{\ ?\ } + \underline{\ ?\ })^2$	Substitute values for AB, AC, and CD.
$y^2 = \underline{\ ?\ } + \underline{\ ?\ }$	Add.
$y^2 = \underline{\ ?\ } + \underline{\ ?\ }$	Multiply.
$y^2 = \underline{\ ?\ }$	Add.
$y = \underline{\ ?\ }$	Find the positive square root.
$y \approx \underline{\ ?\ }$	Round to the nearest tenth.

The value of y is approximately $\underline{\ ?\ }$.

Hands-On Activity

Materials:
- graph paper
- ruler

EXPLORE PYTHAGOREAN TRIPLES

A Pythagorean triple is any set of three whole numbers that satisfy the Pythagorean Theorem equation $c^2 = a^2 + b^2$. The table shows several sets of Pythagorean triples.

a	b	c
3	4	5
5	12	13
7	24	25
12	16	20

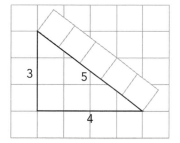

STEP 1 Select one Pythagorean triple from the table. Draw a triangle with legs a units and b units long on a piece of graph paper.

STEP 2 Using a strip of graph paper as a measuring tool, measure the hypotenuse of the triangle. Is it equal to the greatest value in the Pythagorean triple?

STEP 3 Repeat **STEP 1** and **STEP 2** using the other Pythagorean triples in the table.

STEP 4 The converse of the Pythagorean Theorem says that if the sum of the squares of the lengths of the two legs of a triangle equals the square of the length of the hypotenuse, then the triangle is a right triangle. Do your triangle measurements support this statement? Explain.

The Converse of the Pythagorean Theorem.

You have just learned that the square of the hypotenuse of a right triangle is equal to the sum of the squares of the two legs.

In the activity, you have observed the converse of the Pythagorean Theorem.

Converse of the Pythagorean Theorem
If the sum of the squares of the lengths of the two legs of a triangle is equal to the square of the length of the hypotenuse, then the triangle is a right triangle. If $a^2 + b^2 = c^2$, then the triangle is a right triangle.

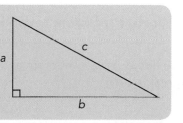

Example 3 **Determine whether a triangle is a right triangle.**

a) Tanya plans to use four triangles like the one shown below to form a diamond shape. For her plan to work, the triangle must be a right triangle. Determine whether the triangle is a right triangle.

Solution

$8^2 + 15^2 \overset{?}{=} 17^2$ Use the converse of the Pythagorean Theorem.

$64 + 225 \overset{?}{=} 289$ Multiply.

$289 = 289$ Simplify.

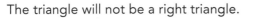

17 cm

15 cm

8 cm

The triangle is a right triangle.

b) Tom wants to form a triangle using pieces of wire that are 4 inches, 7 inches, and 9 inches long. Will it be a right triangle?

Solution

$4^2 + 7^2 \overset{?}{=} 9^2$ Use the converse of the Pythagorean Theorem.

$16 + 49 \overset{?}{=} 81$ Multiply.

$65 \neq 81$ Simplify.

The length of the longest side is 9 inches.

The triangle will not be a right triangle.

Guided Practice

Copy and complete each ___?___ with a value and each ⬚?⬚ with = or ≠.

3 A triangle has side lengths 13 centimeters, 15 centimeters, and 18 centimeters. Is it a right triangle?

$13^2 + 15^2 \overset{?}{=}$ ___?___   Use the Converse of the Pythagorean Theorem.

___?___ + ___?___ $\overset{?}{=}$ ___?___   Multiply.

___?___ ⬚?⬚ ___?___   Simplify.

The triangle ___?___ a right triangle.

 Solve Real-World Problems Involving the Pythagorean Theorem.

You can use the Pythagorean Theorem and its converse to solve many real-world problems.

Based on the information in a problem, you may need to identify, sketch, and label the dimensions of a right triangle.

Example 4

Use the Pythagorean Theorem to solve an indirect measurement problem.

Some students are having a car wash fundraiser. They attach one end of a banner with flags on it to the top of a pole that is 12 feet tall. They attach the other end to the ground. If the banner is 15 feet long, how far from the base of the pole is the banner attached?

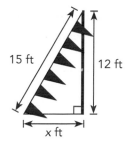

15 ft   12 ft   x ft

> The banner, pole, and segment along the ground form a right triangle. The banner is the hypotenuse, the pole is one leg of the triangle, and the segment along the ground is the other leg.

Solution

Let the length of the segment along the ground be x feet.

$15^2 = 12^2 + x^2$	Substitute values for the lengths of the banner and the pole.
$225 = 144 + x^2$	Multiply.
$225 - \mathbf{144} = 144 + x^2 - \mathbf{144}$	Subtract 144 from both sides.
$81 = x^2$	Simplify.
$x = 9$	Find the positive square root.

The distance between the banner and the base of the pole is 9 feet.

Guided Practice

Complete.

4 A ladder 18 feet long is leaning against a wall. The base of the ladder is 9 feet away from the wall. Find the distance from the top of the ladder to the ground. Round your answer to the nearest tenth.

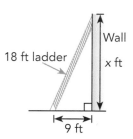

Wall
18 ft ladder   x ft
9 ft

Let the distance from the top of the ladder to the ground be x feet.

$\underline{\ ?\ } = \underline{\ ?\ } + x^2$	Substitute values for the lengths of the ladder and the segment.
$\underline{\ ?\ } = \underline{\ ?\ } + x^2$	Multiply.
$\underline{\ ?\ } - \underline{\ ?\ } = \underline{\ ?\ } + x^2 - \underline{\ ?\ }$	Subtract $\underline{\ ?\ }$ from both sides.
$\underline{\ ?\ } = x^2$	Simplify.
$x = \underline{\ ?\ }$	Find the positive square root.
$x \approx \underline{\ ?\ }$	Round to the nearest tenth.

The distance from the top of the ladder to the ground is approximately __?__ feet.

Example 5   **Use the Pythagorean Theorem to solve a real-world problem.**

Sue Ann hangs a picture frame of width 15 centimeters on the wall. The distance from the nail to the edge of the picture frame is 10 centimeters. Find the length of wire used to hang the picture frame.

> Notice that the wire and the edge of the picture frame form an isosceles triangle that can be divided into two congruent right triangles.

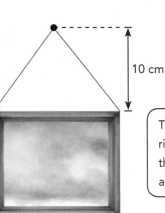

10 cm

> The length of the hypotenuse of each right triangle is half the total length of the wire. The legs are 10 centimeters and half of 15 centimeters long.

Solution

Let the length of half the wire be x centimeters. This represents the length of the hypotenuse of one of the right triangles.

$x^2 = 7.5^2 + 10^2$	Use the Pythagorean Theorem.
$x^2 = 56.25 + 100$	Multiply.
$x^2 = 156.25$	Add.
$x = \sqrt{156.25}$	Find the positive square root.
$x = 12.5$	Simplify.

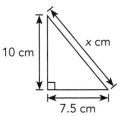

10 cm   x cm

7.5 cm

The length of the hypotenuse is 12.5 centimeters.

To find the total length of wire used, multiply 12.5 by 2.

$2 \cdot 12.5 = 25$ cm

So, the length of wire used is 25 centimeters.

Think Math

Suppose you have 20 centimeters of wire. When you hang the picture frame from the nail, about how far will the edge of the picture frame be from the nail? How did you find the answer?

Guided Practice

Complete.

5 A tree has a shadow length of approximately 9 feet. The distance from the tip of the tree to the tip of the shadow is about 15 feet. How tall is the tree?

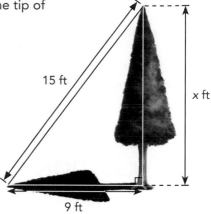

15 ft

x ft

9 ft

Let the height of the tree be x feet.

$$\underline{\ ?\ } = \underline{\ ?\ } + x^2 \qquad \text{Use the Pythagorean Theorem.}$$

$$\underline{\ ?\ } = \underline{\ ?\ } + x^2 \qquad \text{Multiply.}$$

$$\underline{\ ?\ } - \underline{\ ?\ } = \underline{\ ?\ } + x^2 - \underline{\ ?\ } \qquad \text{Subtract } \underline{\ ?\ } \text{ from both sides.}$$

$$\underline{\ ?\ } = x^2 \qquad \text{Simplify.}$$

$$x = \underline{\ ?\ } \qquad \text{Find the positive square root.}$$

$$x = \underline{\ ?\ } \qquad \text{Simplify.}$$

The height of the tree is __?__ feet.

6 The support pole of the tent shown forms one leg of a right triangle. One side of the tent forms the hypotenuse of the right triangle. Find the length of the base of the tent.

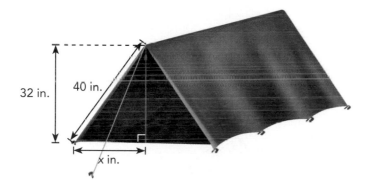

32 in.

40 in.

x in.

Let the length of half the base of the tent be x inches.

$$\underline{\ ?\ } = \underline{\ ?\ } + x^2 \qquad \text{Use the Pythagorean Theorem.}$$

$$\underline{\ ?\ } = \underline{\ ?\ } + x^2 \qquad \text{Multiply.}$$

$$\underline{\ ?\ } - \underline{\ ?\ } = \underline{\ ?\ } + x^2 - \underline{\ ?\ } \qquad \text{Subtract } \underline{\ ?\ } \text{ from both sides.}$$

$$\underline{\ ?\ } = x^2 \qquad \text{Simplify.}$$

$$x = \underline{\ ?\ } \qquad \text{Find the positive square root.}$$

$$x = \underline{\ ?\ } \qquad \text{Simplify.}$$

The length of half the base of the tent is __?__ inches.

$$\underline{\ ?\ } \cdot 24 = \underline{\ ?\ } \text{ in.}$$

So, the length of the base of the tent is __?__ inches.

Practice 7.1

For this practice, you may use a calculator.

Copy the road signs shown below, identify a right triangle in each sign, and label the hypotenuse with an arrow.

1

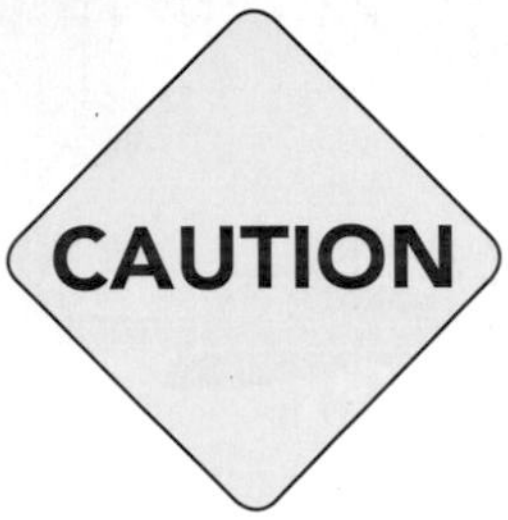
CAUTION

2

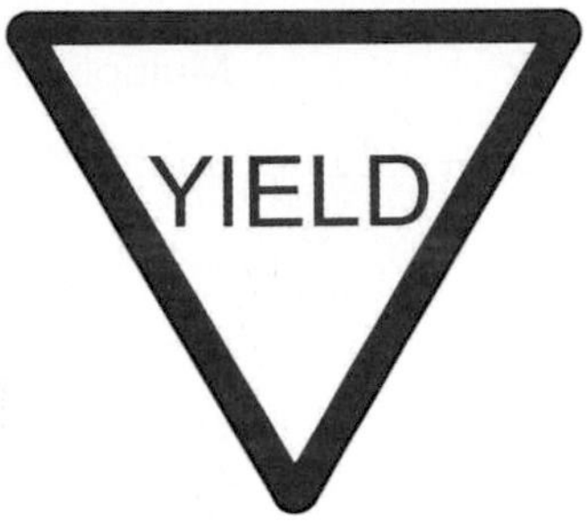
YIELD

Find the value of *x*.

3

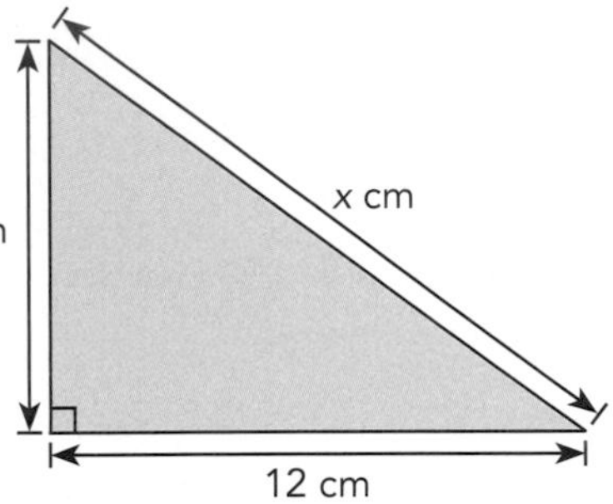
9 cm
x cm
12 cm

4

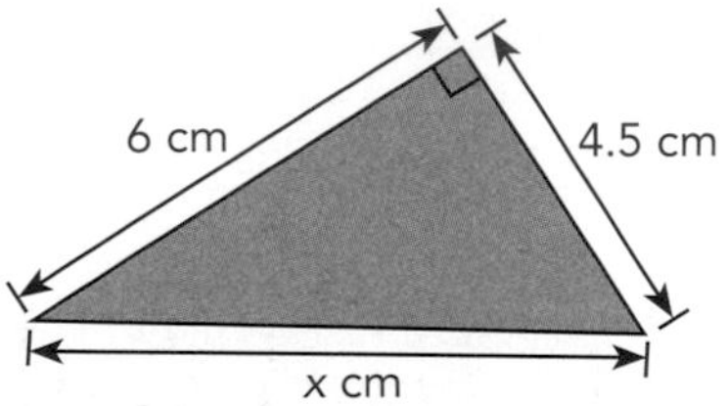
6 cm
4.5 cm
x cm

5

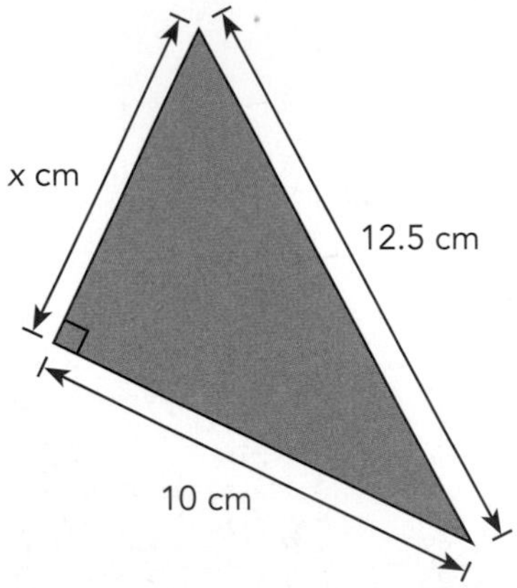
x cm
12.5 cm
10 cm

6

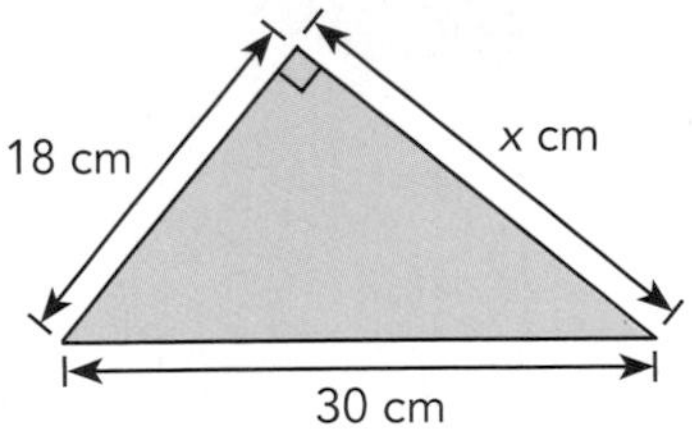
18 cm
x cm
30 cm

Calculate each unknown side length. Round your answer to the nearest tenth.

7

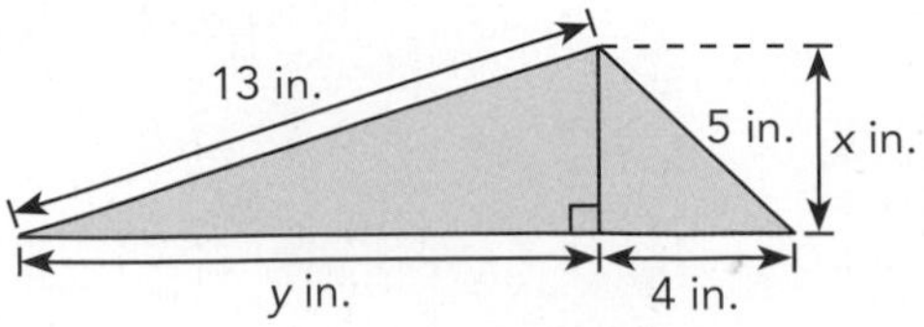
13 in.
5 in.
x in.
y in.
4 in.

8

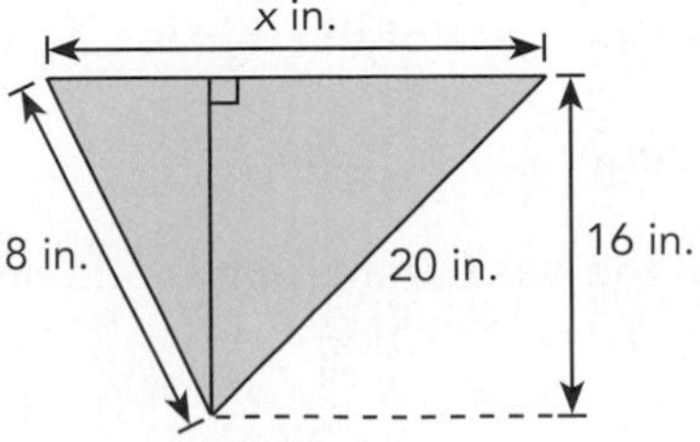
x in.
18 in.
20 in.
16 in.

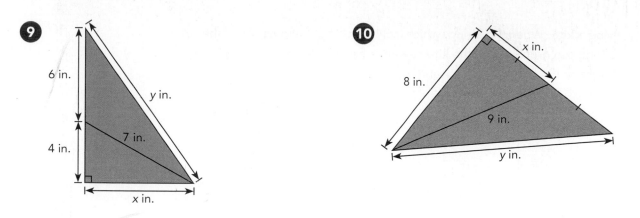

9 6 in. / y in. / 4 in. / 7 in. / x in.

10 x in. / 8 in. / 9 in. / y in.

Solve. Show your work. Round your answer to the nearest tenth.

11 Daniel had two pieces of wire. He bent each piece of wire into the shape of a triangle. Determine which triangle is a right triangle.

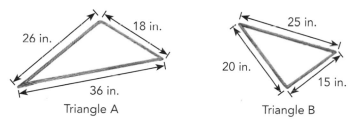

26 in. / 18 in. / 36 in.
Triangle A

25 in. / 20 in. / 15 in.
Triangle B

12 Kendrick wants to build a slide for his son in the backyard. He buys a slide that is 8 feet long. The height of the stairs is 5 feet. Find the distance from the bottom of the stairs to the base of the slide.

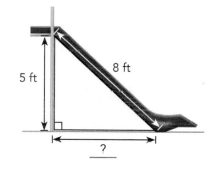

5 ft / 8 ft / ?

13 Mrs. Hanson uses a wheelchair. Her husband decides to build a ramp to make it easier for her to enter and leave the house. Find the length of the ramp.

? / 12 in. / 70 in.

14 A sign is hung outside a shop on the wall of a building. One end of the brace that holds the sign is connected to the wall. The other end of the brace is connected to the wall by a wire. Use the dimensions in the diagram to find the length of the wire.

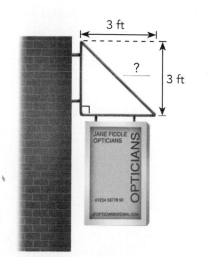

3 ft / ? / 3 ft

JANE FIDDLE OPTICIANS

OPTICIANS

01234 56778 90
OPTICIANS@EMAIL.COM

15 Kelly is flying a kite. When the string, which is 34 feet long, becomes taut, the distance along the ground from the kite to Kelly's hand is 6.5 feet. Find the vertical height of the kite above her hand.

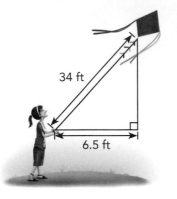

16 In a movie scene, an actor runs up a ramp that leads from the top of one building to the top of another building. The horizontal distance between the two buildings is 8.6 meters. The height of the shorter building is 18 meters while the height of the taller building is 24 meters. Find the length of the ramp.

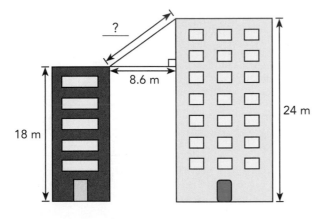

17 The size of a rectangular television screen is given as the length of the diagonal of the screen. Find the size of a television screen that has a height of 38.4 inches and width of 28.8 inches.

18 A ship sailed from Port X to Port Y. It traveled 20 kilometers due north and then 25 kilometers due west. Find the shortest distance between the two ports.

19 Mike wants to build a sailboat. The scale drawing is shown on the right. Find the values of x and y.

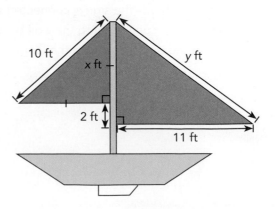

20 The diagonal length of a square window is 40 centimeters. Find the area of the window.

21 Triangles *ABC* and *ACD* are right triangles. *AB* is 28 meters long. *AC* is 21 meters long. Find the lengths of $\overline{BC}$ and $\overline{AD}$.

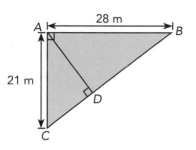

22 The infield of a baseball diamond is a square. Barry measures the distance from home plate to second base and finds that it is about 38.7 meters.

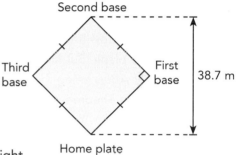

a) Find the approximate distance from home plate to first base.

b) Find the area of the infield.

23 The road sign shown is in the shape of an equilateral triangle. The height of the road sign is 15 inches.

15 in.

a) Find the length of each side.

b) Find the area of the sign.

24 *Math Journal* A salesman selling windows says that a window frame that is 8 feet long and 6.5 feet wide is rectangular. He also says that it has a diagonal length of 12 feet. Danielle thinks that the salesman is wrong in saying that the window is rectangular. Who is right and why?

25 *Math Journal* Fiona buys a triangular table. The sides of the table top are 29.4 inches, 39.2 inches, and 49 inches long. She wants to place the table in a corner of a rectangular room. Will the table fit snugly in the corner? Explain.

Understanding the Distance Formula

Lesson Objectives

- Use the Pythagorean Theorem to find the distance between two points on a coordinate plane.
- Understand the distance formula.

Use the Pythagorean Theorem to Find the Distance Between Two Points on a Coordinate Plane.

You already know how to find the lengths of horizontal and vertical segments in a coordinate plane. But how would you find the length of $\overline{AB}$ shown below? One way is to think of $\overline{AB}$ as being the hypotenuse of a right triangle. Then you can use the Pythagorean Theorem to find the length of $\overline{AB}$.

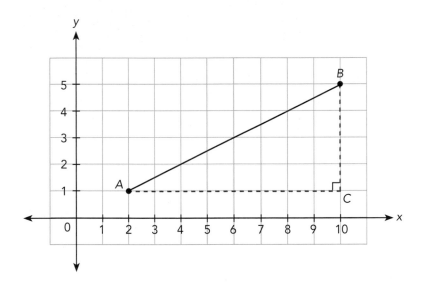

$$AC^2 + BC^2 = AB^2 \qquad \text{Use the Pythagorean Theorem.}$$
$$8^2 + 4^2 = AB^2 \qquad \text{Substitute values for } AC \text{ and } BC.$$
$$64 + 16 = AB^2 \qquad \text{Multiply.}$$
$$80 = AB^2 \qquad \text{Add.}$$
$$\sqrt{80} = AB \qquad \text{Find the positive square root.}$$
$$AB \approx 8.9 \text{ units} \qquad \text{Round to the nearest tenth.}$$

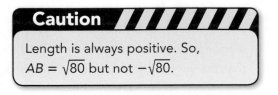

Caution

Length is always positive. So, $AB = \sqrt{80}$ but not $-\sqrt{80}$.

So, the distance between points A and B is exactly $\sqrt{80}$ units and approximately 8.9 units.

Example 6 **Use the Pythagorean Theorem to find a distance on a coordinate plane.**

Solve.

Points $X(1, 1)$ and $Y(5, 5)$ are plotted on a coordinate plane. Find the distance between points X and Y. Find both the exact value and the approximate value to the nearest tenth.

Solution

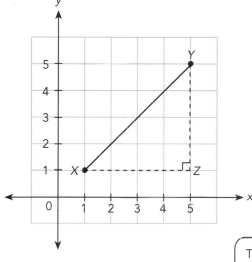

Plot the points and draw the segment connecting them. Plot a point Z to form the third vertex of a right triangle and sketch a right triangle. $\overline{XY}$ is the hypotenuse.

The coordinates of Z are $(5, 1)$. To find XZ, find the absolute value of the difference of the x-coordinates of X and Z. To find YZ, find the absolute value of the difference of the y-coordinates of Y and Z.

First find the lengths of $\overline{XZ}$ and $\overline{YZ}$.

$XZ = |5 - 1|$
$\quad = 4$ units

$YZ = |5 - 1|$
$\quad = 4$ units

Then use the Pythagorean Theorem to find the length of $\overline{XY}$.

$XZ^2 + YZ^2 = XY^2$	Use the Pythagorean Theorem.
$4^2 + 4^2 = XY^2$	Substitute values for XZ and YZ.
$16 + 16 = XY^2$	Multiply.
$32 = XY^2$	Add.
$\sqrt{32} = XY$	Find the positive square root.
$XY \approx 5.7$ units	Round to the nearest tenth.

So, the distance between points X and Y is exactly $\sqrt{32}$ units and approximately 5.7 units.

Guided Practice

Solve.

1 Points $P\,(-5, 3)$ and $Q\,(3, -6)$ are plotted on a coordinate plane. Find the distance between points P and Q. Find both the exact value and an approximate value. Round your answer to the nearest tenth.

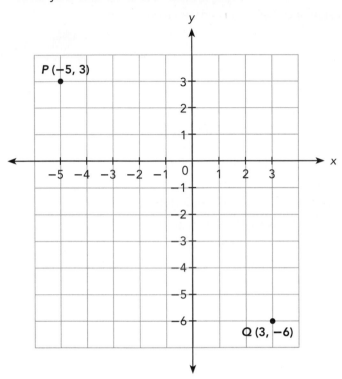

Plot point R ($\underline{\quad?\quad}$, $\underline{\quad?\quad}$) to form a third vertex for triangle PQR.

$PR = |\,\underline{\quad?\quad} - \underline{\quad?\quad}\,|$

$\quad = \underline{\quad?\quad}$ units

$QR = |\,\underline{\quad?\quad} - \underline{\quad?\quad}\,|$

$\quad = \underline{\quad?\quad}$ units

$\underline{\quad?\quad} + \underline{\quad?\quad} = PQ^2$ Use the Pythagorean Theorem.

$\underline{\quad?\quad} + \underline{\quad?\quad} = PQ^2$ Substitute values for PR and QR.

$\underline{\quad?\quad} + \underline{\quad?\quad} = PQ^2$ Multiply.

$\underline{\quad?\quad} = PQ^2$ Add.

$PQ = \underline{\quad?\quad}$ Find the positive square root.

$PQ \approx \underline{\quad?\quad}$ units   Round to the nearest tenth.

So, the distance between points P and Q is exactly $\underline{\quad?\quad}$ units and

approximately $\underline{\quad?\quad}$ units.

Understand the Distance Formula.

The distance between two points A and B on a coordinate plane is the length of the line segment connecting the two points. As you saw earlier, you can first measure the horizontal distance between the points and the vertical distance between the points, and then use the Pythagorean Theorem.

$AB^2 = $ (**Horizontal distance**)$^2 + $ (**Vertical distance**)^2

So, $AB = \sqrt{[(\textbf{Horizontal distance})^2 + (\textbf{Vertical distance})^2]}$.

This equation is usually written using variables for the coordinates of points A and B, as shown below.

The distance formula;
The distance between points A (x_1, y_1) and B (x_2, y_2) is $\sqrt{(x_2 - x_1)^2 + (y_2 - y_1)^2}$.

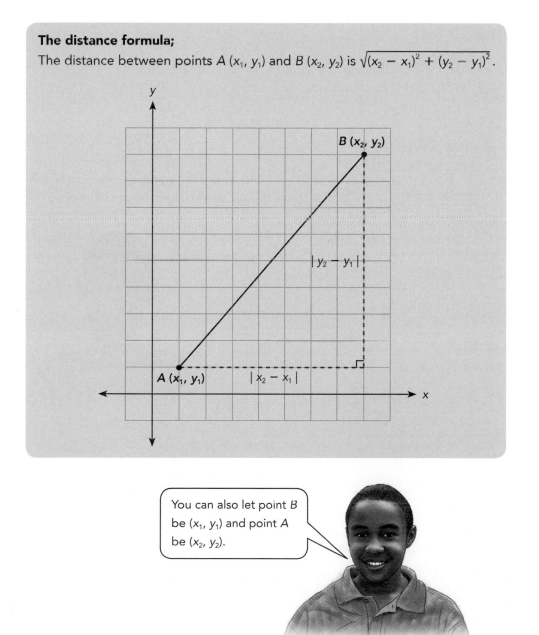

You can also let point B be (x_1, y_1) and point A be (x_2, y_2).

Example 7   Use the distance formula to solve a geometry problem.

Randy plots the points A (0, 5), B (7, 1), and C (4, −2) on graph paper. He joins the three points to form triangle ABC.

a)   Find the lengths of $\overline{AB}$, $\overline{BC}$, and $\overline{AC}$.

Solution

First find the length of $\overline{AB}$.
Let A (0, 5) be (x_1, y_1) and B (7, 1) be (x_2, y_2).

$$\begin{aligned}
\text{Distance from A to B} &= \sqrt{(x_2 - x_1)^2 + (y_2 - y_1)^2} \\
&= \sqrt{(7 - 0)^2 + (1 - 5)^2} \\
&= \sqrt{7^2 + (-4)^2} \\
&= \sqrt{65} \text{ units}
\end{aligned}$$

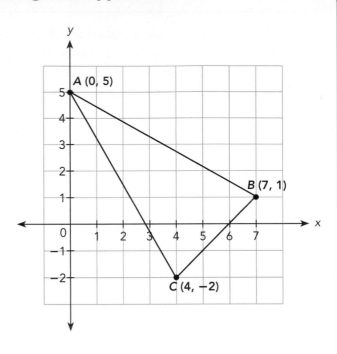

The length of $\overline{AB}$ is $\sqrt{65}$ units.

Next find the length of $\overline{BC}$.
Let B (7, 1) be (x_1, y_1) and C (4, −2) be (x_2, y_2).

$$\begin{aligned}
\text{Distance from B to C} &= \sqrt{(x_2 - x_1)^2 + (y_2 - y_1)^2} \\
&= \sqrt{(4 - 7)^2 + [(-2) - 1]^2} \\
&= \sqrt{(-3)^2 + (-3)^2} \\
&= \sqrt{9 + 9} \\
&= \sqrt{18} \text{ units}
\end{aligned}$$

Triangle ABC has three sides: $\overline{AB}$, $\overline{AC}$, and $\overline{BC}$. To find the length of each side, find the distances between two pairs of points.

The length of $\overline{BC}$ is $\sqrt{18}$ units.

Then find the length of $\overline{AC}$.
Let A (0, 5) be (x_1, y_1) and C (4, −2) be (x_2, y_2).

$$\begin{aligned}
\text{Distance from A to C} &= \sqrt{(x_2 - x_1)^2 + (y_2 - y_1)^2} \\
&= \sqrt{(4 - 0)^2 + [(-2) - 5]^2} \\
&= \sqrt{4^2 + (-7)^2} \\
&= \sqrt{65} \text{ units}
\end{aligned}$$

The length of $\overline{AC}$ is $\sqrt{65}$ units.

b)   Is triangle ABC an isosceles triangle? Explain.

Solution

Because AB = AC, triangle ABC is an isosceles triangle.

Math Note

When you are comparing distances or lengths, such as AB and AC, you do not need to find an approximate value for a square root.

AB = AC = $\sqrt{65}$ units, so the side lengths are equal.

Guided Practice

Solve.

2 Mrs. Smith gives the class the coordinates $D(-1, -2)$, $E(2, 4)$, and $F(5, -1)$ and asks them to join the three points to form triangle DEF.

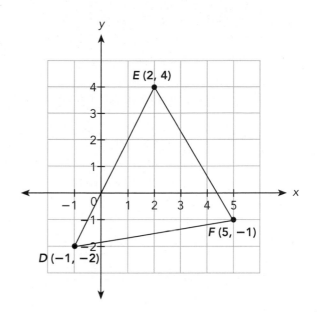

a) Find the length of $\overline{DE}$, $\overline{EF}$, and $\overline{DF}$.

First find the length of $\overline{DE}$.
Let $D(-1, -2)$ be (x_1, y_1) and $E(2, 4)$ be (x_2, y_2).

Distance from D to $E = \sqrt{(x_2 - x_1)^2 + (y_2 - y_1)^2}$

$\qquad = \sqrt{[2 - (-1)]^2 + (4 - \underline{\ ?\ })^2}$

$\qquad = \sqrt{3^2 + \underline{\ ?\ }}$

$\qquad = \underline{\ ?\ }$ units

The length of $\overline{DE}$ is $\underline{\ ?\ }$ units.

Next find the length of $\overline{EF}$.
Let $E(2, 4)$ be (x_1, y_1) and $F(5, -1)$ be (x_2, y_2).

Distance from E to $F = \sqrt{(x_2 - x_1)^2 + (y_2 - y_1)^2}$

$\qquad = \sqrt{(5 - 2)^2 + (\underline{\ ?\ } - 4)^2}$

$\qquad = \sqrt{3^2 + \underline{\ ?\ }}$

$\qquad = \underline{\ ?\ }$ units

> If two of the three sides of a triangle are of the same length, the triangle is an isosceles triangle.

The length of $\overline{EF}$ is $\underline{\ ?\ }$ units.

Then find the length of $\overline{DF}$.
Let $D(-1, -2)$ be (x_1, y_1) and $F(5, -1)$ be (x_2, y_2).

Distance from D to $F = \sqrt{(x_2 - x_1)^2 + (y_2 - y_1)^2}$

$\qquad = \sqrt{[5 - \underline{\ ?\ }]^2 + [\underline{\ ?\ } - (-2)]^2}$

$\qquad = \sqrt{\underline{\ ?\ } + \underline{\ ?\ }}$

$\qquad = \underline{\ ?\ }$ units

The length of $\overline{DF}$ is $\underline{\ ?\ }$ units.

b) Is triangle DEF an isosceles triangle? Explain.

Because $\underline{\ ?\ }$, triangle DEF is $\underline{\ ?\ }$.

Example 8 **Use the distance formula to solve a geometry problem.**

Amy plots the points $X(-4, 2)$, $Y(-1, -5)$, and $Z(3, -1)$ on graph paper. She joins the three points to form triangle XYZ.

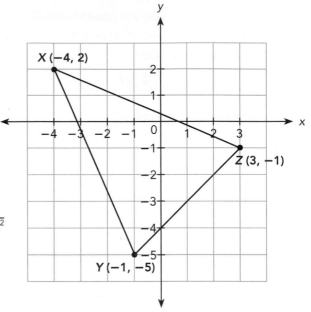

a) Find the lengths of $\overline{XY}$, $\overline{YZ}$, and $\overline{XZ}$.

Solution

First find the length of $\overline{XY}$.

Let $X(-4, 2)$ be (x_1, y_1) and $Y(-1, -5)$ be (x_2, y_2).

$$\begin{aligned}
\text{Distance from } X \text{ to } Y &= \sqrt{(x_2 - x_1)^2 + (y_2 - y_1)^2} \\
&= \sqrt{[(-1) - (-4)]^2 + [(-5) - 2]^2} \\
&= \sqrt{3^2 + (-7)^2} \\
&= \sqrt{58} \text{ units}
\end{aligned}$$

The length of $\overline{XY}$ is $\sqrt{58}$ units.

Next find the length of $\overline{YZ}$.

Let $Y(-1, -5)$ be (x_1, y_1) and $Z(3, -1)$ be (x_2, y_2).

$$\begin{aligned}
\text{Distance from } Y \text{ to } Z &= \sqrt{(x_2 - x_1)^2 + (y_2 - y_1)^2} \\
&= \sqrt{[3 - (-1)]^2 + [(-1) - (-5)]^2} \\
&= \sqrt{4^2 + 4^2} \\
&= \sqrt{32} \text{ units}
\end{aligned}$$

The length of $\overline{YZ}$ is $\sqrt{32}$ units.

Then find the length of $\overline{XZ}$.

Let $X(-4, 2)$ be (x_1, y_1) and $Z(3, -1)$ be (x_2, y_2).

$$\begin{aligned}
\text{Distance from } X \text{ to } Z &= \sqrt{(x_2 - x_1)^2 + (y_2 - y_1)^2} \\
&= \sqrt{[3 - (-4)]^2 + [(-1) - 2]} \\
&= \sqrt{7^2 + (-3)^2} \\
&= \sqrt{58} \text{ units}
\end{aligned}$$

The length of $\overline{XZ}$ is $\sqrt{58}$ units.

b) Is triangle XYZ an isosceles triangle? Explain.

Solution

Because $XY = XZ$, triangle XYZ is an isosceles triangle.

Guided Practice

Solve.

3 Mr. Jacobs gives his students the coordinates $R\,(-3, 3)$, $S\,(-1, -3)$, and $T\,(-5, -4)$ and asks them to join the three points to form triangle RST.

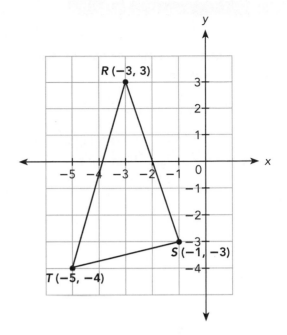

a) Find the lengths of $\overline{RT}$, $\overline{ST}$, and $\overline{RS}$.

First find the length of $\overline{RT}$.
Let $R\,(-3, 3)$ be (x_1, y_1) and $T\,(-5, -4)$ be (x_2, y_2).

$$
\begin{aligned}
\text{Distance from } R \text{ to } T &= \sqrt{(x_2 - x_1)^2 + (y_2 - y_1)^2} \\
&= \sqrt{[(-5) - (-3)]^2 + [(-4) - \underline{\ ?\ }]^2} \\
&= \sqrt{(-2)^2 + \underline{\ ?\ }} \\
&= \underline{\ ?\ } \text{ units}
\end{aligned}
$$

The length of $\overline{RT}$ is $\underline{\ ?\ }$ units.

Next find the length of $\overline{ST}$.
Let $S\,(-1, -3)$ be (x_1, y_1) and $T\,(-5, -4)$ be (x_2, y_2).

$$
\begin{aligned}
\text{Distance from } S \text{ to } T &= \sqrt{(x_2 - x_1)^2 + (y_2 - y_1)^2} \\
&= \sqrt{[(-5) - (-1)]^2 + [\underline{\ ?\ } - (-3)]^2} \\
&= \sqrt{(-4)^2 + \underline{\ ?\ }} \\
&= \underline{\ ?\ } \text{ units}
\end{aligned}
$$

The length of $\overline{ST}$ is $\underline{\ ?\ }$ units.

Then find the length of $\overline{RS}$.
Let $R\,(-3, 3)$ be (x_1, y_1) and $S\,(-1, -3)$ be (x_2, y_2).

$$
\begin{aligned}
\text{Distance from } R \text{ to } S &= \sqrt{(x_2 - x_1)^2 + (y_2 - y_1)^2} \\
&= \sqrt{[\underline{\ ?\ } - (-3)]^2 + [(-3) - 3]} \\
&= \sqrt{\underline{\ ?\ } + (-6)^2} \\
&= \underline{\ ?\ } \text{ units}
\end{aligned}
$$

The length of $\overline{RS}$ is $\underline{\ ?\ }$ units.

b) Is triangle RST an isosceles triangle? Explain.

Because $\underline{\ ?\ }$, triangle RST is $\underline{\ ?\ }$.

For this practice, you may use a calculator. Round your answers to the nearest tenth if necessary.

Solve. Show your work.

1 Points $M(-3, -2)$ and $N(4, 5)$ are plotted on a coordinate plane. Find the exact distance between points M and N.

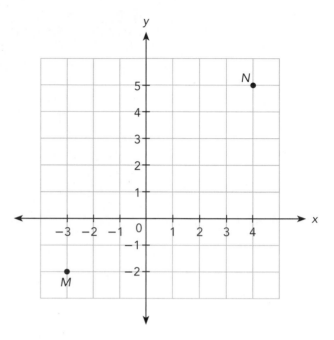

2 Find the distance between each pair of points. Which pair of points are the greatest distance apart?

a) $A(1, 4), B(6, 6)$

b) $C(-4, 7), D(3, 2)$

c) $L(2, -5), N(-3, -1)$

d) $Y(-6, -4), Z(0, 5)$

3 Zack plots the points $R(1, -4)$, $S(-5, 0)$, and $T(5, 2)$ on a coordinate plane. He joins the three points to form triangle RST. Is the triangle an isosceles triangle? Explain.

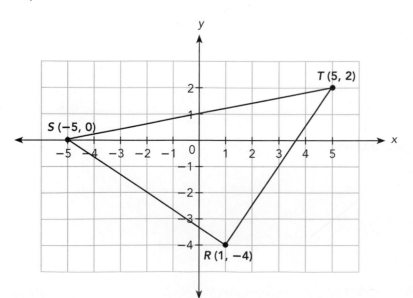

Use the data in the diagram for questions **4** to **6**. Each unit on the grid equals 1 kilometer.

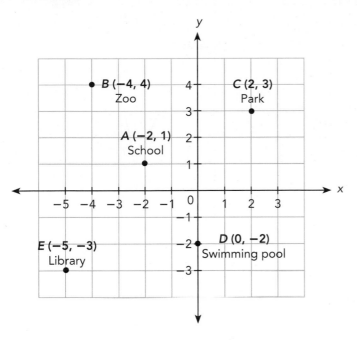

4 Find the approximate distance from the school to each of the following locations.

a) Zoo **b)** Park **c)** Swimming pool **d)** Library

5 Which two locations are the same distance from the school?

6 Which location is farthest from the school?

Solve. Show your work.

7 A ship is located at the point shown in the diagram. The ship needs to stop at a port for refueling on its way to the lighthouse. It can either stop at Port A or Port B. If the captain wants the journey to be as short as possible, which port should the ship stop at?

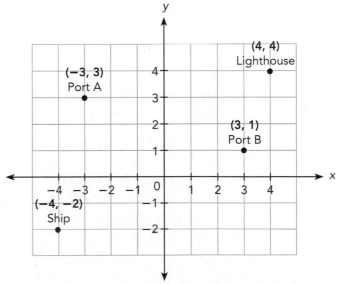

8 Blair drew two triangles on a coordinate plane.

a) Find the lengths of the sides of triangle *XYZ*. Classify the triangle by its side lengths.

b) Blair thinks that triangle *RST* is a right triangle. Do you agree? Why or why not?

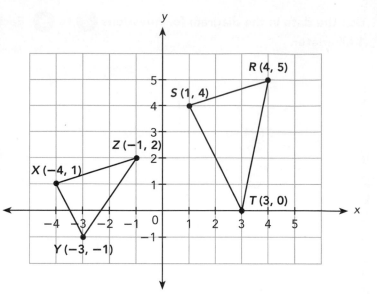

9 The engine on a cruise ship has broken down and the passengers are waiting for a patrol ship to rescue them. The positions of the two ships are shown on the right. Each unit on the grid equals 6 miles.

a) How far is the patrol ship from the cruise ship?

b) If the patrol ship travels at a speed of 50 miles per hour, how long will it take to reach the boat?

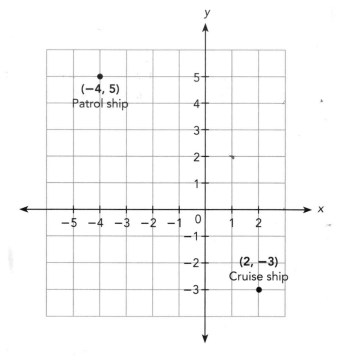

10 *Math Journal* Point *P* (1, 2) is the center of a circle. Three of the following points lie on the circle. Tell which point is not on the circle. Explain your reasoning. *A* (−1, 4), *B* (4, 4), *C* (3, 0), and *D* (3, 4)

11 *Math Journal* Jose found the distance between points *X* and *Y* by first counting grids to find the horizontal and vertical distances. Then he used the Pythagorean Theorem. How is his method different from using the distance formula? How is it the same?

7.3 Understanding the Pythagorean Theorem and Solids

Lesson Objective

- Use the Pythagorean Theorem to solve problems involving solids.

Use the Pythagorean Theorem to Solve Problems Involving Solids.

You can use the Pythagorean Theorem to solve problems involving solids. To do so, you may need to think about a cross section of the solid, and then visualize a right triangle on that cross section.

For instance, the height of the Great Pyramid of Giza is about 480 feet, and the length of a side of its square base is about 756 feet. The drawing below shows how you can visualize a right triangle on a cross section that passes through the vertex of the pyramid and is perpendicular to the base.

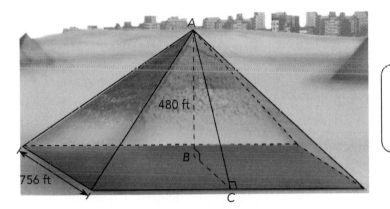

The length of one leg of the right triangle is the height of the pyramid. The length of the other leg is half the length of a side of the base of the pyramid.

You can use the Pythagorean Theorem to find the slant height, $\overline{AC}$, of the Great Pyramid.

$$AB^2 + BC^2 = AC^2 \qquad \text{Use the Pythagorean Theorem.}$$
$$480^2 + 378^2 = AC^2 \qquad \text{Substitute values for } AB \text{ and } BC.$$
$$230{,}400 + 142{,}884 = AC^2 \qquad \text{Multiply.}$$
$$373{,}284 = AC^2 \qquad \text{Add.}$$
$$\sqrt{373{,}284} = AC \qquad \text{Find the positive square root.}$$
$$AC \approx 611.0 \text{ ft} \qquad \text{Round to the nearest tenth.}$$

So, the slant height of the Great Pyramid is exactly $\sqrt{373{,}284}$ feet and approximately 611.0 feet.

Think Math

If you know the slant height of the pyramid, how do you find the lateral surface area of the pyramid?

Example 9 **Use the Pythagorean Theorem to find unknown side lengths.**

Susan uses the cone-shaped paper cup shown to get some water from a water cooler. What is the depth of the paper cup? Round your answer to the nearest tenth.

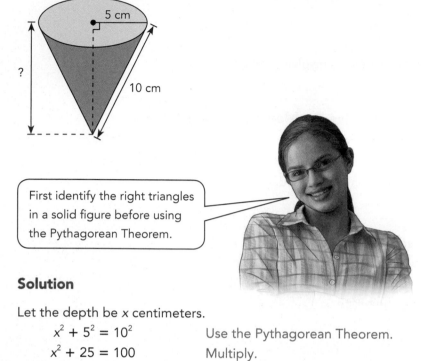

First identify the right triangles in a solid figure before using the Pythagorean Theorem.

Solution

Let the depth be x centimeters.

$x^2 + 5^2 = 10^2$	Use the Pythagorean Theorem.
$x^2 + 25 = 100$	Multiply.
$x^2 + 25 - 25 = 100 - 25$	Subtract 25 from both sides.
$x^2 = 75$	Simplify.
$x = \sqrt{75}$	Find the positive square root.
$x \approx 8.7$	Round to the nearest tenth.

So, the depth of the paper cup is approximately 8.7 centimeters.

Guided Practice

Solve.

1 The radius of a cone-shaped hat is 5 centimeters. The slant length of the hat is 8 centimeters. What is the height of the hat? Round your answer to the nearest tenth.

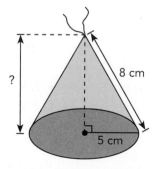

Let the height be x centimeters.

$x^2 + \underline{\ ?\ } = 8^2$	Use the Pythagorean Theorem.
$x^2 + \underline{\ ?\ } = \underline{\ ?\ }$	$\underline{\ ?\ }$
$x^2 + \underline{\ ?\ } - \underline{\ ?\ } = \underline{\ ?\ } - \underline{\ ?\ }$	$\underline{\ ?\ }$
$x^2 = \underline{\ ?\ }$	$\underline{\ ?\ }$
$x = \underline{\ ?\ }$	Find the positive square root.
$x \approx \underline{\ ?\ }$	$\underline{\ ?\ }$ to the nearest tenth.

So, the height of the hat is approximately $\underline{\ ?\ }$ centimeters.

Example 10 **Use the Pythagorean Theorem to find unknown side lengths.**

The figure shows a cubic stool of side length 15 inches. The length of the diagonal of the base, $\overline{EF}$, is $\sqrt{450}$ inches. Find the length of the central diagonal, $\overline{DF}$. Find both the exact value and the approximate value to the nearest tenth.

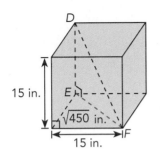

Solution

$$DE^2 + EF^2 = DF^2 \qquad \text{Use the Pythagorean Theorem.}$$
$$15^2 + \sqrt{450}^2 = DF^2 \qquad \text{Substitute values for } DE \text{ and } EF.$$
$$225 + 450 = DF^2 \qquad \text{Multiply.}$$
$$675 = DF^2 \qquad \text{Add.}$$
$$\sqrt{675} = DF \qquad \text{Find the positive square root.}$$
$$DF \approx 26.0 \text{ in.} \qquad \text{Round to the nearest tenth.}$$

So, the length of the central diagonal is exactly $\sqrt{675}$ inches and approximately 26.0 inches.

Guided Practice

Solve.

2 Given the diagonal length, XY, of the end wall of the King's Chamber of the Great Pyramid and the length, XZ, of the chamber, find the length, YZ, of the central diagonal. Find both the exact value and the approximate value to the nearest tenth.

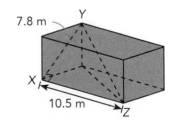

$$\underline{\ ?\ } + \underline{\ ?\ } = YZ^2 \qquad \text{Use the Pythagorean Theorem.}$$
$$\underline{\ ?\ } + \underline{\ ?\ } = YZ^2 \qquad \text{Substitute values for } \overline{XY} \text{ and } \overline{XZ}.$$
$$\underline{\ ?\ } + \underline{\ ?\ } = YZ^2 \qquad \text{Multiply.}$$
$$\underline{\ ?\ } = YZ^2 \qquad \text{Add.}$$
$$\underline{\ ?\ } = YZ \qquad \text{Find the positive square root.}$$
$$YZ \approx \underline{\ ?\ } \text{ m} \qquad \text{Round to the nearest tenth.}$$

So, the length of the central diagonal is exactly $\underline{\ ?\ }$ meters and approximately $\underline{\ ?\ }$ meters.

For this practice, you may use a calculator. Use 3.14 as an approximation for π.
Round your answer to the nearest tenth where necessary.

For each solid, find the value of the variable.

1
10 in.
w in.
6 in.

2
x in.
4 in.
3 in.

3
20 in.
12 in.
y in.

4
10 in.
z in.

Solve. Show your work. Round your answer to the nearest tenth.

5 Find the lateral surface area.

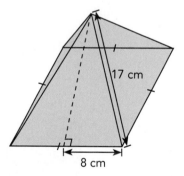

17 cm

8 cm

6 The area of of the lateral surface is πrℓ, where ℓ is the slant height of the cone.
Find the lateral surface area of the cone.

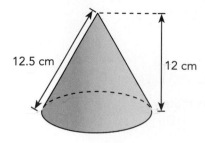

12.5 cm
12 cm

7 A straw that is 16 centimeters long fits inside the glass shown. The height of the glass is 14 centimeters. Find the radius of the glass.

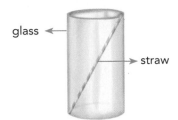

glass ← → straw

8 A spider sits in a corner of a tank shaped like a rectangular prism. The tank is 13 inches long, 6 inches wide, and 8 inches high. The spider starts to make a web by spinning a length of silk that stretches tightly from one corner along a central diagonal to the opposite corner.

a) Find the length of the diagonal of the rectangular floor of the tank.

b) Find the length of the silk the spider spins from one corner of the tank to the other corner.

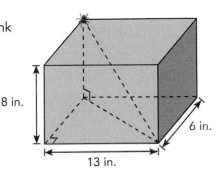

8 in.

6 in.

13 in.

9 A conical party hat is made from a piece of paper as shown. Given that its radius is 3 inches, find the height of the party hat.

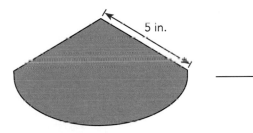

5 in.

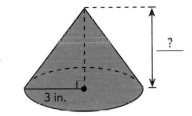

?

3 in.

10 Mindy wants to make a metal paperweight in the shape of a square pyramid. The paperweight will have the dimensions shown.

a) Find the length of a diagonal of the square base.

b) Find the height of the paperweight.

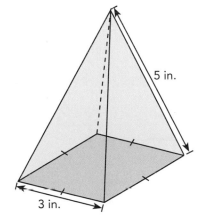

5 in.

3 in.

11 *Math Journal* A box shaped like a rectangular prism is 14.5 centimeters long, 4 centimeters wide, and 3.5 centimeters high. You have a ruler that is 15 centimeters long and 3 centimeters wide. Can it fit inside this box? Explain.

Lesson Objective

- Use the Pythagorean Theorem to find volumes of composite solids.

Use the Pythagorean Theorem to Find Volumes of Composite Solids.

Solids that are made up of more than one of the basic solids are called composite solids. To find the volume of a composite solid, you can find the sum or difference of the volumes of the various solids that make up the composite solid.

Suppose you want to build a birdhouse. For the roof, you use a wooden square pyramid with a base length of 5 inches and an edge length of 6 inches as shown. For the bottom part of the birdhouse, you use a wooden square prism also with a base length of 5 inches and a height of 7 inches. To find the volume of space inside the birdhouse, you can find the volumes of the pyramid and the prism, and then add the two volumes.

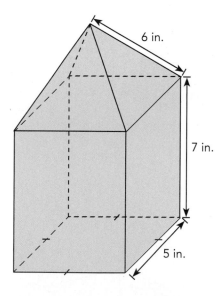

First identify the parts of the composite solid. Then find the volume of each part.

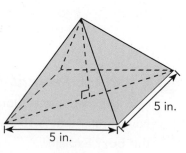

To find the volume of the pyramid, you can use the formula:

$$\text{Volume} = \frac{1}{3} \cdot \text{Area of base} \cdot \text{Height}$$

You know that the area of the base, B, is 25 square inches, but the diagram shows only the length of one slanted edge of the pyramid. To find the height, you can visualize an isosceles triangle inside the pyramid, as shown. This isosceles triangle can be divided into two identical right triangles. The height of the pyramid forms a leg of one of these triangles. The other leg is half the diagonal of the base of the pyramid.

To find the height, you need to use the Pythagorean Theorem two times.

First find the diagonal length of the square bases.

Let d represent the length of the diagonal in inches.

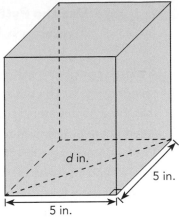

$$d^2 = 5^2 + 5^2$$ Use the Pythagorean Theorem.
$$d^2 = 25 + 25$$ Multiply.
$$d^2 = 50$$ Add.
$$d = \sqrt{50}$$ Find the positive square root.

d in.

5 in.

5 in.

Next find the height of the pyramid.

Let h represent the height of the pyramid in inches.

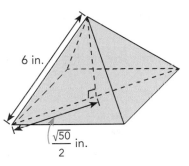

$$6^2 = h^2 + \left(\frac{\sqrt{50}}{2}\right)^2$$ Use the Pythagorean Theorem.
$$36 = h^2 + 12.5$$ Multiply.
$$36 - \mathbf{12.5} = h^2 + 12.5 - \mathbf{12.5}$$ Subtract 12.5 from both sides.
$$23.5 = h^2$$ Simplify.
$$h = \sqrt{23.5}$$ Find the positive square root.

6 in.

$\frac{\sqrt{50}}{2}$ in.

Then find the volume of the pyramid.

Volume of pyramid $= \dfrac{1}{3} \cdot$ Area of base $\cdot$ Height

$\qquad\qquad\qquad\quad = \dfrac{1}{3} \cdot 25 \cdot \sqrt{23.5}$ Use the exact value of height.

$\qquad\qquad\qquad\quad \approx 40.4$ in^3 Round to the nearest tenth.

> The length of the diagonal is exactly $\sqrt{50}$ inches. So half the diagonal length is $\dfrac{\sqrt{50}}{2}$ inches.

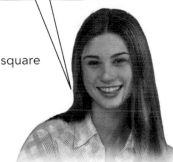

You can use the formula for the volume of a prism to find the volume of the square prism.

Volume $=$ Area of base $\cdot$ Height
$\qquad\quad = 5^2 \cdot 7$
$\qquad\quad = 175$ in^3

Finally, find the combined volume of the composite solid.

Volume of space inside birdhouse
$=$ Volume of square prism $+$ Volume of square pyramid
$\approx 175 + 40.4$
$= 215.4$ in^3

So, the volume of space inside the birdhouse is approximately 215.4 cubic inches.

Example 11 **Use the Pythagorean Theorem to solve problems involving volumes of composite solids.**

A plastic pencil grip is shaped like a triangular prism with a cylindrical hole. The bases are equilateral triangles with sides that are 2 centimeters long. The height of the prism is 4 centimeters. The cylindrical hole has a diameter of 1 centimeter. Find the volume of plastic used in the pencil grip. Round your answer to the nearest tenth. Use 3.14 as an approximation for π.

Solution

First find the height of the base of the triangular prism.

Let h represent the height of the base of the prism in centimeters.

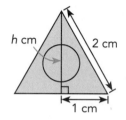

$2^2 = h^2 + 1^2$	Use the Pythagorean Theorem.
$4 = h^2 + 1$	Multiply.
$4 - 1 = h^2 + 1 - 1$	Subtract 1 from both sides.
$h^2 = 3$	Simplify.
$h = \sqrt{3}$	Find the positive square root.

Then find the volume of the prism.

Volume of prism = Area of base · Height

$\quad\quad\quad = \dfrac{1}{2} \cdot 2 \cdot \sqrt{3} \cdot 4$ Use the exact value for the height.

$\quad\quad\quad \approx 6.9 \text{ cm}^3$ Round to the nearest tenth.

Next find the volume of the cylindrical hole.

Volume of cylinder = Area of base · Height

$\quad\quad\quad = \pi \cdot \left(\dfrac{1}{2}\right)^2 \cdot 4$

$\quad\quad\quad \approx 3.14 \cdot \dfrac{1}{4} \cdot 4$

$\quad\quad\quad \approx 3.1 \text{ cm}^3$

Finally, find the volume of plastic used.

Volume of plastic used = Volume of triangular prism – Volume of cylindrical hole

$\quad\quad\quad \approx 6.9 - 3.1$

$\quad\quad\quad = 3.8 \text{ cm}^3$

So, the volume of plastic used is approximately 3.8 cubic centimeters.

Guided Practice

Solve.

1 A solid metal trophy is made up of a cylinder and a cone. The radius of the cylinder is equal to the radius of the cone. Find the volume of metal used to make the trophy. Round your answer to the nearest tenth. Use 3.14 as an approximation for π.

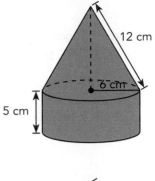

First find the height of the cone.

Let h represent the height of the cone in centimeters.

$$\underline{\ \ ?\ \ } = h^2 + \underline{\ \ ?\ \ }$$ Use the Pythagorean Theorem.

$$\underline{\ \ ?\ \ } = h^2 + \underline{\ \ ?\ \ }$$ Multiply.

$$\underline{\ \ ?\ \ } - \underline{\ \ ?\ \ } = h^2 + \underline{\ \ ?\ \ } - \underline{\ \ ?\ \ }$$ Subtract 36 from both sides.

$$h^2 = \underline{\ \ ?\ \ }$$ Simplify.

$$h = \underline{\ \ ?\ \ }$$ Find the positive square root.

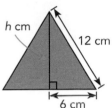

Then find the volume of the cone.

Volume of cone $= \dfrac{1}{3} \cdot$ Area of base $\cdot$ Height

$$= \underline{\ \ ?\ \ }$$ Use the exact value of the height of the cone.

$$\approx \underline{\ \ ?\ \ } \text{ cm}^3$$

Next find the volume of the cylinder.

Volume $=$ Area of base $\cdot$ Height

$$= \underline{\ \ ?\ \ }$$

$$\approx \underline{\ \ ?\ \ } \text{ cm}^3$$

Finally, find the volume of metal used.

Volume of metal used

$=$ Volume of cone $+$ Volume of cylinder

$$\approx \underline{\ \ ?\ \ } + \underline{\ \ ?\ \ }$$

$$= \underline{\ \ ?\ \ } \text{ cm}^3$$

So, the volume of metal used is approximately $\underline{\ \ ?\ \ }$ cubic centimeters.

For this practice, you may use a calculator. Use 3.14 as an approximation for π. Round your answer to the nearest tenth if necessary.

1 Find the volume of each of the following composite solids.

a) A triangular prism with a cylindrical hole cut out of it.

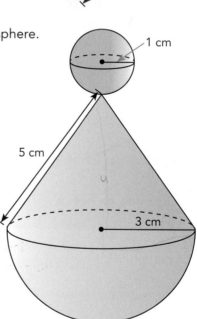

14.1 cm

4 cm

12 cm

10 cm

b) A sphere connected to a cone that sits on top of a hemisphere.

1 cm

5 cm

3 cm

2 A ceramic candle holder in the shape of a cylinder has a radius of 2.40 inches. A hemisphere of radius 1.75 inches is removed from the center of the cylinder. Find the volume of ceramic in the candle holder.

1.75 in.

4 in.

2.40 in.

3 A tent has a conical roof and a cylindrical wall as shown. The cylindrical wall and the conical roof are of the same height. The radius of the tent is 9 meters. Ropes are used to tie the tent to the ground.

a) Find the height of the wall.

b) Find the volume of space inside the tent.

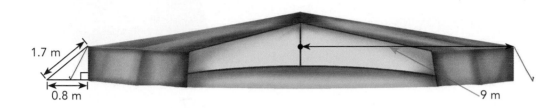

1.7 m

0.8 m

9 m

4 A traffic cone is made up of a cone fixed on top of a square prism base with a height of 1 inch. Find the volume of the traffic cone.

28 in.

19 in.

7.3 in.

1 in.

5 A sculpture is made out of a cone resting on top of a hemisphere. The hemisphere has a radius of 1 meter. Use the information in the diagram below to find the volume of the sculpture.

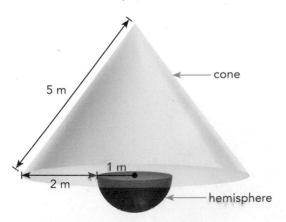

cone

5 m

1 m

2 m

hemisphere

6 A trophy is made of a glass triangular prism attached to a 0.5 inch high wooden block shaped like a square prism. The height of the trophy is 6 inches. The volume of the wooden base is 4.5 cubic inches. Find the volume of the entire trophy, including the base.

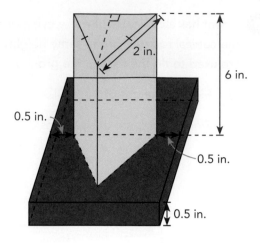

7 A swimming pool is 12 feet long and 10 feet wide. At its deepest, it is 7 feet deep. A slope 5 feet long links the deep end to the shallow end. Jonathan wants to fill the pool with 800 cubic feet of water. Is this possible? Explain.

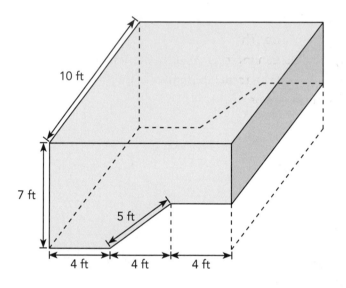

8 A crystal paperweight is shaped like a cylinder with a star-shaped hole. The top of the star-shaped hole is shaped like a square with four points that are identical equilateral triangles. The height of the cylinder is 3 centimeters. Find the volume of the paperweight.

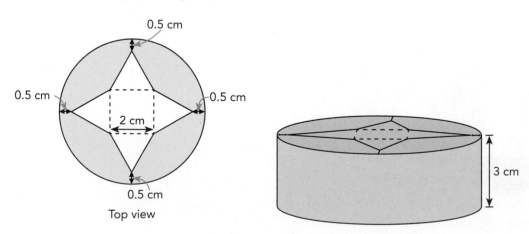

Top view

9 ✏️📓 *Math Journal* The solid shown below is made of a cylinder with two identical cones at the ends of the cylinder. Linda says that if the radius of the cylinder is doubled, the volume of the solid will also be doubled. Is she correct? Why?

Brain @ Work

1 An architect designs a staircase for a new house. There will be 14 steps, and each step will be 17 centimeters high and 25 centimeters wide. The architect will build a railing on both sides of the steps. Find the total length needed for the two railings, not including any vertical support posts.

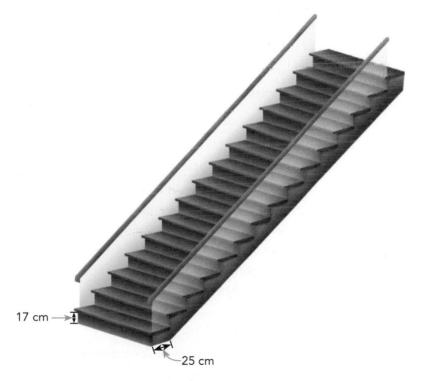

17 cm

25 cm

2 The Colorado river is about 210 meters wide. Brad and John start swimming from the same bank. Brad swims 215 meters against the current to reach a point on the opposite bank. Brad's swimming speed is greater than the speed of the current. John swims 220 meters with the current to reach another point on the opposite bank. Find the distance between the two points.

Chapter Wrap Up

Concept Map

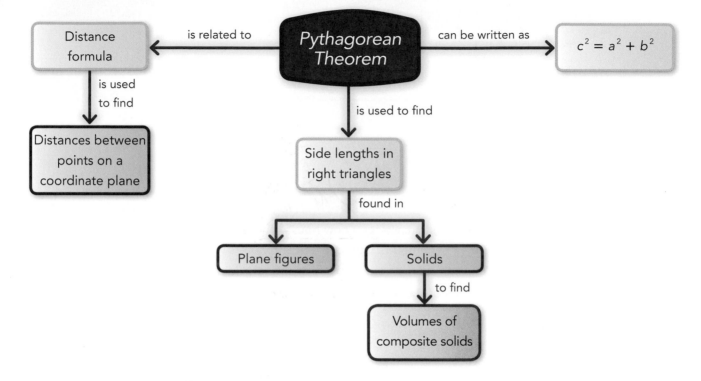

Key Concepts

▶ The Pythagorean Theorem applies only to right triangles.

▶ The relationship between the longest side length c and the other two side lengths, a and b, of a right triangle is given by $c^2 = a^2 + b^2$.

▶ If the sum of the squares of the lengths of the two shortest sides of a triangle is equal to the square of the length of the longest side, then the converse of the Pythagorean Theorem states that the triangle is a right triangle.

▶ The Pythagorean Theorem is related to the distance formula, $\sqrt{(x_2 - x_1)^2 + (y_2 - y_1)^2}$, which is used to find the distance between two points on a coordinate plane.

▶ The Pythagorean Theorem can be used to solve problems in three dimensions, such as finding the volume of a solid.

Chapter Review/Test

Concepts and Skills

For this review, you may use a calculator. Use 3.14 as an approximation for π.
Round your answer to the nearest tenth where necessary.

1 Find the value of x in each of the following diagrams.

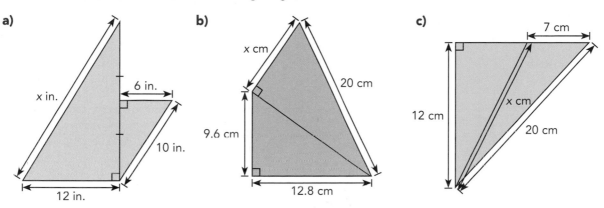

a)

b)

c)

2 Find the distance between each pair of points. Which pair of points are the greatest distance apart?

a) A (5, 2), B (8, 5)

b) C (−3, 2), D (2, 3)

c) L (1, −3), N (−2, −1)

d) Y (−3, −3), Z (0, 4)

3 Find the value of x in each of the following diagrams.

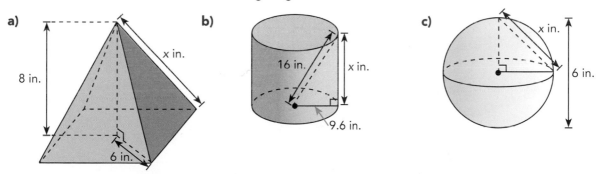

a)

b)

c)

4 Find the volume of each of the following composite solids.

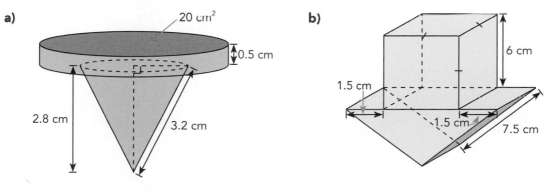

a)

b)

Problem Solving

Solve. Show your work.

An interactive game teaches users how to find the distance between two points on a coordinate plane. Each unit on the grid equals 1 kilometer. Use the grid for questions **5** and **6**.

5 Find the distance between the farmer and each location.

a) River

b) Pond

c) Town

d) Orchard

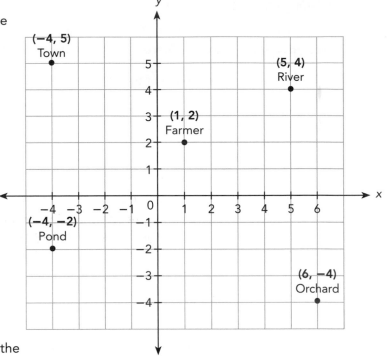

6 The farmer wants to go fishing in either the river or the pond. Which one is closer to his current position? How many kilometers fewer will he walk if he chooses the source that is closer?

7 Candy builds a cage for some chickens out of wood and wire mesh, as shown below. The two slanted sides of the cage are the same size and shape. Find the height of the cage.

40 in.

64 in.

8 A straw that is 12 centimeters long fits inside a glass. The height of the glass is 7.5 centimeters. Find the radius of the glass.

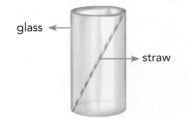

glass

straw

9 Naomi makes a lampshade by making a cone and then cutting off part of the cone, as shown. Find the diameter of the larger opening in the lampshade.

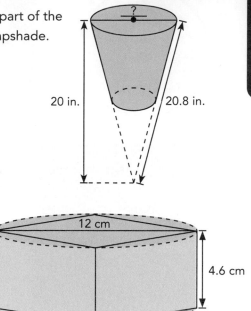

20 in.   20.8 in.

10 Four identical pieces are cut off the sides of a cylinder, as shown. The remaining shape is a square prism. The diagonal of the prism's square base is as long as the diameter of the cylinder. The diameter of the cylinder is 12 centimeters, and the height of the cylinder is 9 centimeters. Find the length of a side of the square base of the prism. Then find an approximate volume of the prism.

12 cm

4.6 cm

11 Ellen's computer screen is a 20 inch screen, which means that the length of the diagonal of the rectangular screen is 20 inches. The screen can be laid flat in a box that is 12 inches wide. How long is the box?

12 An 18-centimeter tall suitcase is shaped like a rectangular prism. The length of the diagonal of one of its largest faces is 30 centimeters. Find the width of the suitcase.

13 Vera kicks a ball 123 feet diagonally across a rectangular playground of width 85 feet. Find the length of the playground.

14 A river is 10.5 meters wide and its banks are parallel to each other. John tries to swim straight across, but the current pushes him downstream so that he lands 14 meters from the spot he wanted to reach. How far did he swim?

15 An extendable ladder 9.8 feet long leans against a wall with the base 3 feet from the wall. Assuming the base of the ladder does not move, about how much higher will the top of the ladder be above the ground when the ladder extended to twice its original length?

16 A doorway is 80 inches tall and 32 inches wide. Can a round tabletop with a diameter of 90 inches fit through the doorway? If not, what is the greatest possible diameter that will fit through the doorway? Explain.

Geometric Transformations

8.1 Translations

8.2 Reflections

8.3 Rotations

8.4 Dilations

8.5 Comparing Transformations

How do animators make characters move?

In video games and cartoons, the characters move in many ways: they change position, size, and angle of observation. In early films, each movement was captured in a sequence of hand-drawn cels.

Today, computer programmers write mathematical instructions that describe the sequence of changes needed to show movement. These changes are made using geometric transformations. Points of a figure are located on the screen using the coordinates of the x and y pixels. By using the rules for a transformation called a translation to these coordinates, for example, the figure can appear to move to the left or right, up or down.

In this chapter, you will learn many ways of moving points in a plane and how to write an algebraic description of these moves.

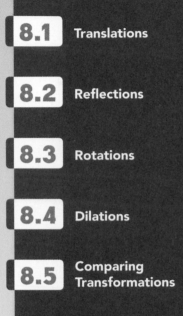

BIG IDEA

▶ Geometric transformations move figures about on a plane. Each type of transformation changes some properties of a figure, but leaves other properties unchanged.

Recall Prior Knowledge

Recognizing a symmetric point on the coordinate plane

A point can be represented on the coordinate plane.

Point A (2, 1) is in the Quadrant I. It is 1 unit from the x-axis and 2 units from the y-axis.

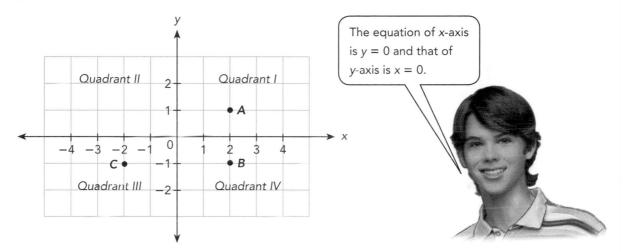

The equation of x-axis is $y = 0$ and that of y-axis is $x = 0$.

Points A and B are symmetrical about the x-axis because if you fold the plane along the x-axis, points A and B will match up. Point A is the reflection of point B. You can also say point B is the reflection of point A. The distances of points A and B from the x-axis are the same. They are both 1 unit from the x-axis.

Points B and C are reflections of each other in the y-axis. They are both 2 units from the y-axis.

 Quick Check

Solve. Show your work.

1 Points W and Z are reflections of each other in the x-axis. If W is the point (4, −3), what are the coordinates of Z?

2 Points P (−2, 5) and Q (−2, −5) are reflections of each other in the line k. What is an equation of line k?

3 Points M (2, −1) and N (−2, −1) are reflections of each other in the line m. What is an equation of line m?

4 If a point S is the reflection of R (1, 4) in the x-axis, what is the length of $\overline{RS}$?

Identifying directly proportional quantities

Two directly proportional quantities x and y are related by an equation of the form
$y = kx$.

The table shows some values of x and y that are related by the equation $y = 3x$.

x	1	2	4
y	3	6	12

For each pair of values, y and x:

$\dfrac{3}{1} = 3 \qquad \dfrac{6}{2} = 3 \qquad \dfrac{12}{4} = 3$

✓ Quick Check

State whether x and y are directly proportional.

5 $y = 1.5x$

6 $y = -\dfrac{x}{2}$

7

x	2	3	4
y	4	9	16

Recognizing perpendicular bisectors

The perpendicular bisector of a line segment is the line
that bisects the line segment and is perpendicular to it.

$\overleftrightarrow{XY}$ is the perpendicular bisector of $\overline{AB}$. So $AX = XB = \dfrac{AB}{2}$,
and $m\angle AXY = m\angle BXY = 90°$.

Any point on the perpendicular bisector of a line segment
is equidistant from the two endpoints of the line segment.
For example, $AY = BY$.

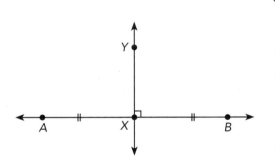

✓ Quick Check

**State whether $\overleftrightarrow{YZ}$ is a perpendicular bisector of the given segment. Justify your
answer. If $\overleftrightarrow{YZ}$ is a perpendicular bisector, name two pairs of distances that are
equal.**

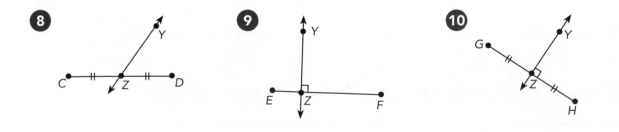

8

9

10

8.1 Translations

Lesson Objectives

- Understand the concept of a translation.
- Draw images after translations.
- Find the coordinates of points after translations.

Understand the Concept of a Translation.

Suppose a chair at position P in a classroom is moved to another position A as shown.

From P, the chair is moved 2 units to the right and 3 units towards the front to position A.

This type of movement is called a translation. In this case, it is 2 units to the right and 3 units forward.

Math Note

A translation can be vertical, horizontal, or a combination of horizontal and vertical motions. You can represent the horizontal and vertical parts of a combination with dashed arrows.

Front of Classroom

A

3 units up

P

2 units to the right

Translation is a commutative movement. This means that the new position is the same whether you translate 2 units to the right then 3 units up or 3 units up then 2 units to the right.

Continue on next page

A translation of 1 unit to the left and 3 units forward describes the movement from *P* to *B*. You can say that the translation **maps** *P* onto *B*.

Likewise, a translation of 2 units down maps *P* to *C*. *C* is called the **image** of *P* under the translation.

P has a different image under each translation. *B* is the image of *P* under the first translation, and *C* is the image of *P* under the second translation.

A **transformation** is a function that maps every point on the plane to another point on the plane. A translation, sometimes called a slide, is one example of a transformation.

An **invariant** point is a point that remains unchanged, or a point that mapped onto itself under a transformation. In a translation, there is no invariant point because every point is moved under the transformation.

Example 1 **Translate a point.**

Marcus walks from a point A (2, 1) in a campsite to point A', as described by a translation of 3 units to the left and 2 units down. Mark the position of A' on the coordinate plane.

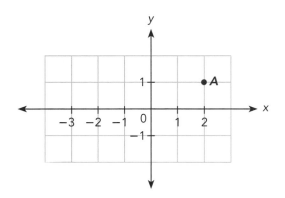

The point A' is read as "A prime."

Solution

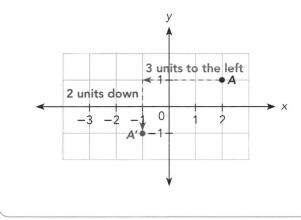

Guided Practice

Copy and complete on graph paper.

1 Abigail jogs from point H (3, 2) in a park to point H', as described by a translation of 5 units to the left and 3 units up. Mark the position of H' on the coordinate plane.

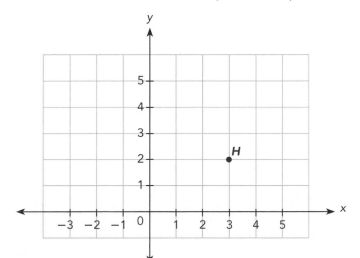

Example 2 | Translate a line segment.

Ronald set up his tent. The position of one side of the base of the tent is represented by $\overline{AB}$. Due to strong wind, he relocated his tent to $\overline{A'B'}$. This movement is described by the translation 3 units to the left and 2 units up. Draw and label $\overline{A'B'}$ on the coordinate plane.

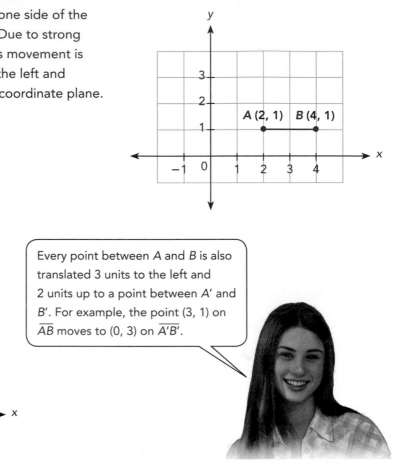

Solution

Every point between A and B is also translated 3 units to the left and 2 units up to a point between A' and B'. For example, the point (3, 1) on $\overline{AB}$ moves to (0, 3) on $\overline{A'B'}$.

Guided Practice

Copy and complete on graph paper.

2 Mr. McBride wanted to set up a barbeque pit in his backyard. He had to move a swing set represented by $\overline{HL}$. He decided to move the swing set by a translation of 4 units to the right and 2 units down to $\overline{H'L'}$. Draw and mark $\overline{H'L'}$ on the coordinate plane.

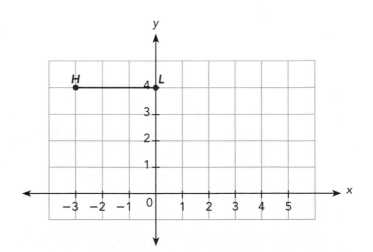

Technology Activity

Materials:
- geometry software

EXPLORE THE PROPERTIES OF TRANSLATIONS WITH GEOMETRY SOFTWARE

STEP 1 Draw a line segment using a geometry software program.

STEP 2 Select the *Translate* function, within the *Transform* menu. Enter the number of units by which you wish to translate the line segment. Translate the line segment to its new position.

STEP 3 How is the length and position of the new line segment related to the original line segment?

> ### Think Math
>
> A horizontal segment is translated horizontally. Is the image parallel to the original segment? Does a translation always map a segment onto a parallel segment? Explain.

STEP 4 Repeat **STEP 2** using a triangle and then a rectangle. Observe how each figure is related to its image.

STEP 5 How do the size and shape of the figures change under a translation? Do the parallel sides of the rectangle remain parallel? Do the perpendicular sides of the rectangle remain perpendicular?

Math Journal Which of these properties does a translation seem to preserve: lengths, shapes, parallel lines, or perpendicular lines? Explain.

Draw Images After Translations.

From the activity, you have observed that translations preserve shape, size, parallelism, and perpendicularity.

When a figure is drawn on a coordinate plane, you can easily draw its image. You need only to find the images of the vertices and connect them appropriately.

Example 3 **Translate polygons.**

Mr. Milano is a builder planning to construct three houses on three nearby lots. He has located the position of the first house on a map of the lots, and plans to locate the other two houses, $A'B'C'D'$ and $A''B''C''D''$, using the following translations.

a) $A'B'C'D'$ is the image of $ABCD$ under the translation: 5 units to the left, 1 unit down.

b) $A''B''C''D''$ is the image of $ABCD$ under the translation: 4 units down.

Copy the diagram, and draw $A'B'C'D'$ and $A''B''C''D''$.

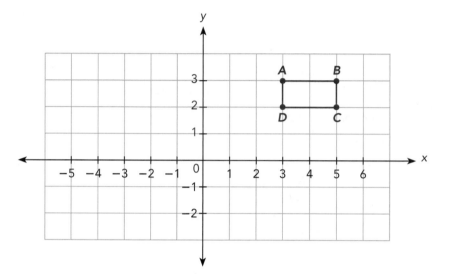

Solution

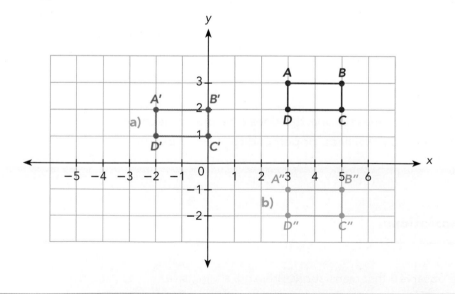

Guided Practice

Complete on graph paper.

3 Tim is creating a wrapping paper design on his computer. He wants to move figure *EFGH* by translating it 5 units to the left and 4 units down. *E, F, G,* and *H* have the coordinates (1, 2), (3, 2), (3, 3), and (1, 3). Draw *EFGH* and *E'F'G'H'* on the same coordinate plane. Use 1 grid square on both axes to represent 1 unit for the interval from −4 to 3. Then complete the following statements.

E (1, 2) is mapped onto *E'* (__?__, __?__).

F (3, 2) is mapped onto *F'* (__?__, __?__).

G (3, 3) is mapped onto *G'* (__?__, __?__).

H (1, 3) is mapped onto *H'* (__?__, __?__).

Find the Coordinates of Points After Translations.

You have learned to translate points on a coordinate plane. You can find the coordinates of the images by simple addition.

For example, to translate *A* (1, 1) by **5** units to the right and **3** units up, the image *A'* (6, 4) is found by (1 + **5**, 1 + **3**). If *A* is translated by **5** units to the left and **3** units down, the image *A"* (−4, −2) is found by (1 + (−5), 1 + (−3)), or (1 − **5**, 1 − **3**).

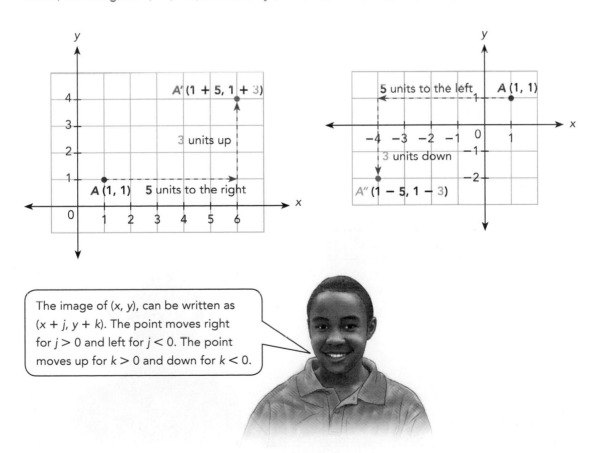

The image of (*x, y*), can be written as (*x + j, y + k*). The point moves right for *j* > 0 and left for *j* < 0. The point moves up for *k* > 0 and down for *k* < 0.

Example 4 **Find the coordinates of points after translations.**

A triangular block of concrete *ABC* at a construction site is to be relocated using the translation: 5 units to the right and 3 units down. The coordinates of *A*, *B*, and *C* are given in the table. Find the coordinates of the relocated block *A'B'C'*. Then state the new coordinates for any point (*x*, *y*) under this translation.

Original Point	Is Mapped Onto
A (1, 1)	A' (?, ?)
B (3, 1)	B' (?, ?)
C (2, 5)	C' (?, ?)
(x, y)	(?, ?)

To find the coordinates of the block after the translation, add 5 units to the *x*-coordinate and subtract 3 units from the *y*-coordinate for each point.

Solution

Original Point	Is Mapped Onto
A (1, 1)	A' (6, −2)
B (3, 1)	B' (8, −2)
C (2, 5)	C' (7, 2)
(x, y)	(x + 5, y − 3)

Guided Practice

Complete.

4 A triangle has coordinates *A* (2, 1), *B* (3, 2), and *C* (1, 4). It is moved under the translation 2 units to the left and 3 units up. Find the coordinates of the image triangle *A'B'C'*. Then state the new coordinates for any point (*x*, *y*) under this translation.

Original Point	Is Mapped Onto
A (2, 1)	A' (?, ?)
B (3, 2)	B' (?, ?)
C (1, 4)	C' (?, ?)
(x, y)	(?, ?)

To find the coordinates of *A'*, *B'*, and *C'*, subtract 2 units from the *x*-coordinate and add 3 units to the *y*-coordinate of *A*, *B*, and *C*.

Find the coordinates of the image under each translation.

 1 P (0, 2) is translated by 8 units to the left.

2 Q (−3, 5) is translated by 3 units to the right and 10 units up.

3 R (−4, −2) is translated by 1 unit to the left and 6 units up.

Copy each diagram on graph paper and draw the image under each translation.

4 $\overline{AB}$ is translated 5 units to the right and 1 unit down.

5 Triangle *DEF* is translated 3 units to the left and 2 units up.

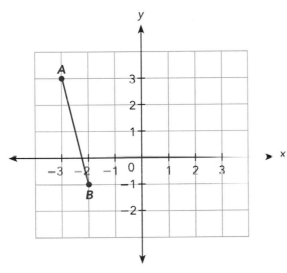

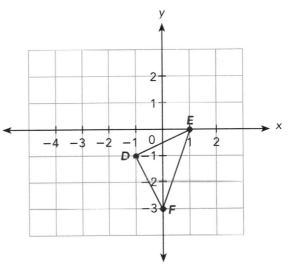

Find the coordinates of each point using the given translation. Label the images on a coordinate plane.

6 Jon's apartment is located at A (2, 2). He uses the translations described in **a)** to **d)** to visit each of his neighbors.

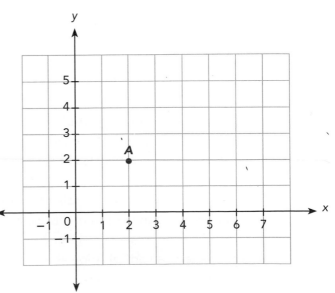

  a) From A (2, 2), translate by 3 units to the right, 2 units up to B.

  b) From B, translate by 2 units to the left, 1 unit up to C.

  c) From C, translate by 1 unit to the right, 2 units down to D.

  d) From D, translate by 2 units to the left, 3 units down to E.

Solve. Show your work.

 7 The base of a box is at *ABCD*. It is moved by a translation to a new position *A'B'C'D'*. The table shows the position to which *A* was mapped. Find the new position of the other three vertices of the base. Copy and complete the table.

Original Point	A (4, 1)	B (6, 1)	C (6, −1)	D (4, −1)
Is Mapped Onto	A' (0, −2)	B' (_?_, _?_)	C' (_?_, _?_)	D' (_?_, _?_)

8 A crane moved a cargo pallet from *ABCD* to other positions on the ship's deck.

a) Find the coordinates of *A'B'C'D'* under a translation that moves each point (*p, q*) to (*p* + 4, *q* + 1). Copy and complete the table. Draw *A'B'C'D'* on a graph paper.

Original Point	A (−2, 1)	B (0, 3)	C (2, 1)	D (0, −1)
Is Mapped Onto	A' (_?_, _?_)	B' (_?_, _?_)	C' (_?_, _?_)	D' (_?_, _?_)

b) The position of *A"B"C"D"* is shown on the coordinate plane. State the new coordinates of any point (*x, y*) under the translation from *ABCD* to *A"B"C"D"*.

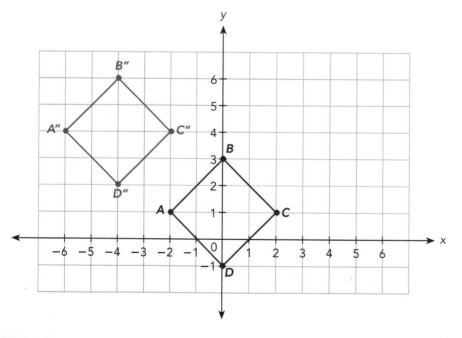

9 A computer program *T* instructs a robotic arm to move an object on the coordinate plane 2 units to the right and 3 units down. The object at point *P* is translated by *T* to point *P'*. Find the coordinates of *P* if point *P'* is (3, 3).

10 A line has the equation *y* = *x*. It is translated up by 3 units. What is the equation of the new line? How do the slopes of the line and its image compare?

11 In a wallpaper pattern, a vertical stripe at *x* = −1 is copied by moving it to *x* = 1. Describe the translation of this stripe both verbally and algebraically.

8.2 Reflections

Lesson Objectives

- Understand the concept of a reflection.
- Draw images after reflections.
- Find the coordinates of points after reflections.

Vocabulary

reflection

line of reflection

Understand the Concept of a Reflection.

Have you ever seen a reflection in the water, such as the one in the river above? You see that the reflected image looks the same as the object that is reflected.

Ms. Jenkins is making a painting with water colors. She makes a dot **A** on a piece of paper with a paintbrush. When the paint is wet, she folds the paper into half. What will she get on the paper?

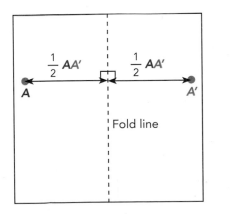

Ms. Jenkins gets another dot **A'** on the paper. The fold line is halfway between the dots. The fold line is the perpendicular bisector of $\overline{AA'}$.

Continue on next page ➡

You can say that **A′** is a reflection of **A** in the **line of reflection** or that **A′** is the image of **A** under the reflection. The line of reflection may also be called the line of symmetry.

You may have studied "flips" in other math classes. These are the same thing as reflections.

Think Math

What is the relationship between $\overline{AA'}$ and the line of reflection?

Example 5 **Reflect a point.**

To make a paper mask, Kathy folds a paper into half and marks a point A for an eyehole. She then cuts through the folded paper at A to make two eyeholes A and A'. If $AA' = 4$ centimeters, find the distance between A and the fold line.

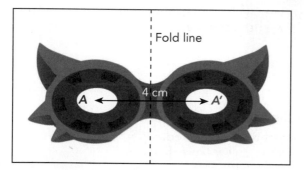

Fold line

4 cm

A A'

The fold line is the line of reflection. The mask is symmetric about the fold line. The eyeholes are at the same distance from the line of reflection.

Solution

Distance between A and the fold line: $\dfrac{4}{2} = 2$ cm

The distance between A and the fold line is 2 centimeters.

Guided Practice

Solve.

1. Andrew wants to hang a square poster on his bedroom wall. He knows that to get the poster to balance properly, he needs to place a second picture hanger at W', with the dotted vertical line as the line of symmetry. If the distance between W and the vertical line is 3 inches, find WW'.

3 in.

W

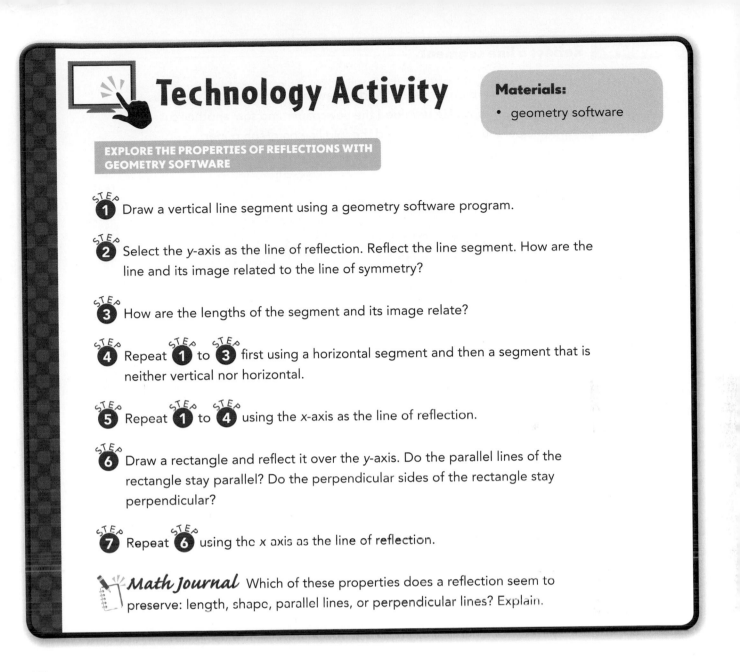

Technology Activity

Materials:
- geometry software

EXPLORE THE PROPERTIES OF REFLECTIONS WITH GEOMETRY SOFTWARE

STEP 1 Draw a vertical line segment using a geometry software program.

STEP 2 Select the y-axis as the line of reflection. Reflect the line segment. How are the line and its image related to the line of symmetry?

STEP 3 How are the lengths of the segment and its image relate?

STEP 4 Repeat **STEP 1** to **STEP 3** first using a horizontal segment and then a segment that is neither vertical nor horizontal.

STEP 5 Repeat **STEP 1** to **STEP 4** using the x-axis as the line of reflection.

STEP 6 Draw a rectangle and reflect it over the y-axis. Do the parallel lines of the rectangle stay parallel? Do the perpendicular sides of the rectangle stay perpendicular?

STEP 7 Repeat **STEP 6** using the x-axis as the line of reflection.

Math Journal Which of these properties does a reflection seem to preserve: length, shape, parallel lines, or perpendicular lines? Explain.

Draw Images After Reflections.

In the activity, you may have observed the following:

Reflections preserve shape and size. They also preserve parallelism and perpendicularity.

All polygons and combinations of polygons are made up of line segments joined at their endpoints. When you reflect these figures, you reflect all the line segments joined at their endpoints. The images of all these line segments and their endpoints combine to form the whole image.

Example 6 **Reflect a line segment.**

Jayden made a straight cut $\overline{AB}$ on a piece of folded newspaper on two occasions, as shown in the following diagrams. He unfolded the newspaper and saw another cut line $\overline{A'B'}$. Draw and label the two cut lines and the fold line on graph paper.

a)

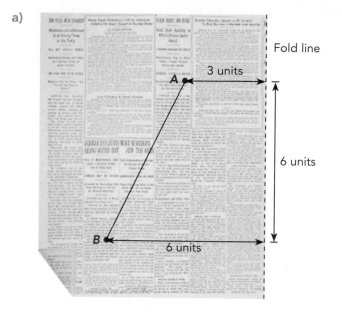

Solution

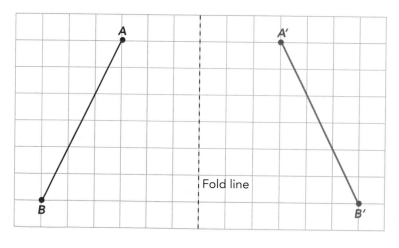

The distance from A to the fold line equals the distance of A' to the fold line. Likewise, the distance of B to the fold line equals the distance of B' to the fold line.

b)

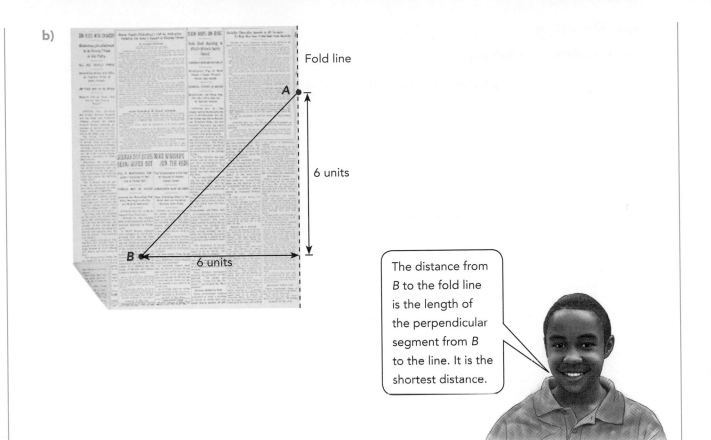

Fold line

A

6 units

B ← 6 units →

> The distance from *B* to the fold line is the length of the perpendicular segment from *B* to the line. It is the shortest distance.

Solution

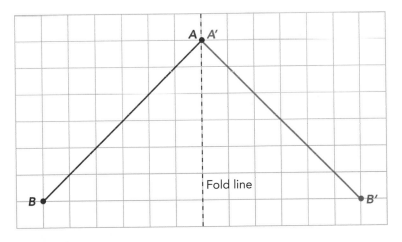

A *A′*

Fold line

B • • *B′*

Math Note

Notice that point *A* is mapped onto itself, that is, points *A* and *A′* are the same point. Point *A* is an invariant point. All points on the line of reflection are invariant, because each one maps onto itself.

Guided Practice

Copy and complete on graph paper.

2 Each line segment is reflected in $\overleftrightarrow{MN}$. On a copy of the diagram, draw each image.

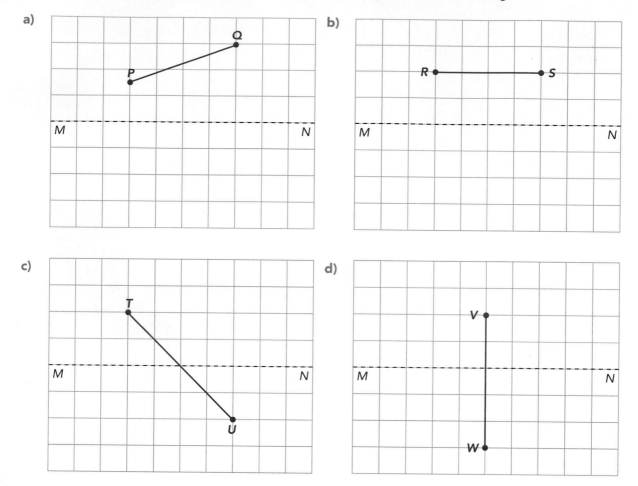

Example 7 **Reflect a figure in the x-axis.**

Susan placed a cup on a table. She then placed cardboard on top of the cup and another cup on top of the cardboard. The side view of *ABCD*, the cup below the cardboard, is shown. The cardboard is aligned with the x-axis.

The side view of cup *A′B′C′D′* is the reflection of the side view of cup *ABCD*. Draw and label the side view of cup *A′B′C′D′*.

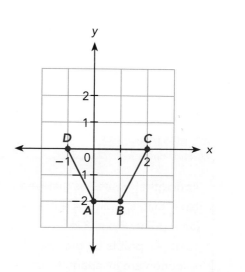

Solution

$A'B'C'D'$ is the reflection of $ABCD$ in the x-axis.

Vertices	Distance from the x-axis
A and A'	2
B and B'	2
C and C'	0
D and D'	0

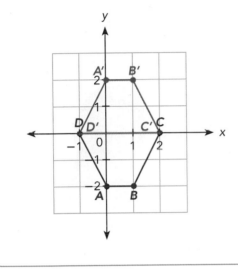

The x-coordinates of each point of $ABCD$ and its image of $A'B'C'D'$ are the same. The y-coordinates are opposites. That is, (x, y) is mapped onto $(x, -y)$. The invariant points of this figure are all the points of $\overline{CD}$, because they are on the line of reflection.

Guided Practice

Copy and complete on graph paper.

3 Layla is designing a star-shaped figure for a stencil. She wants the bottom half to be a reflection of the top half. She will reflect it across the x-axis to draw the other half. Complete the design for her.

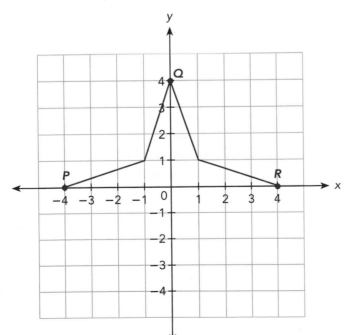

Example 8   **Reflect a figure in the *y*-axis.**

Ally draws shape with the following coordinates for its vertices.

A (0, 2), *B* (2, 2), *C* (2, 1), *D* (1, 1), *E* (1, −1), and *F* (0, −1).

She reflects it in the *y*-axis to get an alphabet letter. Draw the letter on the coordinate plane.

Solution

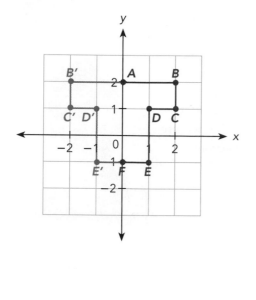

Points *A* and *F* are the invariant points of this figure because they are on the line of reflection. You can see that a reflection in the *x*-axis maps (*x*, *y*) onto (*x*, −*y*) and a reflection in the *y*-axis maps (*x*, *y*) onto (−*x*, *y*).

Guided Practice

Complete.

4 A figure has vertices *P* (0, 2), *Q* (−1, 0), *R* (−2, 1), *S* (−1, −2), and *T* (0, −2), is reflected in the *y*-axis. Draw the figure and its image on the coordinate plane.
Use 1 grid square on both axes to represent 1 unit for the interval from −2 to 2.

Find the Coordinates of Points After Reflections.

You have seen how figures are reflected in a line. The perpendicular distance of each point of the figure from the line of reflection is the same as the perpendicular distance of the image point from the line of reflection. That is, the line of reflection is the perpendicular bisector of the segment joining each point to its image.

You can apply this property of reflections to find the coordinates of points after reflections.

Example 9 **Find the coordinates of points after a reflection.**

State the coordinates of the points.

$A'B'C'D'$ is a reflection of $ABCD$ in the y-axis.

a) What are the coordinates of A, B, C, and D?

Solution

The coordinates are A (1, 1), B (3, 2), C (3, 3), and D (1, 4).

b) What are the coordinates of A', B', C', and D'?

Solution

The coordinates are A' (−1, 1), B' (−3, 2), C' (−3, 3), and D' (−1, 4).

> Each point and its image is the same distance from the line of reflection, the y-axis. For example, A and A' are each 1 unit from the y-axis. Their x-coordinates are opposites, and their y coordinates are the same.

Think Math

What is the reflection of $A'B'C'D'$ in the y-axis? How do you know?

Guided Practice

Complete.

 Mr. Patterson is building a double bird house, one next to the other. The vertices of the front of one houses have coordinates P (3, 0), Q (5, 3), R (3, 6), and S (1, 3). The front of the other bird house, $P'Q'R'S'$, is a reflection of the first one in the y-axis.

The x-coordinates of vertices of $PQRS$ and $P'Q'R'S'$ are __?__, and their y-coordinates are __?__.

P (3, 0) is mapped onto P' (__?__, __?__).

Q (5, 3) is mapped onto Q' (__?__, __?__).

R (3, 6) is mapped onto R' (__?__, __?__).

S (1, 3) is mapped onto S' (__?__, __?__).

Any point (x, y) is mapped onto (__?__, __?__) when reflected in the y-axis.

Copy each diagram on graph paper and draw the image using the given reflection.

1 In the x-axis

2 In the y-axis

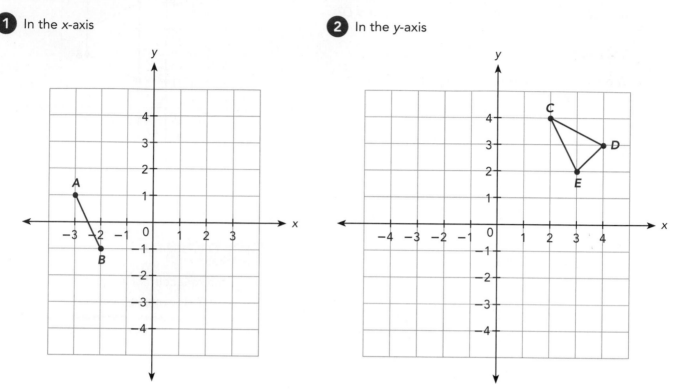

3 Ethan placed six sticks on a table. Three of the sticks, $\overline{PQ}$, $\overline{RS}$, and $\overline{TU}$ are shown on the coordinate plane. The other sticks are images of the three sticks, with $x = 0$ as the line of reflection. On a copy of the graph, draw the sticks not shown on the coordinate plane.

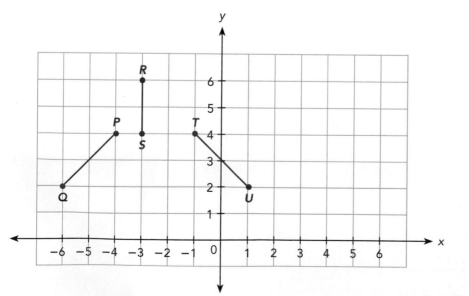

Solve.

4 A pattern is drawn on the coordinate plane and then repeated by first reflecting it in the x-axis and reflecting the original pattern in the y-axis.

a) Copy and complete the table by finding the position of each of the other tiles. On a copy of the coordinate plane, indicate the positions of the images.

Locations	Reflection in the x-axis	Reflection in the y-axis
A (4, 5)	A' ?	A" ?
B (4, 4)	B' ?	B" ?
C (5, 4)	C' ?	C" ?
D (3, 3)	D' ?	D" ?
E (3, 2)	E' ?	E" ?
F (4, 2)	F' ?	F" ?

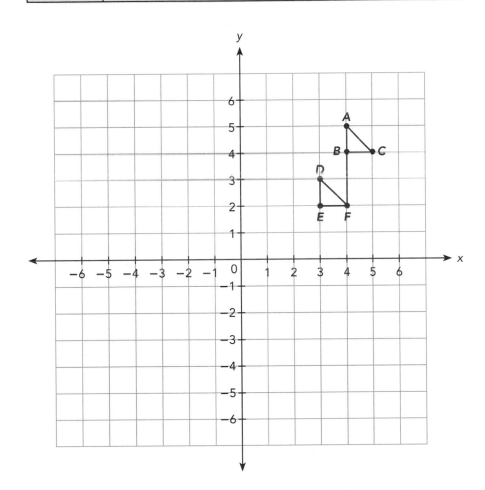

b) Reflect A', B', and C' in the y-axis. What are the coordinates of the image?

c) Reflect A", B", and C" in the x-axis. What are the coordinates of the image? How do these coordinates compare to those in **b)**?

Copy and complete on graph paper.

5 Isabella painted a water color design on graph paper. Some of the points were at A (−4, 8), B (−2, 8), C (−1, 6), D (−2, 4), E (−4, 4), and F (−5, 6). She folded the paper along $y = 3$ to reflect the design. The image points are A', B', C', D', E', and F'.

a) Draw the line $y = 3$.

b) Find the coordinates of A', B', C', D', E', and F'.

c) Draw the image and label A', B', C', D', E', and F'.

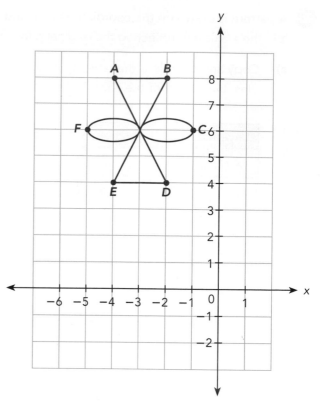

Solve.

6 The image of a butterfly with its wings symmetrically spread out is outlined on the coordinate plane. The uppermost tips of the wings are at (4, 5) and (−2, 5). The lowermost tip of one wing is at (2, 0).

a) Find an equation of the line of reflection.

b) Find the position of the lower tip of the other wing.

7 *Math Journal* Point A' is the image of point A under a reflection. How do you find the line of reflection, without the use of a coordinate grid?

8 A tablecloth has two red dots on it. They are at positions (−3, −1) and (−1, −3). The cloth is folded in half, so that the dots touch each other. What is an equation for the line along which the tablecloth was folded?

9 A leaf is symmetric about its midvein, the central vein that runs the length of the leaf. The leaf is outlined in the coordinate plane with its midvein on the line $y = -x$.

a) A side vein has a length of 6 units on the grid. What is the length of its symmetric counterpart?

b) The endpoint of another side vein is at (4, 3). What is the endpoint of its symmetric counterpart?

8.3 Rotations

Lesson Objectives

- Understand the concept of a rotation.
- Draw images after rotations.
- Find the coordinates of points after rotations.

Vocabulary

rotation	center of rotation
clockwise	counterclockwise
angle of rotation	half turn

Understand the Concept of a Rotation.

Emma is taking a ride on a Ferris wheel. She was at position A five minutes ago. As the Ferris wheel turns, she is now at position A'.

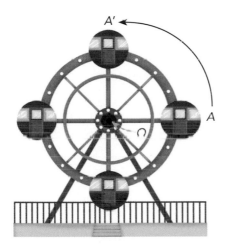

A rotation is sometimes called a "turn."

Emma has gone through a movement known as rotation.

A rotation maps an object about the **center of rotation** through a given angle either **clockwise** (⌐) or **counterclockwise** (⌐).

In the diagram above, point A is rotated about the center O to A'. The **angle of rotation** is $\angle AOA'$. The measure of $\angle AOA'$ is a 90°. The direction of rotation is counterclockwise. The direction opposite to counterclockwise is clockwise. You can say that a rotation of 90° counterclockwise about the point O maps A to A'.

> **Math Note**
>
> Each point and its image are at the same distance from the center of rotation.

Example 10 **Rotate a point.**

A fruit platter is on a rotating plate. A strawberry at position *R* rotates clockwise to *R'*. The center of rotation is the origin, *O*. State the angle of rotation.

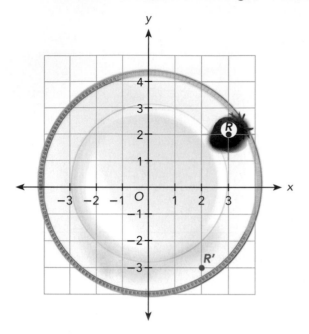

Solution

Join *R* and *R'* to the origin, *O*.

Measure ∠*ROR'*. It is 90°. So, the angle of rotation is 90°.

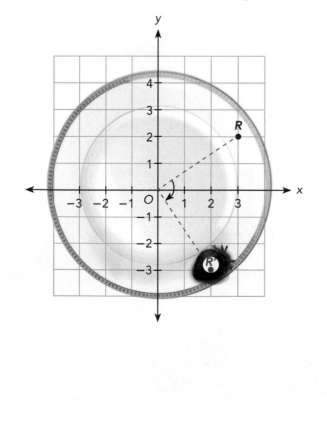

Think Math

If the fruit platter is rotating counterclockwise, what is the angle of rotation? Explain.

Guided Practice

Solve. Show your work.

1 *P* is rotated counterclockwise to *P'* about the origin. State the angle of rotation.

a)

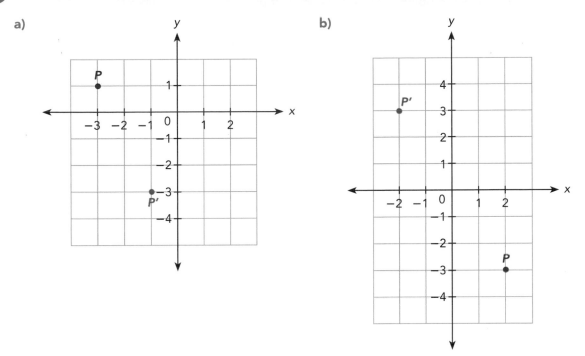

b)

2 The tip of a fan blade for a ceiling fan rotates from position *W* to *W'*. The angle of rotation is 180°.

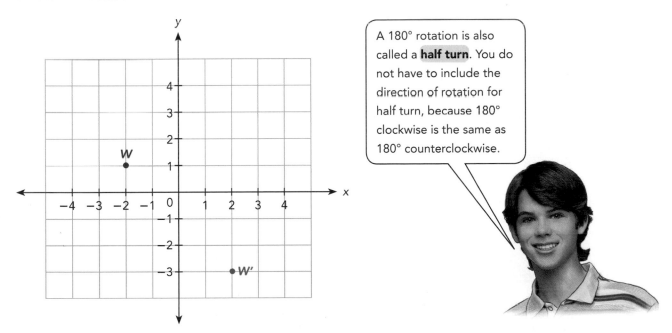

A 180° rotation is also called a **half turn**. You do not have to include the direction of rotation for half turn, because 180° clockwise is the same as 180° counterclockwise.

a) On a copy of the graph, mark and label the center of rotation as *T*.

b) *W'* is rotated 90° clockwise to *W''* about the center *T*. Label *W''* on the graph in **a)**.

Example 11 | **Rotate a line segment.** ──────────────

The windshield wiper on a car is swept through a counterclockwise rotation from *A* to *A'* about the origin, *O*. *B* is the point at (0, 3). If m∠*AOB* = 60°, what is the angle of rotation?

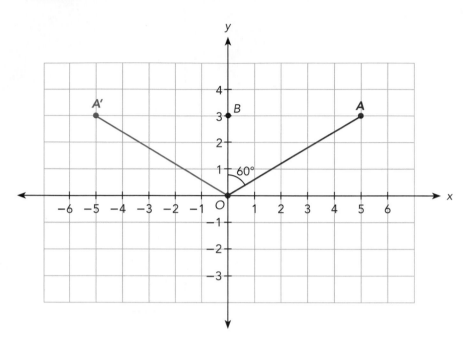

Solution

OA = *OA'*. Triangle *OAA'* is an isosceles triangle with *y*-axis as the line of symmetry.

m∠*AOB* = m∠*A'OB* = 60°

So, the angle of rotation is 120°.

> **Think Math**
>
> Both *A* and *A'* are 3 units from the
> *x*-axis and 6 units from the *y*-axis.
> Can you explain why?

Guided Practice

Complete.

3 The hour hand of a clock turns through an angle from 12 noon to 4 P.M.
State the following.

   a) The center of rotation

   b) The angle and direction of rotation

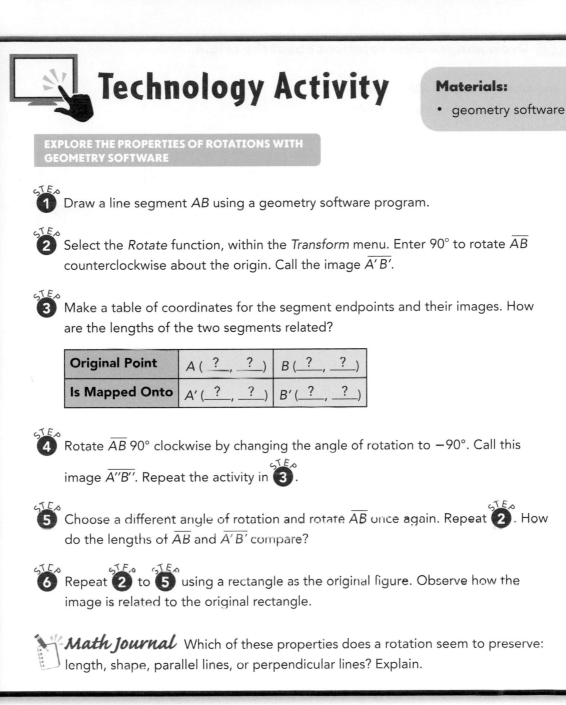

Technology Activity

Materials:
• geometry software

EXPLORE THE PROPERTIES OF ROTATIONS WITH GEOMETRY SOFTWARE

STEP 1 Draw a line segment AB using a geometry software program.

STEP 2 Select the *Rotate* function, within the *Transform* menu. Enter 90° to rotate $\overline{AB}$ counterclockwise about the origin. Call the image $\overline{A'B'}$.

STEP 3 Make a table of coordinates for the segment endpoints and their images. How are the lengths of the two segments related?

Original Point	A (? , ?)	B (? , ?)
Is Mapped Onto	A' (? , ?)	B' (? , ?)

STEP 4 Rotate $\overline{AB}$ 90° clockwise by changing the angle of rotation to −90°. Call this image $\overline{A''B''}$. Repeat the activity in **STEP 3**.

STEP 5 Choose a different angle of rotation and rotate $\overline{AB}$ once again. Repeat **STEP 2**. How do the lengths of $\overline{AB}$ and $\overline{A'B'}$ compare?

STEP 6 Repeat **STEP 2** to **STEP 5** using a rectangle as the original figure. Observe how the image is related to the original rectangle.

✎ *Math Journal* Which of these properties does a rotation seem to preserve: length, shape, parallel lines, or perpendicular lines? Explain.

Draw Images After Rotations.

In the activity, you may have observed the following:

Rotations preserve shape and size. They also preserve parallelism and perpendicularity.

You have seen how a line segment can be rotated. A rotation can be described as a transformation that rotates all points on a line or figure clockwise or counterclockwise angle about the center of rotation. You will see in the next example how to find the image of a figure after a rotation.

Example 12 **Draw images after rotations about the origin.**

Draw and label the image *A'B'C'* under each rotation. Then complete the table of coordinates.

A triangular flag *ABC* is connected to a rotating shaft. The shaft is positioned at the origin, *O*.

Original Point	A (2, 1)	B (4, 0)	C (2, 0)
Is Mapped Onto	A' (?, ?)	B' (?, ?)	C' (?, ?)

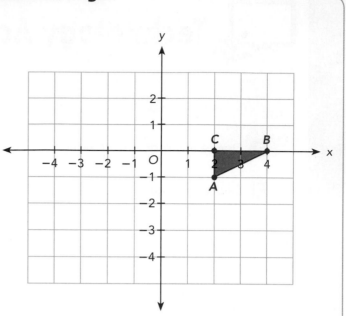

a) 90° clockwise about the origin

Solution

The steps to rotate point *A* are as follows:

STEP 1 Join *O* to *A*.

STEP 2 With *O* as the center, measure 90° clockwise from $\overline{OA}$.

STEP 3 Mark *A'* such that *OA'* = *OA*.

STEP 4 Repeat the steps for points *B* and *C* to locate the images *B'* and *C'*. Join the points to complete the image.

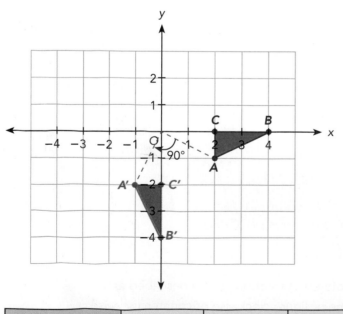

Original Point	A (2, −1)	B (4, 0)	C (2, 0)
Is Mapped Onto	A' (−1, −2)	B' (0, −4)	C' (0, −2)

b) 180° about the origin, O

Original Point	A (2, −1)	B (4, 0)	C (2, 0)
Is Mapped Onto	A″ (?, ?)	B″ (?, ?)	C″ (?, ?)

Solution

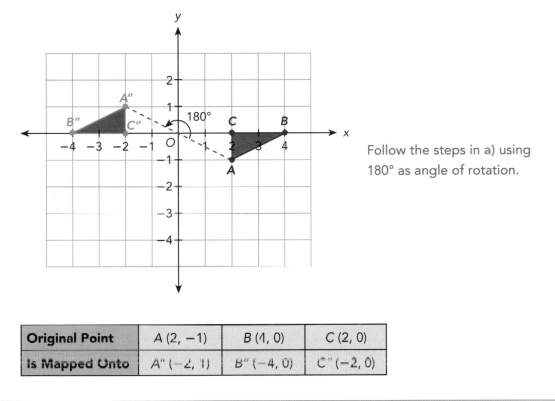

Follow the steps in **a)** using 180° as angle of rotation.

Original Point	A (2, −1)	B (4, 0)	C (2, 0)
Is Mapped Onto	A″ (−2, 1)	B″ (−4, 0)	C″ (−2, 0)

Guided Practice

Copy and complete on graph paper.

4 A rotation of △ABC 90° clockwise about the origin, O, produces the image △A′B′C′.
Draw and label the image △A′B′C′.

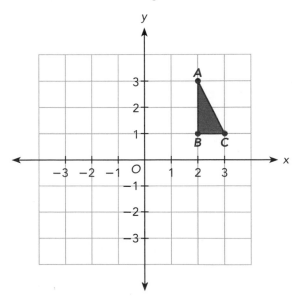

Original Point	Is Mapped Onto
A (2, 3)	A′ (_?_, _?_)
B (2, 1)	B′ (_?_, _?_)
C (3, 1)	C′ (_?_, _?_)

△ABC is read as "triangle ABC."

Find the Coordinates of Points After Rotations.

You have seen that a point can be rotated about a center through a certain angle.

Take the case of the Ferris wheel. If Emma is at coordinates (2, 0), a rotation 90° counterclockwise about the origin, O, will take her to (0, 2). A rotation of 180° about the origin would result in an image at (−2, 0). A rotation 90° clockwise about the origin would produce an image at (0, −2).

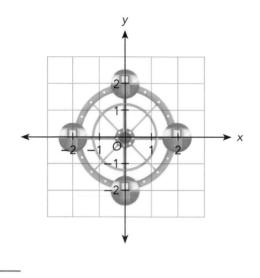

Example 13 | **Find the coordinates of points after rotations.**

A rod is rotating counterclockwise about the origin, O. A square flag is connected to the rotating rod. The position of the flag is at A (2, 2), B (3, 3), C (4, 2), and D (3, 1) as shown. Find the coordinates of the image under each angle of rotation.

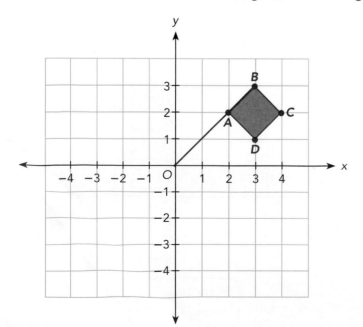

a) 180°

Solution

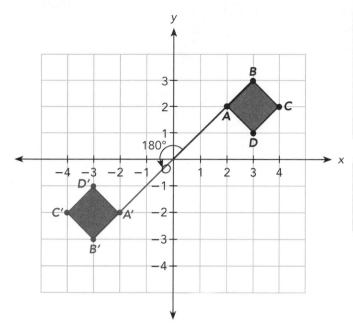

Original Point	Is Mapped Onto
A (2, 2)	A' (−2, −2)
B (3, 3)	B' (−3, −3)
C (4, 2)	C' (−4, −2)
D (3, 1)	D' (−3, −1)

Notice that a point P (x, y) when rotated 180° about the origin is mapped onto the point P' (−x, −y).

b) 270° in a counterclockwise direction

Solution

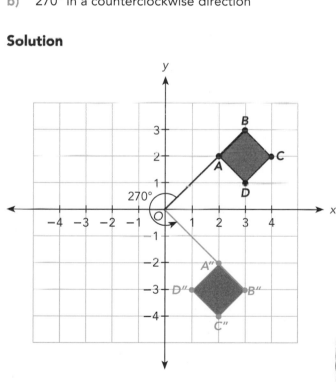

Original Point	Is Mapped Onto
A (2, 2)	A" (2, −2)
B (3, 3)	B" (3, −3)
C (4, 2)	C" (2, −4)
D (3, 1)	D" (1, −3)

Because the sum of all angles around a point is 360°, a 90° clockwise rotation is the same as a 270° counterclockwise rotation. You can measure 90° in a clockwise direction, when you use a protractor.

Guided Practice

Copy and complete on graph paper.

5 An animation artist draws a fish on the coordinate plane and marks the points *A*, *B*, *C*, and *D*. Then the artist rotates the fish 180° about the origin, *O*. Complete the table of coordinates to show the coordinates of the image points *A'*, *B'*, *C'*, and *D'*.

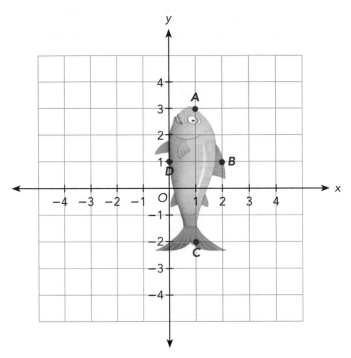

Original Point	Is Mapped Onto
A (1, 3)	A' (__?__, __?__)
B (2, 1)	B' (__?__, __?__)
C (1, −2)	C' (__?__, __?__)
D (0, 1)	D' (__?__, __?__)

6 *DEFG* is rotated 90° counterclockwise about *O*.

a) Draw and label the image *D'E'F'G'*.

b) Complete the table of coordinates for *DEFG* and its image *D'E'F'G'*.

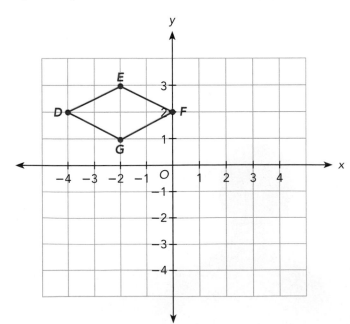

Original Point	Is Mapped Onto
D (−4, 2)	D' (__?__, __?__)
E (−2, 3)	E' (__?__, __?__)
F (0, 2)	F' (__?__, __?__)
G (−2, 1)	G' (__?__, __?__)

Practice 8.3

Solve. Show your work.

1 A rotation of point *P* clockwise about *O* maps onto *P'*. State the angle of rotation.

a)

b)

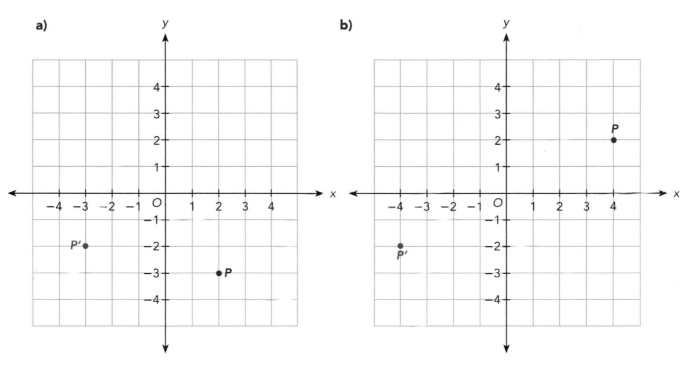

2 $\overline{ON}$ is rotated about the origin, *O* to form the image $\overline{ON'}$. State the angle and direction of each rotation.

a)

b)

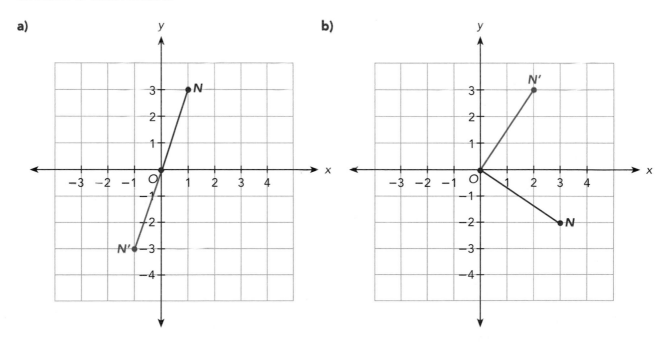

Solve. Show your work.

3 At an amusement park, Olivia is riding the carousel at point *P*. She is rotated from *P* by each of the following rotations. Mark and label her position after each rotation from *P* on a copy of the graph.

a) *A*: 90° counterclockwise about the origin

b) *B*: 90° clockwise about the origin

c) *C*: 270° counterclockwise about the origin

d) *D*: Half turn about the origin

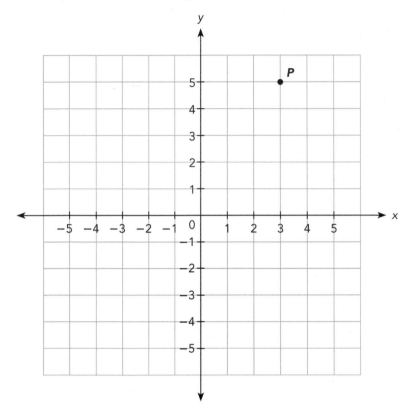

4 A cam of an automobile rotates about a shaft at the origin, *O*. Point *P* on the cam rotates to point *Q*.

a) Describe the rotation.

b) A point (−5, 4) undergoes the same rotation. Find the coordinates of the image.

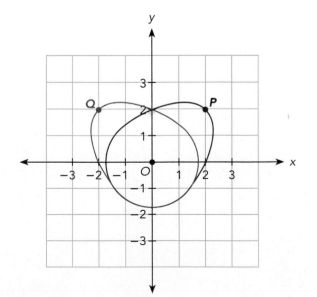

5 The hinges on a door are at (0, 0), looking down from above. Its keyhole is at position (2, 4) when the door is closed. The door swings open. Find the position of the keyhole under each rotation below.

a) 90° clockwise

b) 90°counterclockwise

c) 180°

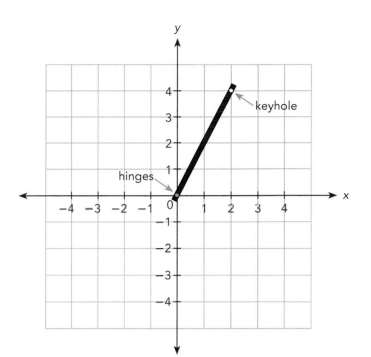

6 Pentagon *ABCDE* is drawn on the coordinate plane.

a) *ABCDE* is rotated 90° clockwise about the origin, *O*. Draw and label the image *A'B'C'D'E'*.

b) State the coordinates of *A'*, *B'*, *C'*, *D'*, and *E'*.

c) *ABCDE* is rotated 90° counterclockwise about the origin, *O*. Draw the image *A"B"C"D"E"*. State the coordinates for *A"B"C"D"E"*.

d) How are *A'B'C'D'E'* and *A"B"C"D"E"* related?

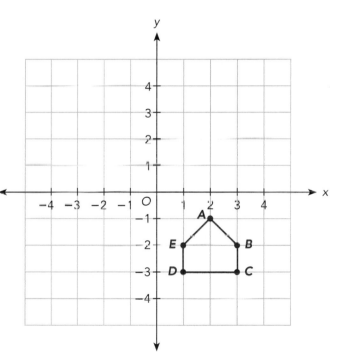

7 A regular hexagon *ABCDEF* is rotated about its center, *O*, so that its appearance stays the same, but the vertices are rotated to different positions. For example in one rotation, A moves to B, B to C, and so on. Which clockwise rotations will cause this effect?

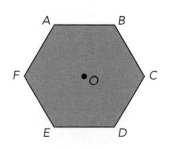

8 *Math Journal* Which points are invariant under a rotation? Explain.

8.4 Dilations

Lesson Objectives

- Understand the concept of a dilation.
- Find the dimensions of figures after dilations.
- Draw images after dilations.
- Find the center of dilations.

Understand the Concept of a **Dilation**.

Suppose a picture and its frame are both squares. Each side of the picture is 4 units long. The picture frame has sides that are 8 units long.

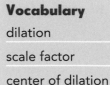

The shape of the picture frame's border is said to be a dilation of the picture's border. The shape of the two figures is the same, but the side lengths of the picture frame are twice the side lengths of the picture. A dilation maps an object onto an image by scaling its size up or down.

A dilation with center O maps a point P of a figure to the corresponding point P' of the image. The distance OP' is k times the distance OP, where k is the **scale factor** ($k \neq 0$). The length of each side of the image is also k times the length of the corresponding side in the figure.

Corresponding sides of the two figures consist of a side and its image after a transformation.

$$\text{Scale factor} = \frac{\text{Distance from the center of dilation to image}}{\text{Distance from the center of dilation to original point}}$$

In the diagram, point **A** on the picture is mapped onto point **A'** on the picture frame about the **center of dilation** O. Points O, **A**, and **A'** are on the same straight line.

Example 14 **Understand the concept of dilation.**

Mrs. Tonelli cuts three triangles from colored papers and pastes them on a board. Which triangles are dilations of one another?

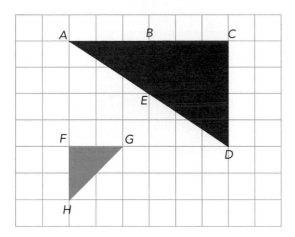

Solution

△ABE and △ACD are dilations of one another, because they have a center of dilation, A, and the sides of △ACD are twice as long as the sides of △ABE.

△FGH is not a dilation of the other two triangles, since it does not share a center of dilation with them.

Guided Practice

Solve.

1 Which triangles are dilations of one another? Explain.

a)

b)

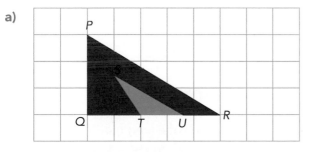

Find the Dimensions of Figures After Dilations.

Look again at the picture and picture frame.

The sides of the picture when enlarged to twice their length will be the same size as the picture frame. The scale factor of this dilation is 2.

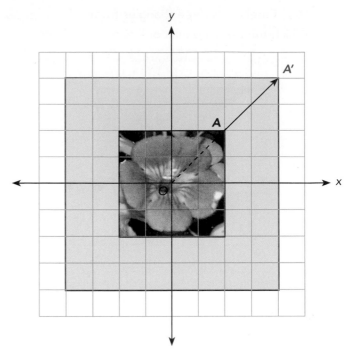

To find the scale factor, compare the lengths of a side and its image. The ratio of the image length to the original length is the scale factor.

Scale factor = $\dfrac{\text{Length of picture frame}}{\text{Length of picture}}$

$= \dfrac{8}{4}$

$= 2$

The center of dilation O and points **A** and **A'** are on the same straight line, and

Scale factor = $\dfrac{\text{Distance from center of dilation to a point on image}}{\text{Distance from center of dilation to corresponding point of figure}}$

$= \dfrac{OA'}{OA}$

$= 2$

Supposed you do not know the length of the picture frame but you know that the picture has side lengths of 12 inches. The picture is dilated with center O and scale factor 2. This forms the image of the picture frame.

Length of picture frame = Length of picture · Scale factor

$= 12 \cdot 2$

$= 24$ in.

So, you can say that the lengths of the sides of the picture frame are 24 inches.

This answer is reasonable, because a dilation with a scale factor greater than 1 enlarges a figure. A dilation with a scale factor between 0 and 1 reduces a figure.

Think Math

If you know the length of the sides of the picture frame is 16 inches, how can you find the side length of the picture?

Example 15 **Find the dimensions of figures after dilations.**

Mrs. Marquez is making pancakes on a griddle. At first, the pancake batter forms a 4-inch circle. It flows to become a bigger circle. The scale factor of the dilation is 1.5. Find the diameter of the pancake.

Solution

The pancake is a dilated image of the pancake batter.

Diameter of pancake = Diameter of pancake batter · Scale factor

$$= 4 \cdot 1.5$$
$$= 6 \text{ in.}$$

The diameter of the pancake is 6 inches.

Guided Practice

Copy and complete.

2 A rectangle has coordinates A (5, 1), B (3, 1), C (3, 4), and D (5, 4).

a) Find the length and width of $ABCD$.

The length of $ABCD$ is __?__ units. Its width is __?__ units.

b) Find the length and width of the image of $ABCD$ when dilated with scale factor 2.

Length of image: __?__ · __?__ = __?__ units

Width of image: __?__ · __?__ = __?__ units

c) Find the length and width of the image of $ABCD$ when dilated with scale factor $\frac{1}{2}$.

Length of image: __?__ · __?__ = __?__ units

Width of image: __?__ · __?__ = __?__ units

d) What are the coordinates of the image rectangle under each dilation if the center of dilation is at the origin?

	Scale Factor 2	Scale Factor $\frac{1}{2}$
A maps onto	(_?_, _?_)	(_?_, _?_)
B maps onto	(_?_, _?_)	(_?_, _?_)
C maps onto	(_?_, _?_)	(_?_, _?_)
D maps onto	(_?_, _?_)	(_?_, _?_)

You may want to draw the rectangle and its images on the coordinate plane to solve **c)**.

Technology Activity

Materials:
- geometry software

EXPLORE THE PROPERTIES OF DILATIONS WITH GEOMETRY SOFTWARE

STEP 1 Draw a line segment *AB* using a geometry software program.

STEP 2 Select the *Dilate* function, within the *Transform* menu. Enter the scale factor 2 to dilate the line segment about the origin. Record your results in a table of coordinates.

Original Point	?	?
Is Mapped Onto	?	?

STEP 3 Describe how the image of $\overline{AB}$ is related to $\overline{AB}$.

STEP 4 Repeat **STEP 1** to **STEP 3** using a rectangle as the original figure. For **STEP 2**, enter the scale factor $\frac{1}{2}$.

STEP 5 Repeat **STEP 1** to **STEP 3** using a rectangle as the original figure. For **STEP 2**, enter the scale factor −2.

Math Journal Observe any changes in the size or shape of the figure after the dilation. Which of these properties does a dilation preserve: lengths, shape, parallel lines, or perpendicular lines? Explain.

Draw Images After Dilations.

You have seen that the size of a figure can be reduced or enlarged depending on the scale factor *k*. Each length of the image is *k* times that of the original figure.

Think Math

If the scale factor of a dilation is *k* = 1, how does the size of the image compare with that of the object?

From the activity, you have observed that a dilation preserves the shape of a figure, but it may change the figure's size. It also preserves parallelism and perpendicularity.

If the absolute value of the scale factor *k* > 1, the image is larger than the original figure.

If the absolute value of the scale factor *k* is between 0 and 1, the image is smaller than the original figure.

A scale factor of *k* = 0 is not allowed.

Example 16 **Draw images after dilations.**

Draw △ABC and each of its images on a coordinate plane.

△ABC has coordinates A (1, 1), B (2, 1), and C (1, 2). It is transformed by each of the following dilations with their centers at the origin, O.

a)   △ABC is mapped onto △A′B′C′ by a dilation with scale factor 3.

Solution

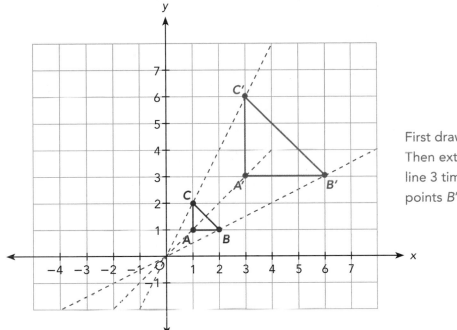

First draw a line from O to A. Then extend the length of the line 3 times to point A′. You find points B′ and C′ in the same way.

Check that each side length of △A′B′C′ is 3 times the corresponding side length of △ABC.

Caution ///////

Only if the center of the dilation is at the origin can you multiply the coordinates of the original figure by the scale factor to find the coordinates of the image. When using a different center, you may want to draw the image to find its coordinates.

Continue on next page

b) △ABC is mapped onto △A″B″C″ by a dilation with scale factor −1.

Solution

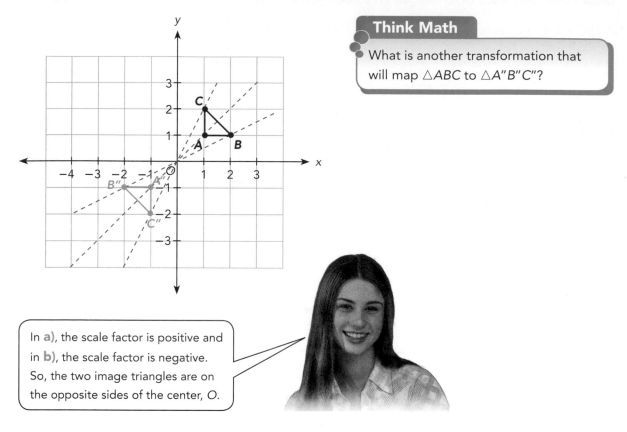

> **Think Math**
>
> What is another transformation that will map △ABC to △A″B″C″?

In **a)**, the scale factor is positive and in **b)**, the scale factor is negative. So, the two image triangles are on the opposite sides of the center, O.

Guided Practice

Copy and complete on graph paper.

3 The management of a swimming pool built a springboard above the pool. The height of the springboard is a dilation of the depth of the pool with center at the origin, O and scale factor $-\frac{1}{3}$.

The depth of the pool is 4.5 meters, represented by $\overline{ST}$ on the coordinate plane. The floor is represented by the positive x-axis and the surface of the water is represented by the negative x-axis. Draw the location and height of the stand for the springboard, $\overline{UV}$, on a copy of this vertical cross section of the pool.

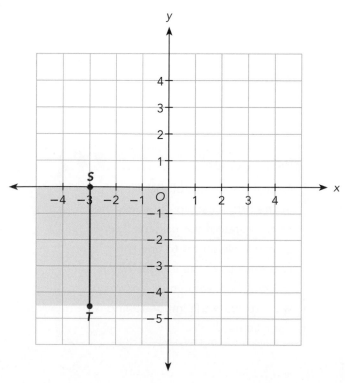

Find the Center of a Dilation.

You have learned how to find the scale factor of a dilation from a figure and its image. You can also find the center of the dilation from the same information.

In two figures related by a dilation, suppose you are given two points A and B of the figure and their images A' and B'. Use these steps to find the center of the dilation.

STEP 1 Draw a line through A and A'. Draw another line through B and B'.

STEP 2 Find where the two lines intersect. This is the center of the dilation.

The following examples that map $\overline{AB}$ onto its image by a dilation illustrate this.

A dilation in which $k > 0$

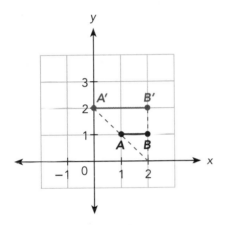

The intersection of lines AA' and BB' is at (2, 0).
So, the center of this dilation is (2, 0).

A dilation in which $k < 0$

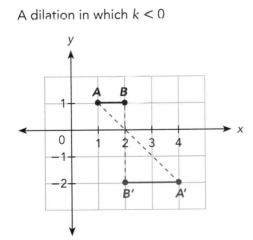

> ### Math Note
>
> The scale factor of a dilation also depends on whether it is positive or negative, that is, whether the image of each point is on the same side of the center as the original point or not.

The intersection of lines AA' and BB' is at (2, 0).
So, the center of this dilation is (2, 0).

The magnitude of the scale factor can be found by either of the following:

$$\text{Scale factor's magnitude} = \frac{\text{Distance from center of dilation to image}}{\text{Distance from center of dilation to original point}}$$

$$\text{Scale factor's magnitude} = \frac{\text{Length of image segment}}{\text{Length of original segment}}$$

Example 17 **Find the center of a dilation.**

The tables show the coordinates for each triangle and their corresponding images. The triangles are each mapped onto their images by a dilation. Draw each triangle and its image on a coordinate plane. Then mark and label *P* as the center of dilation. Find the scale factor for each triangle. Then describe the transformation.

a)

Original Point	A (0, 1)	B (4, 1)	C (4, 3)
Is Mapped Onto	A′ (−1, −1)	B′ (1, −1)	C′ (1, 0)

Solution

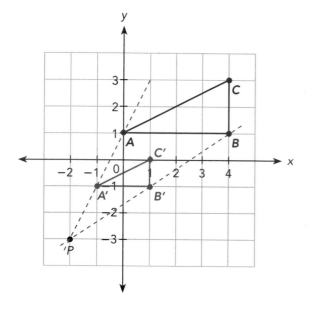

You can also join *C* to *C′* and find the point of intersection with another line to locate the center of dilation.

> The image is smaller than the original figure when the scale factor is between −1 and 1.

A is joined to *A′* and *B* is joined to *B′*. Both lines intersect at the center of dilation, which is at (−2, −3).

Scale factor $= \dfrac{A'B'}{AB} = \dfrac{2}{4} = \dfrac{1}{2}$

So, △*ABC* is mapped onto △*A′B′C′* by a dilation with center *P*, (−2, −3) and scale factor $\dfrac{1}{2}$.

Think Math

There are six ratios that you can use to find the scale factor when △*ABC* is mapped onto △*A′B′C′*. List the five other ratios.

b)

Original Point	D (−1, 7)	E (−1, 3)	F (−3, 5)
Is Mapped Onto	D' (2, 1)	E' (2, 3)	F' (3, 2)

Solution

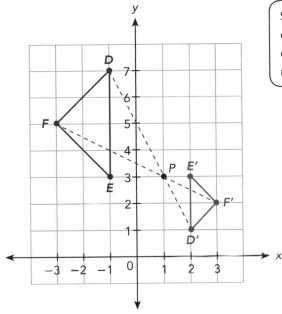

Since △DEF and its image are on opposite sides of the center of dilation. The scale factor will be negative.

D is joined to D' and F is joined to F'. Both lines intersect at the center of dilation which is at (1, 3).

$$\text{Scale factor} = -\frac{D'E'}{DE} = -\frac{2}{4} = -\frac{1}{2}$$

So, △DEF is mapped onto △D'E'F' by a dilation with center P (1, 3) and scale factor $-\frac{1}{2}$.

Guided Practice

Use graph paper. Use 1 grid square on both axes to represent 1 unit for the interval from −7 to 4.

 The triangles are each mapped onto their images by a dilation. Draw each triangle and its image on a coordinate plane. Then mark and label C as the center of dilation. Find the scale factor for each triangle.

a)

Original Point	S (1, 3)	T (0, 1)	U (2, 0)
Is Mapped Onto	S' (−5, −3)	T' (−3, 1)	U' (−7, 3)

b)

Original Point	P (1, 3)	Q (1, 2)	R (2, 1)
Is Mapped Onto	P' (−3, 1)	Q' (−3, −2)	R' (0, −5)

Practice 8.4

Tell whether each transformation is a dilation. Explain.

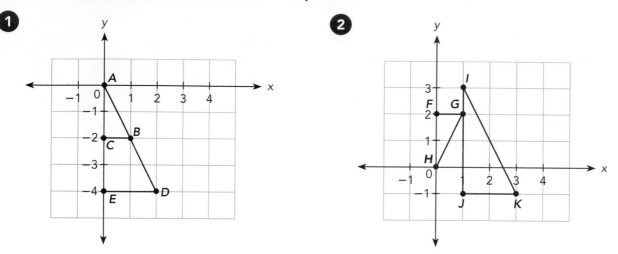

Solve. Show your work.

3 Nikita wants to make a mosaic for a T-shirt's design. She makes some dilated copies of a drawing with a photocopier. The drawing is 6 inches by 4 inches. Find the length and width of each copy with the scale factor given in **a)** to **d)**. State whether each copy is an enlargement or reduction of the drawing.

a) 1.5

b) 2

c) $\dfrac{1}{4}$

d) 140%

Copy and complete on graph paper.

4 Timothy uses a lens to view a 2-inch pencil that is represented by $\overline{AB}$ on the coordinate plane. $\overline{AB}$ is mapped onto $\overline{A'B'}$ by a dilation with center at the origin, O. Draw each image for the given scale factor.

a) Scale factor −0.5

b) Scale factor 0.5

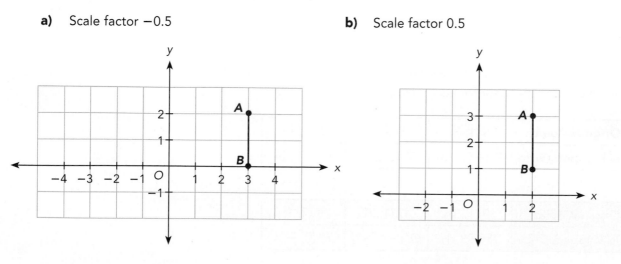

5 Each figure is each mapped onto its image by a dilation with its center at the origin, O. On a copy of the coordinate plane, draw each image.

a) Triangle *LMN* is mapped onto triangle *L'M'N'* with scale factor $-\frac{1}{2}$

b) Rectangle *PQRS* is mapped onto rectangle *P'Q'R'S'* with scale factor 3

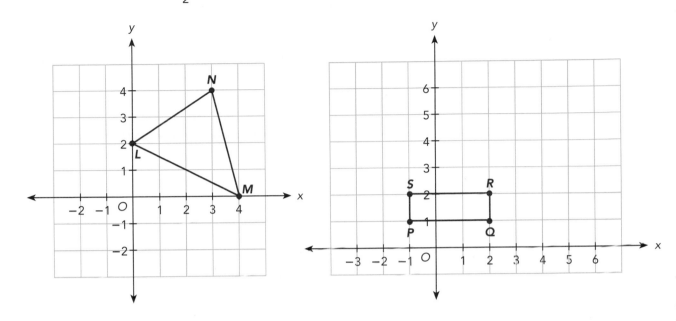

Solve on graph paper. Show your work.

6 In a room, a flashlight is used to illuminate objects and cast their shadows on a wall. Each shadow is a dilation of the object's profile.

a) A pen at point (4, 2) is mapped onto its shadow at (6, 3) with the origin as the center of dilation. Find the scale factor.

b) The shadow of a circular disc has its center at (6, 2) and radius 3 units. The circular disc has center at (2, 2) and radius 1 unit. Find the center of dilation.

7 Each figure is mapped into its image by a dilation. Draw each figure and its image on the coordinate plane. Then mark and label *C* as the center of dilation. Find the scale factor for each figure. Use 1 grid square on both axes to represent 1 unit for the interval from −8 to 6.

a) Quadrilateral *WXYZ*

Original Point	W (−2, −1)	X (−1, −1)	Y (−1, 1)	Z (−2, 1)
Is Mapped Onto	W' (−6.5, 0.5)	X' (−4, 0.5)	Y' (−4, 5.5)	Z' (−6.5, 5.5)

b) Triangle *PQR*

Original Point	P (3, 1)	Q (5, −2)	R (6, 4)
Is Mapped Onto	P' (0, 2.5)	Q' (−1, 4)	R' (−1.5, 1)

8  *Math Journal* What are the invariant points of a dilation? Explain.

8.5 Comparing Transformations

Lesson Objective

- Compare translations, reflections, rotations, and dilations.

Materials:

- geometry software

COMPARE TRANSFORMATIONS WITH GEOMETRY SOFTWARE

STEP 1 Draw two line segments intersecting at a common endpoint using a geometry software program. Call the angle formed ∠AOB.

STEP 2 Measure their lengths and the angles they make with the x-axis. Record your results in the "before" cells of the second column in the following table.

Description	Translation	Reflection	Rotation	Dilation
Length of $\overline{AO}$ before transformation	?	?	?	?
Length of $\overline{AO}$ after transformation	?	?	?	?
Measure of ∠AOB before transformation	?	?	?	?
Measure of ∠AOB after transformation	?	?	?	?

STEP 3 Translate the angle in both the horizontal and vertical directions. Complete the second column of the table.

STEP 4 Reflect the angle in either the x- or y-axis. Complete the third column of the table.

STEP 5 Rotate the angle about the origin. Complete the fourth column of the table.

STEP 6 Dilate the angle by any nonzero scale factor and with any center. Complete the last column of the table.

STEP 7 Note which transformations preserve angle measure. Why does this guarantee that perpendicular lines will be preserved? Why does this guarantee that parallel lines will be preserved?

Math Journal Compare translations, reflections, rotations, and dilations. Discuss which ones preserve lengths, angle measures, perpendicular lines, and parallel lines.

Compare Translations, Reflections, Rotations, and Dilations.

Of the four types of transformation you studied, all of them preserve shape, angle measures, parallel lines and perpendicular lines. But only three preserve lengths: translations, reflections, and rotations. These three types of transformation are called **isometries**.

Dilations do not preserve length, unless the scale factor is 1 or −1. A scale factor with absolute value greater than 1 enlarges the original length but reduces the original length if the absolute value is less than 1.

The word "isometry" comes from two Greek words: *iso-* meaning "equal," and *-metry* meaning "measure."

Think Math

If a line segment is first rotated 90° counterclockwise about the origin, then dilated with center at the origin and scale factor −0.5, how would the lengths of the line segment and its image be related? Justify your answer.

Example 18 Compare transformations of plane figures.

Triangle A is mapped onto triangle B and triangle C.

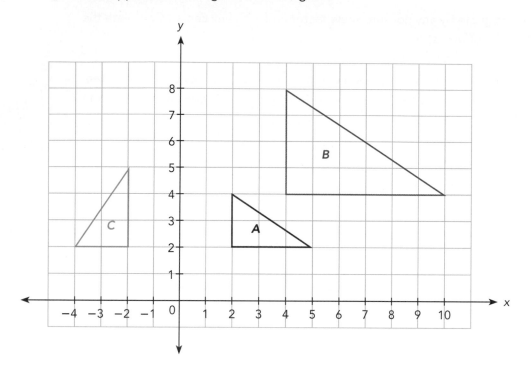

a)   What is the transformation that maps triangle A onto triangle B?

Solution

Triangles A and B have different sizes, but the same shape, so look for a dilation.

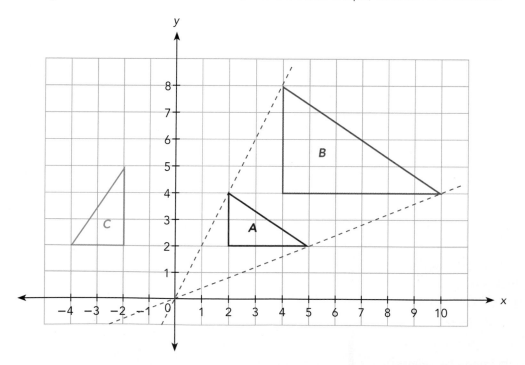

The lines passing through the corresponding vertices of triangles A and B, intersect at the origin, (0, 0). So, the center of dilation is the origin.

Scale factor = $\dfrac{\text{Length of vertical side of triangle } B}{\text{Length of vertical side of triangle } A}$

$\qquad\quad = \dfrac{4}{2}$

$\qquad\quad = 2$

You need to draw lines through two pairs of corresponding vertices and find their intersection. This is the center of the dilation.

Triangle A is mapped onto triangle B by a dilation with center at the origin and scale factor 2.

b) What is the transformation that maps triangle A onto triangle C?

Solution

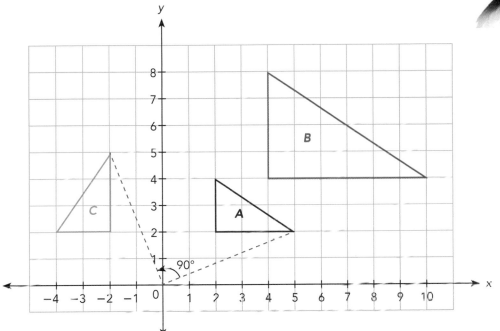

Triangles A and C have the same size and shape. However, triangle A is "turned" to obtain triangle C. So, the transformation is a rotation. You will need to find the center, the angle, and the direction of rotation.

Joining the corresponding vertices, A_1 (5, 2) and C_1 (−2, 5) of triangles A and C to the origin, O, you can see that $OA_1 = AC_1$. So, the origin is the center of rotation. The angle of rotation is the measure of $\angle A_1OC_1$, which is 90°.

Triangle A is mapped onto triangle C by a rotation 90° counterclockwise about the origin.

Continue on next page

c) Compare the two transformations in terms of the shape and size of the triangles.

Solution

The dilation preserves the shape, but not the size of triangle A. The rotation preserves the shape and size.

Guided Practice

Solve on graph paper. Show your work.

1 △ABC is mapped onto △PQR, △LMN, and △XYZ as shown on the coordinate plane. State which transformation was used to obtain each image. Justify your answers.

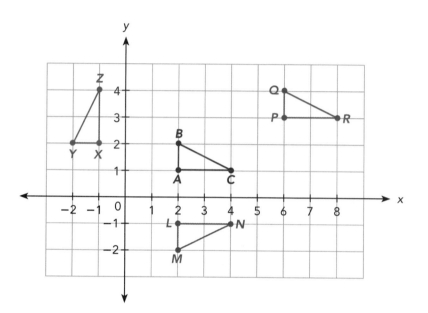

a) What transformation maps △ABC onto △PQR?

b) What transformation maps △ABC onto △LMN?

c) What transformation maps △ABC onto △XYZ?

d) Compare the three transformations in terms of preserving lengths and angle measures.

You can use two vertices and their images to identify a transformation of one triangle onto another. But you should also use the third vertex and its image to check that other points of the figure are related by this transformation.

Copy and complete on graph paper.

1 A curtain is made from a printed fabric with many pentagonal figures on it. One of the pentagons has coordinates *A* (1, 2), *B* (3, 2), *C* (4, 4), *D* (2, 6), and *E* (0, 4). Four other pentagons are images of *ABCDE* after each of the transformations in **a)** to **d)**.

a) *ABCDE* is mapped onto *FGHIJ* by a translation of 8 units down. Draw *FGHIJ*.

b) *ABCDE* is mapped onto *KLMNP* by a reflection about the *y*-axis. Draw *KLMNP*.

c) *ABCDE* is mapped onto *QRSTU* by a rotation 90° clockwise about the origin, *O*. Draw *QRSTU*.

d) *ABCDE* is mapped onto *VWXYZ* by a dilation with center at the origin and scale factor 1.5. Draw *VWXYZ*.

e) Compare the four transformations in terms of lengths and angle measures of the pentagons.

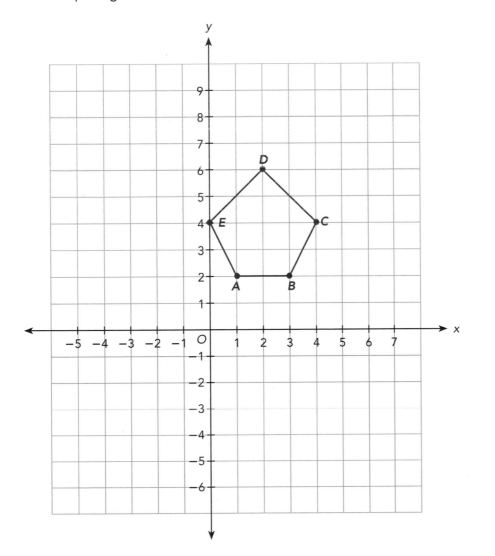

2 Quadrilateral *P* with coordinates (3, 2), (4, 5), (5, 5), and (6, 3) is mapped onto quadrilateral *Q* and *R* shown on the coordinate plane.

a) Describe the transformation from *P* to *Q*.

b) Quadrilateral *P* is mapped onto *R* by a half turn about the origin, *O*. Draw quadrilateral *R*.

c) The transformation that maps quadrilateral *P* onto quadrilateral *R* can be described in another way. Describe the transformation.

d) Compare the transformations in **a)** to **c)** in terms of the preservation of the shape and size of quadrilateral *P*.

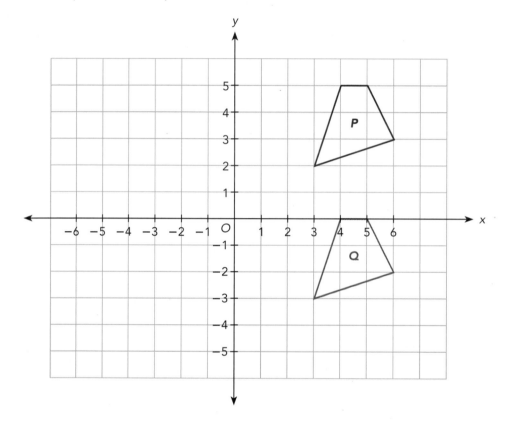

3 There are three arrow signs *J*, *K*, and *L* on a street. Jennifer is standing at the origin, *O*.

a) Arrow *J* tells Jennifer where the Kodak Theatre is. Arrow *K* is the reflection of arrow *J* in the line *y* = 3. Label arrow *J*.

b) Jennifer sees arrow *L* that is an image of arrow *J*. Describe the transformation that maps arrow *J* onto arrow *L*.

c) Compare the two transformations in terms of the shape and size of the arrows.

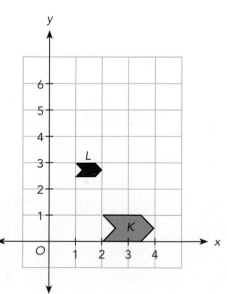

Solve on graph paper. Show your work.

4 Triangle *ABC* is mapped onto triangle *A'B'C'* and triangle *A"B"C"* as shown on the coordinate plane.

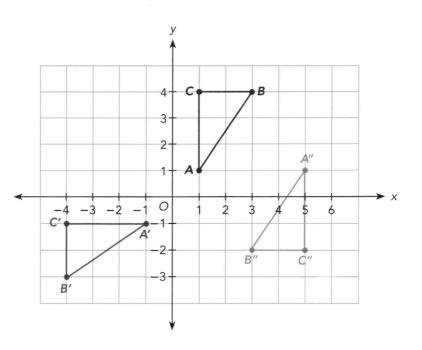

a) Triangle *ABC* is mapped onto triangle *A'B'C'* by a reflection in the line *l*. On a copy of the graph, draw line *l* and label its equation.

b) Triangle *ABC* is mapped onto triangle *A"B"C"* by a dilation with scale factor −1. Mark and label *T* as the center of dilation on the coordinate plane in **a)**.

c) Describe another transformation that maps triangle *ABC* onto triangle *A"B"C"*.

d) Compare the transformations that mapped triangle *ABC* onto triangle *A'B'C'* and *A"B"C"* in terms of preservation of the shape and size of triangle *ABC*.

5 △*ABC* is mapped onto △*A'B'C'* and △*A"B"C"*. The table of coordinates for the triangles is shown.

Original Point	Is Mapped Onto	Is Mapped Onto
A (−4, 3)	A' (4, 3)	A" (−1.5, 7)
B (−3, −1)	B' (3, 1)	B" (−3, 4)
C (−2, −3)	C' (2, 3)	C" (−4.5, 7)

a) Draw △*ABC*, △*A'B'C'*, and △*A"B"C"*. Use 1 grid square on both axes to represent 1 unit for the interval from −5 to 7.

b) △*ABC* is mapped onto △*A'B'C'* by a dilation with center at the origin, *O*, and scale factor −1. Describe another transformation that maps △*ABC* onto △*A'B'C'*.

c) What is the transformation that maps △*ABC* onto △*A"B"C"*?

d) Compare the transformations that mapped △*ABC* onto △*A'B'C'* and △*A"B"C"* in terms of preservation of the shape and size of △*ABC*.

6 *Math Journal* How do you describe a transformation that maps an equilateral triangle onto itself using each of the following: translation, reflection, rotation, and dilation?

Brain @ Work

1. A two-blade table fan is coded with two digits for easy identification. Each blade in the horizontal position shown in the picture is painted with the two-digit number. What number should be used so that when the blades make a half turn, the number will be read correctly?

2. Line P with equation $y = x + 2$ maps onto line Q with equation $y = -x + 4$.

   a) Describe a reflection that maps line P onto line Q.

   b) Describe a rotation that maps line P onto line Q.

3. Triangle ABC is mapped onto triangle XYZ by a rotation 270° clockwise about center P. Both triangles are shown on the coordinate plane below. On a copy of the graph, mark and label the center P. What are the coordinates of center P? Explain how you found your answer.

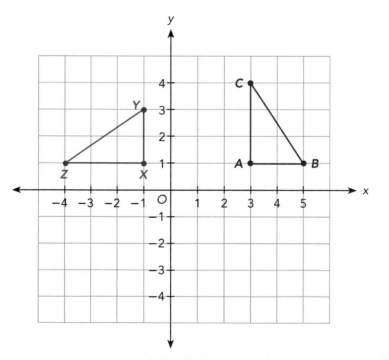

4. After a rain, a circular puddle shrunk steadily for two days in the sun. The puddle was 8 inches in diameter initially. It shrunk by a scale factor each day. After two days, the diameter of the puddle was 6.48 inches. What is the scale factor of dilation? Explain how you found your answer.

Chapter Wrap Up

Concept Map

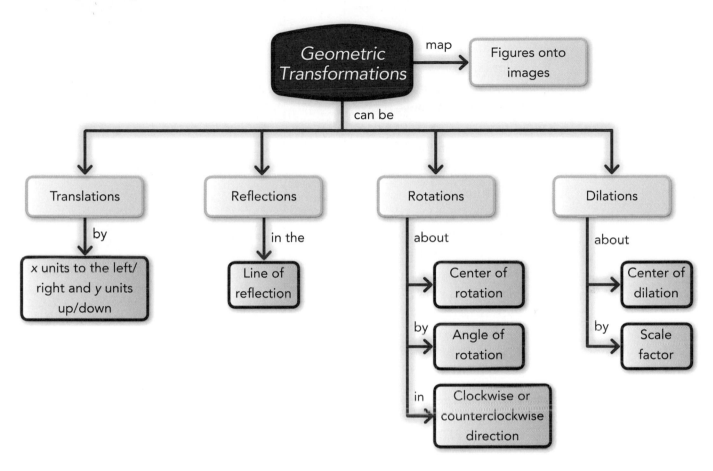

Key Concepts

▶ A transformation is a function that assigns to every point of the plane another point of the plane. Some points are assigned to themselves, and are called invariant points under the transformation.

▶ The isometries are translations, reflections, and rotations. They preserve the shape and size of a figure. Translations, or slides, move every point of a figure by a fixed distance in the same direction. Reflections, or flips, move every point of a figure to its mirror image in the line of reflection. Rotations, or turns, move every point of a figure through a given angle in a clockwise or counterclockwise direction about the center of the rotation.

▶ Dilations enlarge or reduce the size of a figure by a scale factor about the center of dilation. They do not preserve lengths, except for the scale factors of 1 and −1. If the scale factor is between −1 and 1, the dilation is a reduction. If the scale factor is greater than 1 or less than −1, it is an enlargement.

Transformation	Summary	Example mapping $\overline{AB}$ onto $\overline{A'B'}$
Translation Key description: • translate j units to left/right and k units up/down	• Translation j units left/right maps (x, y) onto $(x + j, y)$. For $j > 0$, point moves right. For $j < 0$, point moves left. • Translation k units up/down maps (x, y) onto $(x, y + k)$. For $k > 0$, point moves up. For $k < 0$, point moves down. • There is no invariant point under translation.	Translation of 1 unit to the right and 2 units up
Reflection Key description: • line of reflection	• Reflection in the x-axis maps (x, y) onto $(x, -y)$. • Reflection in the y-axis maps (x, y) onto $(-x, y)$. • Reflection in the line $y = x$ maps (x, y) onto (y, x). • Reflection in the line $y = -x$ maps (x, y) onto $(-y, -x)$. • Points on the line of reflection are invariant.	Reflection in the x-axis
Rotation Key description: • angle • direction (except for 180°) • center of rotation	• Rotation of 180° about the origin maps (x, y) onto $(-x, -y)$. • Rotation of 90° clockwise about the origin maps (x, y) onto $(y, -x)$. • Rotation of 90° counterclockwise about the origin maps (x, y) onto $(y, -x)$. • The center is the only invariant point.	Rotation 90° clockwise about the origin
Dilation Key description: • center of dilation • scale factor	• A dilation with center at the origin and scale factor k maps (x, y) onto (kx, ky). • For $k > 0$, $\overline{AB}$ and $\overline{A'B'}$ are on the same side of the center. For $k < 0$, they are on opposite sides of the center. • The center is the only invariant point.	Dilation with center at the origin and scale factor 2

Chapter Review/Test

Concepts and Skills

State whether a rotation, translation, or a combination of both is involved in each activity.

1 A turning blade of a windmill

2 Pressing the keys on a computer keyboard

3 A printer head moving left and right

4 Wheels on a moving bicycle

Describe the translations.

5 Climbing up 8 steps of a staircase (assume horizontal and vertical distances of each step are the same)

6 Taking an elevator from level 2 to level 5 of a building

Write an equation of the line(s) of reflection.

7

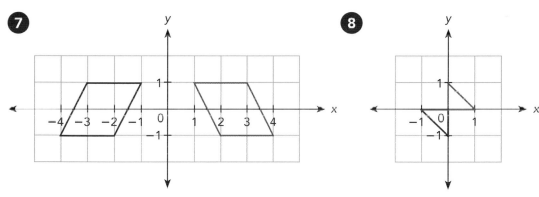

8

9

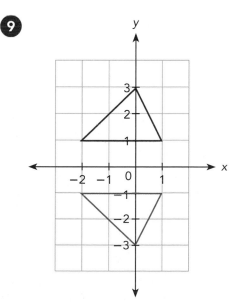

10

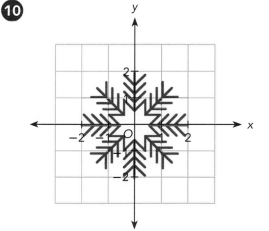

Each diagram shows a figure and its line of reflection. On a copy of the graph, draw the image.

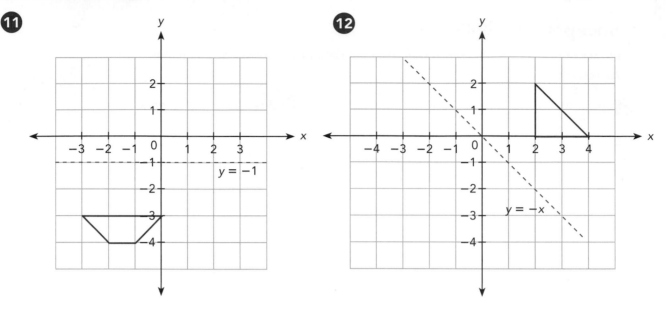

11

$y = -1$

12

$y = -x$

Solve on graph paper. Show your work.

13 $\overline{AB}$ is dilated with center at the origin and scale factor 2. Draw $\overline{AB}$ and its image $\overline{A'B'}$. Use 1 grid square on the horizontal axis to represent 1 unit for x interval from −4 to 10, and 1 grid square on the vertical axis to represent 1 unit for the y interval from −2 to 4.

a) A (2, 1) and B (5, 2)

b) A (1, −1) and B (−2, 2)

14 The table shows the coordinates for △XYZ and its images using two transformation. Use 1 grid square on both axes to represent 1 unit for the interval from −3 to 9.

Original Point	X (1, 3)	Y (1, 1)	Z (2, 1)
Is Mapped Onto	X' (3, 6)	Y' (3, 2)	Z' (5, 2)
Is Mapped Onto	X" (5, 9)	Y" (5, 3)	Z" (8, 3)

a) △XYZ is mapped onto △X'Y'Z' and △X"Y"Z" by a dilation. Draw each triangle and its image on the same coordinate plane. Then mark and label D as the center of dilation.

b) △XYZ is mapped onto △ABC by a rotation 90° counterclockwise about the origin. Draw △ABC on the coordinate plane.

c) △XYZ is mapped onto △PQR by a translation 3 units to the left and 4 units up. Draw △PQR on the coordinate plane.

d) Compare the transformations that mapped △XYZ onto △ABC and △PQR in terms of preservation of the shape and size of △XYZ.

Problem Solving

Solve. Show your work.

15 Jane had lunch with her friends from 1 P.M. to 2 P.M. Describe the geometric transformation of the hour hand of the clock.

16 A scientist used a sensor to track the movement of a mouse. It moved from the point (–2, 3) to the point (8, 6). State the new coordinates of any point (x, y) under this translation.

17 Mrs. Morales outlined a clover with four identical leaflets, as shown, on a coordinate plane. The center of the clover is at (1, 0).

a) How many lines of symmetry does the clover have? Sketch them on a copy of the clover leaf.

b) Find an equation of each line of reflection.

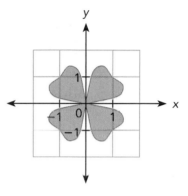

18 A circular mold in a Petri dish had a diameter of $\frac{1}{2}$ inch. The diameter grew by 32% in a day.

a) What is the scale factor of dilation?

b) Find the diameter of the mold after a day.

19 A figurine of the Statue of Liberty is 10 inches tall. The height of the Statue of Liberty is 150 feet. What is the scale factor of the dilation if the figurine is the image of the statue?

20 A spotlight is placed 2 feet from a 1-foot tall vase. A shadow 5 feet tall is cast on a wall as shown in the diagram. Find the distance of the vase from the wall.

Congruence and Similarity

 9.1 **Understanding and Applying Congruent Figures**

 9.2 **Understanding and Applying Similar Figures**

 9.3 **Relating Congruent and Similar Figures to Geometric Transformations**

How tall is a water tower?

The water tower in the town of Luling, Texas, is shaped like a giant watermelon. To find the height of the tower, you don't need to climb all the way up to the top. Instead, you can make some measurements down on the ground. Then you can use the fact that the ratio of your height to the tower's height, and the ratio of the length of your shadow to the length of the tower's shadow are equal.

In this chapter, you'll learn how to use proportional relationships to make indirect measurements.

BIG IDEA

▶ Congruent figures have the same shape and size. Similar figures have the same shape but need not be the same size. Two congruent figures or two similar figures are related by a series of geometric transformations.

Recall Prior Knowledge

Identifying the scale factor in diagrams

A scale factor is the ratio of the length of a line segment in a scale drawing to the actual length of the line segment. The scale factor is also known as the constant of proportionality.

Actual tree house

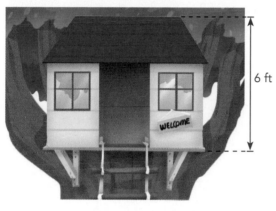

6 ft

Tree house model

2 ft

A model of a tree house is built by reducing all lengths by the same ratio. If the height of the tree house is reduced from 6 feet to 2 feet, the scale factor or constant of proportionality is found by dividing the final height by the original height, that is $\frac{2}{6} = \frac{1}{3}$.

✓ Quick Check

Complete.

1

Scale Factor	Original Length	Scaled Length
2	__?__	16 ft
__?__	5 cm	5 cm
__?__	8 m	4 m
$\frac{1}{4}$	4 in.	__?__

Solve.

2 Shawn built a model of a ship whose length was 4,500 inches. His model was 15 inches long. Find the scale factor.

3 A line segment is 4 centimeters long. When projected on a screen, the line segment is 20 centimeters long. Find the scale factor.

Solving problems involving scale drawings or models

When you know the scale or scale factor, you can find the length of an object in a scale drawing or the actual length of the object. You can also find the area of the object in the scale drawing or the actual area of the object.

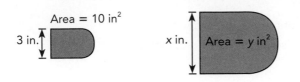

Area = 10 in²

3 in.

x in.   Area = y in²

The length of the figure on the left is enlarged by a scale factor of 2 to produce the figure on the right. Use the scale factor to find the missing length.

$\frac{x}{3} = 2$ The ratio of the two lengths equals the scale factor.

$\frac{x}{3} \cdot 3 = 2 \cdot 3$ Multiply both sides by 3.

$x = 6$ Simplify.

The side length in the larger figure is 6 inches.

Two figures related by a scale factor of 2 have their areas related by a factor of 4. Use this factor to find the area of the larger figure.

$\frac{y}{10} = 2^2$ The ratio of the two areas equals the square of the scale factor.

$\frac{y}{10} \cdot 10 = 4 \cdot 10$ Multiply both sides by 10.

$y = 40$ Simplify.

The area of the larger figure is 40 square inches.

Quick Check

Solve.

4 A model plane is built with a scale factor of $\frac{1}{180}$. The actual length of the plane is 210 feet (2,520 inches). Find the length of the model.

5 The scale of a map is 2 inches : 3 kilometers. The length of a road on the map is 3 inches. Find the actual length of the road.

6 The diagram shows a plot of land *ABCD* drawn on a map.

    a) On the map, $\overline{CD}$ is $1\frac{3}{4}$ inches. Find the scale of the map.

    b) Find the area of *ABCD* on the map.

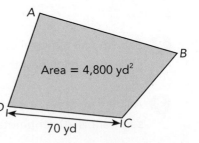

Area = 4,800 yd²

70 yd

Finding the measures of the interior and exterior angles of a triangle

The sum of the angle measures of a triangle is 180°.

$m\angle 1 + m\angle 2 + m\angle 3 = 180°$

The measure of an exterior angle of a triangle is equal to the sum of the measures of the two interior angles that are not adjacent to the exterior angle.

$m\angle 1 + m\angle 2 = m\angle 4$

$m\angle 1 + m\angle 3 = m\angle 5$

$m\angle 2 + m\angle 3 = m\angle 6$

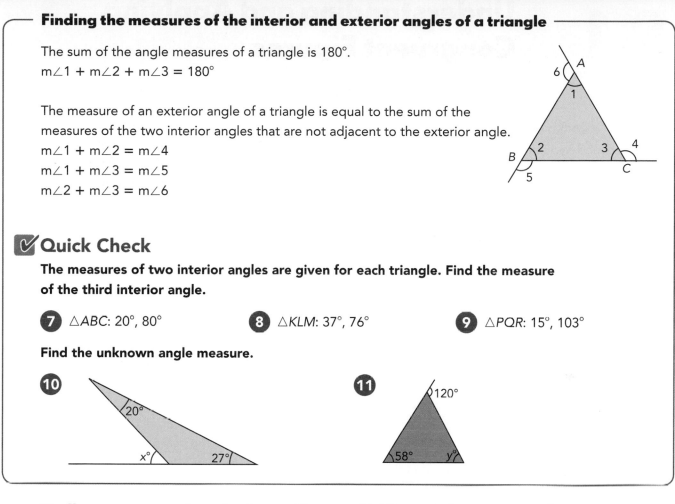

☑ Quick Check

The measures of two interior angles are given for each triangle. Find the measure of the third interior angle.

7 $\triangle ABC$: 20°, 80°

8 $\triangle KLM$: 37°, 76°

9 $\triangle PQR$: 15°, 103°

Find the unknown angle measure.

10
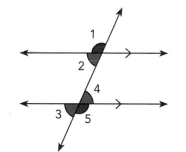

11

Finding measures of angles formed by parallel lines and a transversal

Angles formed by parallel lines and a transversal include alternate interior angles, alternate exterior angles, and corresponding angles.

The figure shows an example of each angle pair.

$\angle 2$ and $\angle 4$ are alternate interior angles.

$\angle 1$ and $\angle 5$ are alternate exterior angles.

$\angle 2$ and $\angle 3$ are corresponding angles.

$m\angle 2 = m\angle 4$, $m\angle 1 = m\angle 5$, and $m\angle 2 = m\angle 3$.

☑ Quick Check

Solve for each variable.

12

13

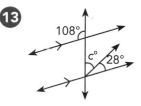

Lesson Objectives

- Understand and apply the concept of congruence.
- Use tests for congruent triangles.

Understand the Concept of Congruence.

Mrs. McWilliams has a curtain with the pattern of cubes shown. What do you notice about the cubes in each block of color?

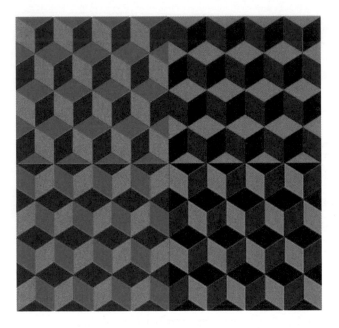

Although the cubes have different colors in different blocks, each has the same shape and size.

Figures with the same shape and size are congruent.

> Congruent figures can be related by a translation, reflection or rotation, or a combination of these motions. You will learn more about this in Lesson 9.3.

Example 1 **Identify congruent figures.**

Identify the figures that seem congruent. Explain why they seem so.

A   B   C   D   E   F

Solution

Figure B and D are congruent. They are regular hexagons and have the same size.

> An easy way to compare the shape and size of two figures is to place one figure on top of the other.

Guided Practice

Identify the figures that seem congruent. Explain why they seem so.

1   A   B   C   D   E   F

2   A   B   C   D   E

Apply the Concept of Congruence.

Megan folds a piece of tracing paper into halves. She draws △ABC on the left half. Then she traces △ABC to draw △DEF on the right half. She unfolds the paper and gets the following diagram.

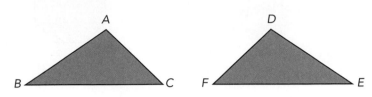

∠A and ∠D are **corresponding angles**. ∠B and ∠E are also corresponding angles. Can you name the last pair of corresponding angles?

$\overline{AB}$ and $\overline{DE}$ are one pair of **corresponding sides** of △ABC and △DEF. $\overline{AC}$ and $\overline{DF}$ are another pair of corresponding sides. Can you name the last pair of corresponding sides?

△ABC is congruent to △DEF since they have the same shape and size. So, their corresponding angles are congruent angles and their corresponding sides are congruent sides. Congruent angles have the same measure and congruent sides have the same length.

As shown below, you can use tick marks on corresponding sides to show they are congruent. You can also use arcs on corresponding angles to show they are congruent.

> When you say that △ABC and △DEF are congruent, the order of the vertices also tells you the correspondence between the vertices.

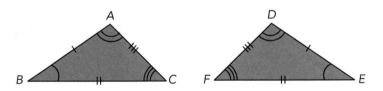

Congruent Angles	Congruent Sides
m∠A = m∠D	AB = DE
m∠B = m∠E	BC = EF
m∠C = m∠F	AC = DF

You can use the congruence symbol ≅ to show △ABC is congruent to △DEF. That is, △ABC ≅ △DEF. This is known as the **statement of congruence**.

Think Math

Two congruent triangles have three pairs of congruent sides and three pairs of congruent angles. How many pairs of congruent sides and congruent angles do two congruent quadrilaterals have? Explain.

Example 2 **Name congruent figures.**

The triangles below are congruent. Write the statement of congruence.

a)

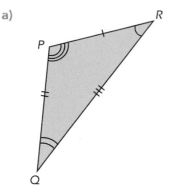

Solution

From the arcs on the angles of the triangles,

∠P corresponds to ∠Z,

∠Q corresponds to ∠Y, and

∠R corresponds to ∠X.

So, the statement of congruence is △PQR ≅ △ZYX.

Math Note

The statement of congruence can also be written as △PRQ ≅ △ZXY and five other ways. Any order that matches up corresponding vertices is correct.

b)

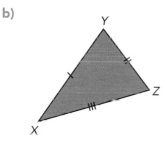
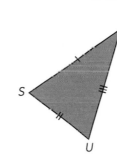

Solution

From the tick marks on the sides of the triangles,

Corresponding Sides	Corresponding Angles
$\overline{XY}$ and $\overline{TS}$	∠X and ∠T
$\overline{YZ}$ and $\overline{SU}$	∠Y and ∠S
$\overline{XZ}$ and $\overline{TU}$	∠Z and ∠U

In △XYZ, vertex X is common to the sides with one tick mark and three tick marks. The vertex in △STU with this property is T.

So, the statement of congruence is △XYZ ≅ △TSU.

Guided Practice

Complete.

3 The quadrilaterals below are congruent. Write the statement of congruence.

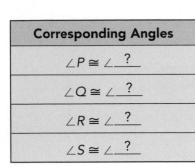

Corresponding Angles
∠P ≅ ∠ __?__
∠Q ≅ ∠ __?__
∠R ≅ ∠ __?__
∠S ≅ ∠ __?__

So, the statement of congruence is *PQRS* ≅ __?__.

Example 3   **Find unknown measures in congruent figures.**

Chloe cut a piece of rectangular paper along one of its diagonals. She formed two congruent triangles △*ABC* and △*DEF*. Find the values of *x* and *y*.

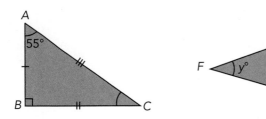

Solution

Corresponding Angles
m∠A = m∠D
m∠B = m∠E
m∠C = m∠F

$x = 55$ ∠A and ∠D have the same measure.

$y° = 180° - 90° - 55°$ ∠ sum of triangle
$y = 35$ Simplify.

So, the value of *x* is 55 and *y* is 35.

Guided Practice

Complete.

4 To make two congruent quadrilaterals, Wendy cut two pieces of cardboard, one on top of the other. She measured the lengths of some sides of the quadrilaterals.

a) Find the values of the variables x, y, and z. All lengths are in inches.

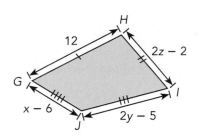 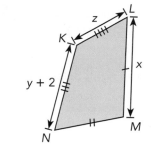

Corresponding Sides
$GH = $ ___?___
$HI = $ ___?___
$IJ = $ ___?___
$JG = $ ___?___

Solve for x:

$x = $ ___?___ $LM = $ ___?___

Solve for y:

$2y - 5 = $ ___?___ $IJ = $ ___?___

$2y - 5 + 5 = $ ___?___   Add 5 to both sides.

$2y = $ ___?___   Simplify.

$2y - y = $ ___?___   Subtract y from both sides.

$y = $ ___?___   Simplify.

Solve for z:

$x - 6 = $ ___?___ $JG = $ ___?___

___?___ $- 6 = $ ___?___   Substitute $x = $ ___?___.

___?___ $= z$ Simplify.

So, the value of x is ___?___, y is ___?___, and z is ___?___.

b) What is the length of each side of *GHIJ*? of *NKLM*?

$GH = $ ___?___ in., $HI = $ ___?___ in., $IJ = $ ___?___ in., $JG = $ ___?___ in.

$NK = $ ___?___ in., $KL = $ ___?___ in., $LM = $ ___?___ in., $MN = $ ___?___ in.

Technology Activity

Materials:
- geometry software

OBSERVE THE CONGRUENCE IN TRIANGLES

STEP 1 Draw △ABC and △DEF so that m∠CAB = m∠FDE, AB = DE, and AC = DF. Draw the two triangles such that point A is 10 units to the left of point D.

STEP 2 Translate △ABC 10 units to the right. Select the *Translate* function within the *Transform* menus. Do the two triangles overlap? Are the two triangles congruent?

STEP 3 Repeat **STEP 1** and **STEP 2** for triangles with different dimensions. Which pairs of corresponding parts did you specify to be congruent? Was this sufficient to make the triangles congruent?

STEP 4 Repeat **STEP 1** to **STEP 3** with △ABC and △DEF so that m∠CAB = m∠FDE, AB = DE, and m∠CBA = m∠FED.

STEP 5 Repeat **STEP 1** to **STEP 3** with △ABC and △DEF so that BC = EF, AB = DE, and AC = DF.

STEP 6 Repeat **STEP 1** to **STEP 3** with △ABC and △DEF so that m∠CAB = m∠FDE = 90°, BC = EF, and AC = DF.

✏️ *Math Journal* How are △ABC and △DEF related in each case? What are the four sets of the minimum conditions for two triangles to be congruent?

Use Tests for Congruent Triangles.

The minimum conditions for identifying congruent triangles comes from drawing unique triangles from given information. In the Technology Activity, you found you could construct unique triangles given the following.

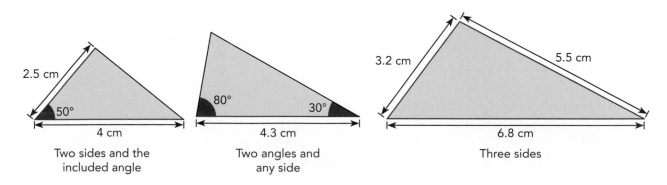

2.5 cm, 50°, 4 cm	80°, 30°, 4.3 cm	3.2 cm, 5.5 cm, 6.8 cm
Two sides and the included angle	Two angles and any side	Three sides

You have learned what congruence is and how to apply the concept of congruence. To assess whether two triangles are congruent, you need not know all three pairs of corresponding sides and all three pairs of corresponding angles are congruent.

The sets of minimum conditions for two congruent triangles are as follows. Two triangles are congruent if they satisfy any of the sets of conditions.

1. **Side-Angle-Side (SAS) Test**
   Two pairs of corresponding sides are congruent and the included angle between one pair is congruent to the corresponding angle.

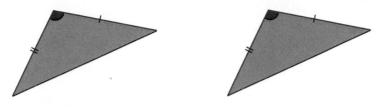

2. **Angle-Angle-Side or Angle-Side-Angle (AAS or ASA) Test**
   Two pairs of corresponding angles are congruent and any side of one triangle is congruent to the corresponding side of the other triangle.

3. **Side-Side-Side (SSS) Test**
   All three pairs of corresponding sides are congruent.

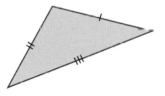 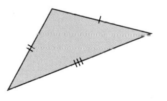

4. **Hypotenuse-Leg (HL) Test**
   The hypotenuse of a right triangle is congruent to the hypotenuse of the other right triangle. Another side of the right triangle is congruent to the corresponding side of the other right triangle.

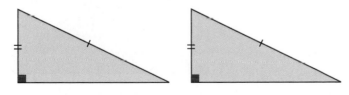

> **Caution** ///////
> You cannot use the side-side-angle (SSA) test, except the hypotenuse-leg (HL) test, to test for congruent triangles.

Example 4 **Identify congruent triangles.**

Identify the congruent triangles. Write the statement of congruence and state the test used.

a) *ABCD* is a parallelogram.

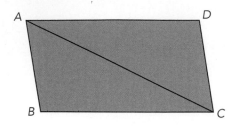

Solution

AB = *CD*, *BC* = *DA*, because opposite sides of a parallelogram are congruent. *AC* = *AC*, because $\overline{AC}$ is a common side of both triangles.

By the SSS test, △*ABC* ≅ △*CDA*.

> **Caution** ///////
>
> Be sure the vertices are in the corresponding order when writing the statement of congruence.

b) $\overline{AD}$ is the angle bisector of ∠*A* and ∠*D*.

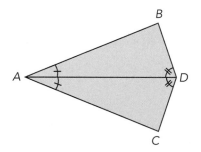

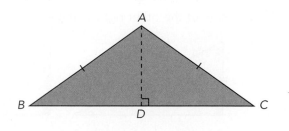

> The angle bisector of ∠*WXY* is the ray $\overrightarrow{XZ}$ in the interior of ∠*WXY* that separates it into two congruent angles.

Solution

m∠*BAD* = m∠*CAD* and m∠*BDA* = m∠*CDA*, because an angle bisector divides an angle into two congruent angles. *AD* = *AD*, because $\overline{AD}$ is a common side of the triangles.

By the ASA test, △*ABD* ≅ △*ACD*.

c) $\overline{AD}$ is perpendicular to $\overline{BC}$.

Solution

△*ADB* and △*ADC* are right triangles. *AB* = *AC*, that is the hypotenuse of △*ADB* is congruent to the hypotenuse of △*ADC*. *AD* = *AD*, because $\overline{AD}$ is a common side of both triangles.

By the HL test, △*ADB* ≅ △*ADC*.

Guided Practice

Complete.

 Justify whether the triangles are congruent. If they are congruent, write the statement of congruence and state the test used.

a)

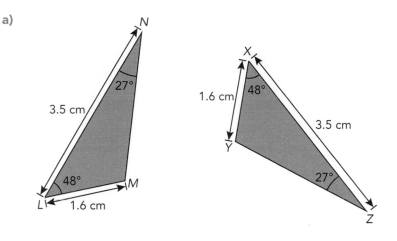

$LN =$ __?__, $m\angle$__?__ $= m\angle$__?__, and $LM =$ __?__.

By the SAS test, $\triangle LMN \cong$ __?__.

> **Caution**
>
> In the SAS test, the angle congruent to its corresponding angle must be the included angle, which is the angle between the congruent corresponding sides.

b)

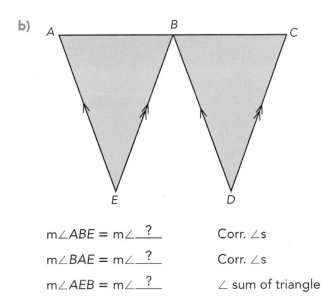

$m\angle ABE = m\angle$ __?__　　　　Corr. $\angle$s

$m\angle BAE = m\angle$ __?__　　　　Corr. $\angle$s

$m\angle AEB = m\angle$ __?__　　　　$\angle$ sum of triangle

Three pairs of congruent angles do not ensure that the triangles are __?__.

Name the figures that are congruent. Name the corresponding congruent line segments and angles.

1 *ABCD* is a parallelogram with diagonal $\overline{BD}$.

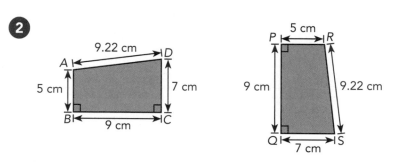

2

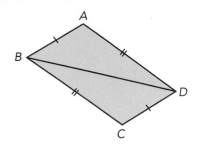

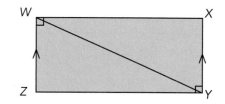

Solve. Show your work.

3 *WXYZ* is a rectangle with diagonal $\overline{WY}$. Explain, using the given test for congruent triangles, why △*WXY* is congruent to △*YZW*.

a) SSS

b) SAS

c) ASA

d) HL

4 *ABCDE* is a regular pentagon with congruent diagonals $\overline{BE}$ and $\overline{BD}$.

a) Justify △*ABE* ≅ △*CBD* with a test for congruent triangles.

b) Name a pair of congruent quadrilaterals.

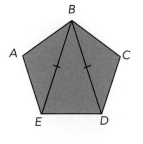

5 △ABC is congruent to △PQR. Find the values of x, y, and z.

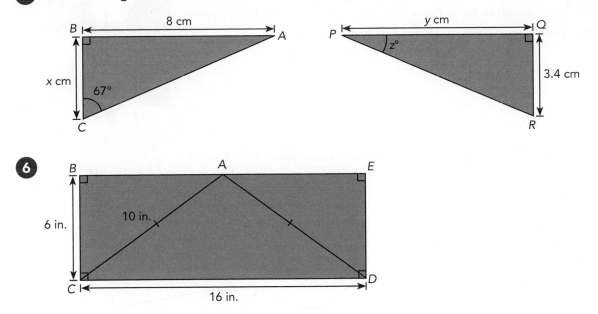

6

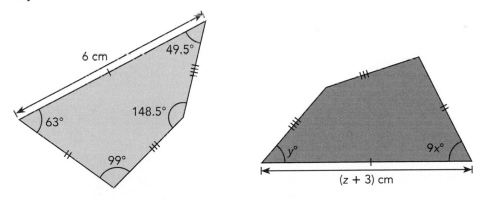

a) Name the figure that is congruent to trapezoid *BADC*.

b) Find the length of each side of the trapezoid you named in **a)**.

7 A piece of fabric has many printed shapes of congruent triangles and congruent quadrilaterals on it.

a) The pieces of fabric shown are congruent quadrilaterals. Find the value of x, y, and z.

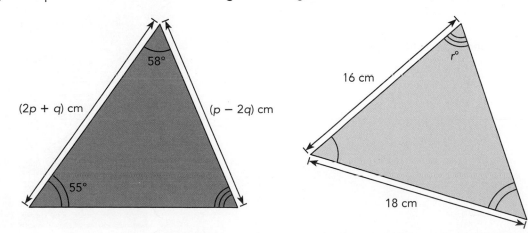

b) The pieces of fabric shown are congruent triangles. Find the value of p, q, and r.

8 The origami cornflower is formed by making symmetrical folds in a paper square. In the diagram, $AB = BC = DE = EF$ and $OA = OC = OD = OF$. Write two possible statements of congruence for $ABCO$.

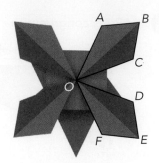

9 In making this suspension bridge, engineers connected two cables at the same point P on the concrete piers and at the same distance from the base of the concrete piers at R.

a) Which congruence test ensures that $\triangle PQR$ is congruent to $\triangle PSR$? Explain.

b) How many other pairs of congruent triangles are attached to each concrete pier? Explain.

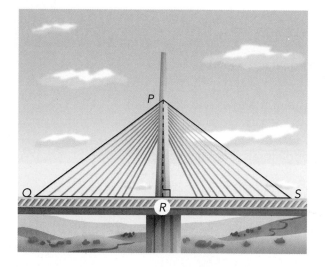

10 This skyscraper has several symmetric triangles overlaid on a grid of horizontal and vertical lines. In each direction, these lines are parallel.

a) This face of the building is symmetric about $\overline{GK}$, so $AB = CD$, $AX = CX$, and $BX = DX$. Give the statement of congruence for $\triangle ABX$ and tell which congruence test you used.

b) Is $\triangle EFG$ congruent to $\triangle HJK$? Explain.

9.2 Understanding and Applying Similar Figures

Lesson Objectives

- Understand and apply the concept of similarity.
- Use tests for similar triangles.

Vocabulary

similarity

Understand the Concept of Similarity.

Mr. Phillips' hobby is collecting stamps. He uses a magnifying glass to see small details on his stamps.

Under the magnifying glass, he sees an enlarged image of the stamp. The image has the same shape as the stamp but is a different size. You can say the stamp and its image are similar. This is the basic idea behind similar figures in mathematics.

Example 5 Identify similar figures.

Identify the figures that seem similar. Explain why.

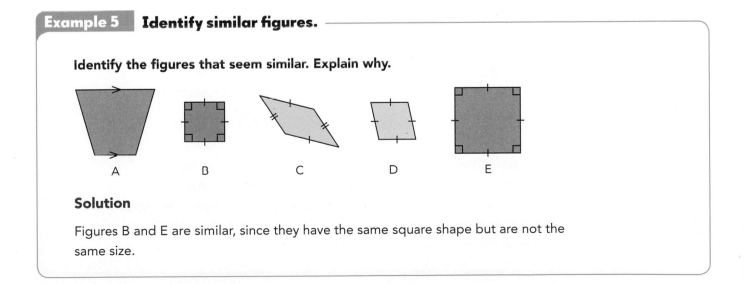

A   B   C   D   E

Solution

Figures B and E are similar, since they have the same square shape but are not the same size.

Guided Practice

Identify the figures that seem similar. Explain why.

1

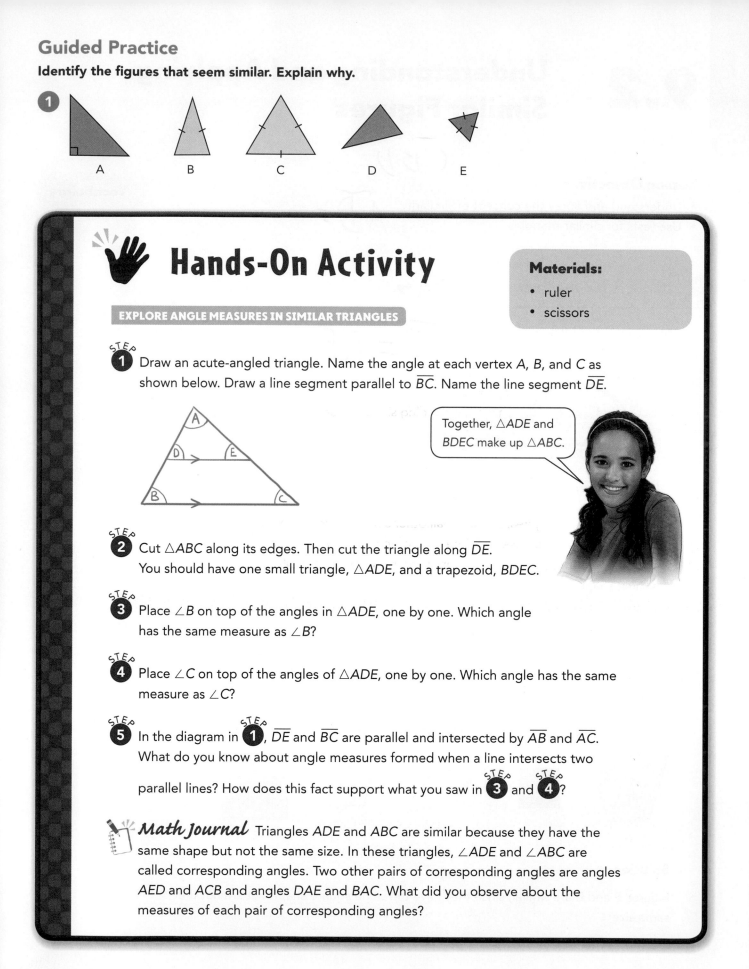

A   B   C   D   E

Hands-On Activity

EXPLORE ANGLE MEASURES IN SIMILAR TRIANGLES

Materials:
- ruler
- scissors

STEP 1 Draw an acute-angled triangle. Name the angle at each vertex A, B, and C as shown below. Draw a line segment parallel to $\overline{BC}$. Name the line segment $\overline{DE}$.

> Together, △ADE and BDEC make up △ABC.

STEP 2 Cut △ABC along its edges. Then cut the triangle along $\overline{DE}$. You should have one small triangle, △ADE, and a trapezoid, BDEC.

STEP 3 Place ∠B on top of the angles in △ADE, one by one. Which angle has the same measure as ∠B?

STEP 4 Place ∠C on top of the angles of △ADE, one by one. Which angle has the same measure as ∠C?

STEP 5 In the diagram in **STEP 1**, $\overline{DE}$ and $\overline{BC}$ are parallel and intersected by $\overline{AB}$ and $\overline{AC}$. What do you know about angle measures formed when a line intersects two parallel lines? How does this fact support what you saw in **STEP 3** and **STEP 4**?

Math Journal Triangles ADE and ABC are similar because they have the same shape but not the same size. In these triangles, ∠ADE and ∠ABC are called corresponding angles. Two other pairs of corresponding angles are angles AED and ACB and angles DAE and BAC. What did you observe about the measures of each pair of corresponding angles?

Apply the Concept of Similarity.

Look at the two similar stamps shown below.

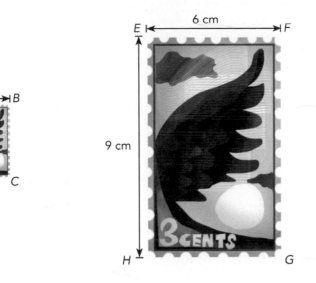

The ratios of the length of the corresponding sides can be calculated as follows.

$$\frac{EF}{AB} = \frac{6}{2} = 3$$

$$\frac{EH}{AD} = \frac{9}{3} = 3$$

In these two similar figures, as well as all other similar figures, the ratios of corresponding lengths are equal. The ratio of the corresponding lengths of similar figures is known as the **scale factor** or **constant of proportionality**.

Think Math

What happens when the scale factor is 1? Are all congruent figures similar?

Caution

Two rectangles are not necessarily similar just because they are both rectangles. The ratios of their corresponding side lengths must also be equal.

You can use the symbol ~ to denote similarity. $ABCD \sim EFGH$ means $ABCD$ is similar to $EFGH$ with corresponding vertices A and E, B and F, C and G, and D and H.

The corresponding angles of similar polygons have the same measure. The lengths of their corresponding sides are proportional.

Establishing the correspondence between vertices is an important first step in finding unknown lengths or angle measures as shown in Example 6 and Example 7.

Continue on next page

Consider two similar rectangles.

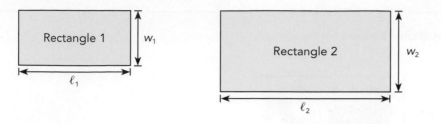

The lengths and widths of similar rectangles have the ratio k. So you can write

$$\frac{\ell_2}{\ell_1} = \frac{w_2}{w_1} = k.$$

So, $\dfrac{\text{Area of rectangle 2}}{\text{Area of rectangle 1}} = \dfrac{\ell_2 w_2}{\ell_1 w_1}$

$$= \frac{\ell_2}{\ell_1} \cdot \frac{w_2}{w_1}$$

$$= k \cdot k$$

$$= k^2$$

This relationship applies to any pair of geometrically similar figures.

> If the ratio of the corresponding lengths of two similar figures is k, then the ratio of their areas is k^2.

Example 6 Find unknown lengths in similar figures.

Solve.

a) $\triangle UVW$ is similar to $\triangle XYZ$. Find the length of $\overline{XY}$.

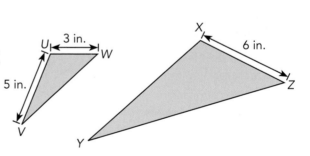

Solution

According to the order of the vertices, U corresponds to X, V corresponds to Y, and W corresponds to Z. So, $\overline{UW}$ corresponds to $\overline{XZ}$ and $\overline{UV}$ corresponds to $\overline{XY}$.

$\dfrac{UW}{XZ} = \dfrac{UV}{XY}$ Set up a proportion since the ratios of corresponding lengths are equal.

$\dfrac{3}{6} = \dfrac{5}{XY}$ Substitute the known values.

$\dfrac{1}{2} = \dfrac{5}{XY}$ Simplify.

$XY \cdot 1 = 5 \cdot 2$ Write the cross product.

$XY = 10$ Multiply.

The length of $\overline{XY}$ is 10 inches.

b) Noah is enlarging a photograph of his pet. The original photo is 6 inches long and 4 inches wide. The enlarged photo is similar to the original and is 15 inches long. How wide is the enlarged photo?

Solution

Method 1

From 6 inches to 15 inches, the scale factor is $\dfrac{15}{6} = \dfrac{5}{2} = 2.5$.

Width of enlarged photo: $4 \cdot 2.5 = 10$ in.

Method 2

Let the width of the enlarged photo be w inches.

Ratio of widths: $\dfrac{w}{4}$

Ratio of lengths: $\dfrac{15}{6}$

$\dfrac{w}{4} = \dfrac{15}{6}$ Set up a proportion since the ratios of corresponding lengths are equal.

$\dfrac{w}{{}_1\cancel{4}} \cdot \cancel{4}^{\,1} = \dfrac{\cancel{15}^{\,5}}{\cancel{6}_{\,2}} \cdot \cancel{4}^{\,2}_{\,1}$ Multiply both sides by 4.

$w = 10$ Simplify.

The enlarged photo is 10 inches wide.

Guided Practice

Solve.

2 Triangle *ABC* and triangle *DEF* are similar triangles.
Find the value of *x*.

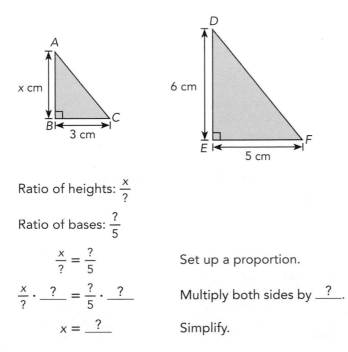

Ratio of heights: $\dfrac{x}{?}$

Ratio of bases: $\dfrac{?}{5}$

$\dfrac{x}{?} = \dfrac{?}{5}$ Set up a proportion.

$\dfrac{x}{?} \cdot \underline{\ \ ?\ \ } = \dfrac{?}{5} \cdot \underline{\ \ ?\ \ }$ Multiply both sides by $\underline{\ ?\ }$.

$x = \underline{\ \ ?\ \ }$ Simplify.

Example 7 **Find unknown lengths and angle measures in similar figures.**

Solve.

a) Find the length of $\overline{PQ}$.

Solution

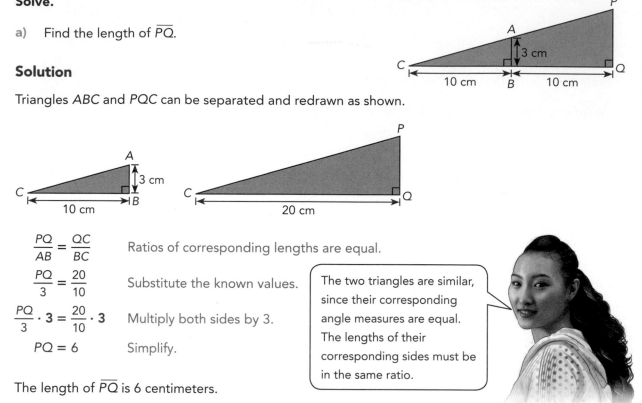

Triangles *ABC* and *PQC* can be separated and redrawn as shown.

$$\frac{PQ}{AB} = \frac{QC}{BC} \qquad \text{Ratios of corresponding lengths are equal.}$$

$$\frac{PQ}{3} = \frac{20}{10} \qquad \text{Substitute the known values.}$$

$$\frac{PQ}{3} \cdot \mathbf{3} = \frac{20}{10} \cdot \mathbf{3} \qquad \text{Multiply both sides by 3.}$$

$$PQ = 6 \qquad \text{Simplify.}$$

> The two triangles are similar, since their corresponding angle measures are equal. The lengths of their corresponding sides must be in the same ratio.

The length of $\overline{PQ}$ is 6 centimeters.

b) $\triangle PQR$ is similar to $\triangle STU$. Find the value of *x* and *y*.

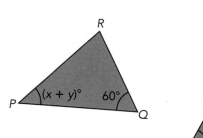
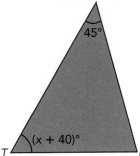

Solution

From the similarity statement, *P* corresponds to *S*, *Q* corresponds to *T*, and *R* corresponds to *U*.

$$m\angle Q = m\angle T \qquad \text{Corresponding angles of similar triangles have equal measures.}$$

$$60 = x + 40 \qquad \text{Write an equation.}$$

$$60 - \mathbf{40} = x + 40 - \mathbf{40} \qquad \text{Subtract 40 from both sides.}$$

$$20 = x \qquad \text{Simplify.}$$

$$m\angle P = m\angle S \qquad \text{Corresponding angles of similar triangles have equal measures.}$$

$$x + y = 45 \qquad \text{Write an equation.}$$

$$20 + y = 45 \qquad \text{Substitute 20 for } x.$$

$$20 + y - \mathbf{20} = 45 - \mathbf{20} \qquad \text{Subtract 20 from both sides.}$$

$$y = 25 \qquad \text{Simplify.}$$

c) $\triangle XUV$ is similar to $\triangle XYZ$. $\triangle XUV$ has area 4 square inches and $\triangle XYZ$ has area 36 square inches. $\overline{UV}$ is 1.5 inches long. Find the length of $\overline{YZ}$.

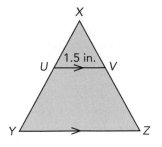

Solution

Use the ratio of the areas to find the ratio of corresponding side lengths.

$$k^2 = \frac{\text{Area of } \triangle XYZ}{\text{Area of } \triangle XUV}$$

$$= \frac{36}{4}$$

$$= 9$$

$$k = 3$$

Use the ratio of corresponding side lengths to find the length of $\overline{YZ}$.

$$\frac{YZ}{UV} = 3 \qquad \text{The ratio of corresponding side lengths equals } k.$$

$$\frac{YZ}{1.5} \cdot 1.5 = 3 \cdot 1.5 \qquad \text{Multiply both sides by 1.5.}$$

$$YZ = 4.5 \qquad \text{Simplify.}$$

The length of $\overline{YZ}$ is 4.5 inches.

Guided Practice

Solve.

3 An engineer wants to make a bridge across a river at $\overline{PR}$. The diagram shows the known measurements. $\overline{SP}$ and $\overline{TR}$ are straight lines and triangle RPQ is similar to triangle TSQ. Find the width x of the river.

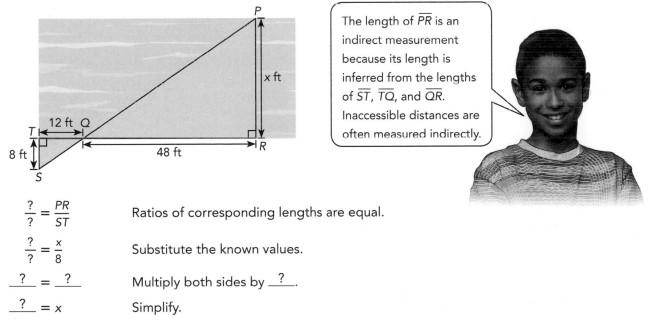

The length of $\overline{PR}$ is an indirect measurement because its length is inferred from the lengths of $\overline{ST}$, $\overline{TQ}$, and $\overline{QR}$. Inaccessible distances are often measured indirectly.

$$\frac{?}{?} = \frac{PR}{ST} \qquad \text{Ratios of corresponding lengths are equal.}$$

$$\frac{?}{?} = \frac{x}{8} \qquad \text{Substitute the known values.}$$

$$\frac{?}{} = \frac{?}{} \qquad \text{Multiply both sides by } \underline{\ ?\ }.$$

$$\frac{?}{} = x \qquad \text{Simplify.}$$

The width of the river is $\underline{\ ?\ }$ feet.

Continue on next page

Solve.

4 △ABC and △DEF are similar triangles. Find m∠D, m∠E, and m∠F.

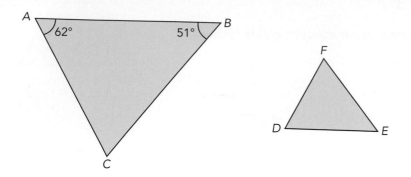

The corresponding angles of similar triangles have __?__ measures.

So m∠D = m∠ __?__ = __?__ ,

m∠E = m∠ __?__ = __?__ ,

and m∠F = 180° − __?__ − __?__   ∠ sum of triangle

     = __?__

5 The area of △AXY is 12 square centimeters. Find the area of △ABC.

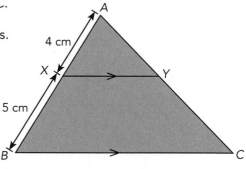

Use the ratio of corresponding lengths to find the ratio of the areas.

$$k^2 = \frac{\text{Area of } \triangle ABC}{\text{Area of } \triangle AXY}$$

$$= \left(\frac{AB}{?}\right)^2$$

$$= \left(\frac{?}{?}\right)^2$$

$$= \frac{?}{?}$$

Let the area of △ABC be x square centimeters.
Use the ratio of the areas to find x.

$$\frac{x}{12} = k^2$$ The ratio of the areas equals k^2.

$$\frac{x}{12} = \frac{?}{?}$$ Substitute __?__ for k^2.

$$\frac{x}{12} \cdot 12 = \frac{?}{?} \cdot \underline{?}$$ Multiply both sides by __?__.

$$x = \underline{?}$$ Simplify.

The area of △ABC is __?__ square centimeters.

Hands-On Activity

Materials:

- two similar triangles
- protractor
- ruler

EXPLORE A MINIMUM CONDITION FOR TWO SIMILAR TRIANGLES

STEP 1 Measure the side lengths of the triangles. Find out if △ABC is similar to △PQR by finding the ratios of the corresponding side lengths.

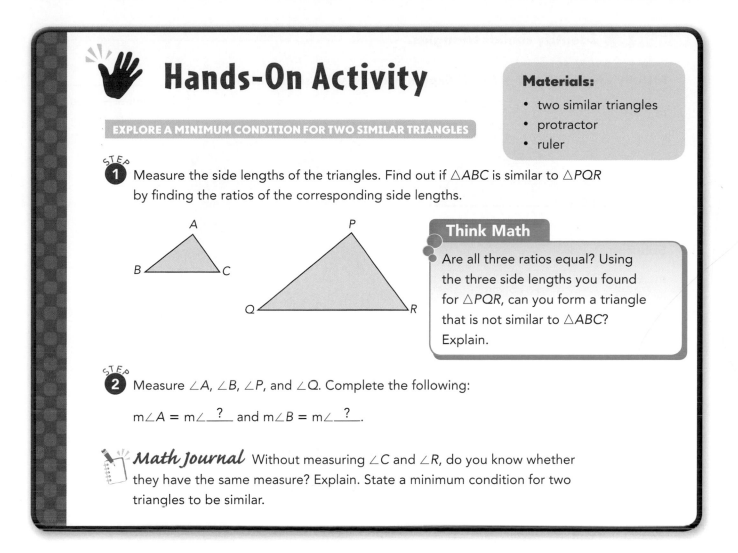

Think Math

Are all three ratios equal? Using the three side lengths you found for △PQR, can you form a triangle that is not similar to △ABC? Explain.

STEP 2 Measure ∠A, ∠B, ∠P, and ∠Q. Complete the following:

m∠A = m∠_?_ and m∠B = m∠_?_.

Math Journal Without measuring ∠C and ∠R, do you know whether they have the same measure? Explain. State a minimum condition for two triangles to be similar.

Use Tests for Similar Triangles.

You have learned that similar polygons have congruent corresponding angles and corresponding sides of proportional lengths. To determine whether two triangles are similar, you need not know the measures of all the corresponding sides and angles, as the preceding activity showed.

Two triangles are similar if they satisfy any of these minimum conditions:

1. Two pairs of corresponding angles have equal measures.

2. All three pairs of corresponding side lengths have the same ratio.

3. Two pairs of corresponding side lengths have the same ratio and the included angles have the same measure.

You use one of the minimum conditions to test for similar triangles.

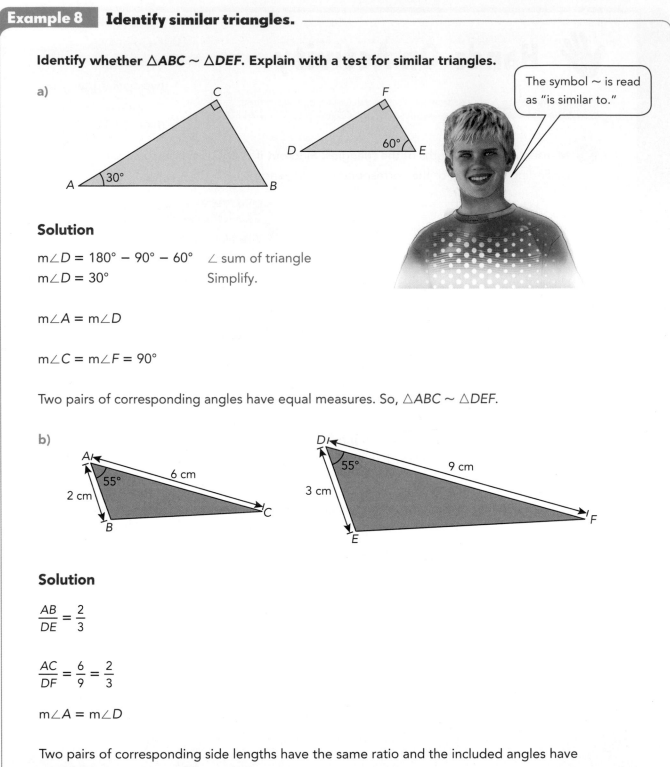

Example 8 | Identify similar triangles.

Identify whether △ABC ~ △DEF. Explain with a test for similar triangles.

a)

The symbol ~ is read as "is similar to."

Solution

m∠D = 180° − 90° − 60°   ∠ sum of triangle
m∠D = 30°   Simplify.

m∠A = m∠D

m∠C = m∠F = 90°

Two pairs of corresponding angles have equal measures. So, △ABC ~ △DEF.

b)

Solution

$\frac{AB}{DE} = \frac{2}{3}$

$\frac{AC}{DF} = \frac{6}{9} = \frac{2}{3}$

m∠A = m∠D

Two pairs of corresponding side lengths have the same ratio and the included angles have equal measures. So, △ABC ~ △DEF.

Guided Practice

Identify whether △ABC is similar to △DEF. Explain with a test for similar triangles.

6

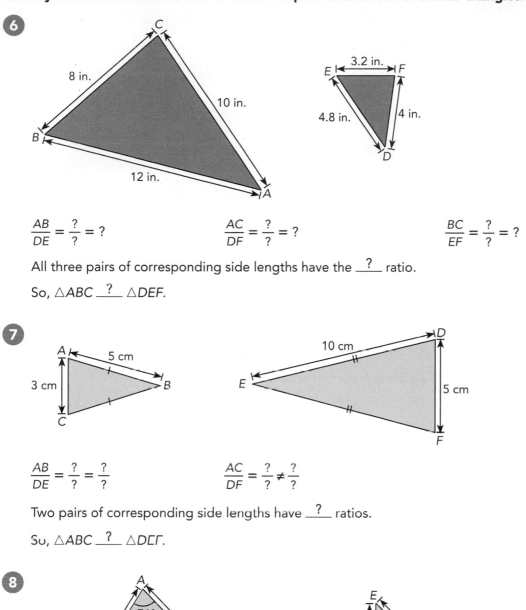

$\dfrac{AB}{DE} = \dfrac{?}{?} = ?$

$\dfrac{AC}{DF} = \dfrac{?}{?} = ?$

$\dfrac{BC}{EF} = \dfrac{?}{?} = ?$

All three pairs of corresponding side lengths have the __?__ ratio.

So, △ABC __?__ △DEF.

7

$\dfrac{AB}{DE} = \dfrac{?}{?} = \dfrac{?}{?}$

$\dfrac{AC}{DF} = \dfrac{?}{?} \neq \dfrac{?}{?}$

Two pairs of corresponding side lengths have __?__ ratios.

So, △ABC __?__ △DEF.

8

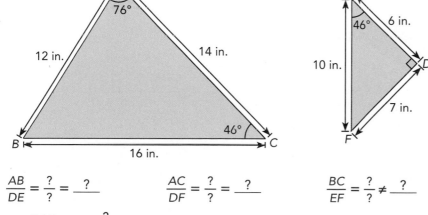

$\dfrac{AB}{DE} = \dfrac{?}{?} = \underline{\ ?\ }$

$\dfrac{AC}{DF} = \dfrac{?}{?} = \underline{\ ?\ }$

$\dfrac{BC}{EF} = \dfrac{?}{?} \neq \underline{\ ?\ }$

m∠BAC ≠ m∠__?__

Two pairs of corresponding side lengths have the __?__ ratio and the included
angles have __?__ measures.

So, △ABC __?__ △DEF.

Identify the figures that seem similar. Explain why.

1

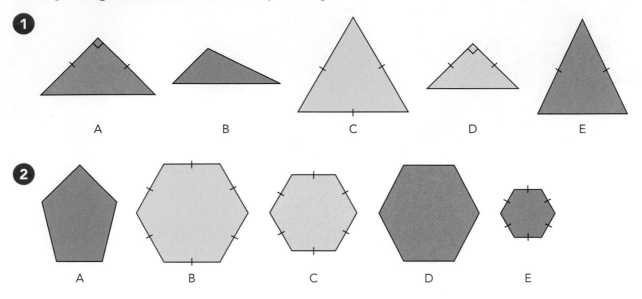

A   B   C   D   E

2

A   B   C   D   E

Triangle *ABC* is similar to triangle *PQR*. Find the scale factor by which △*ABC* is enlarged to △*PQR*.

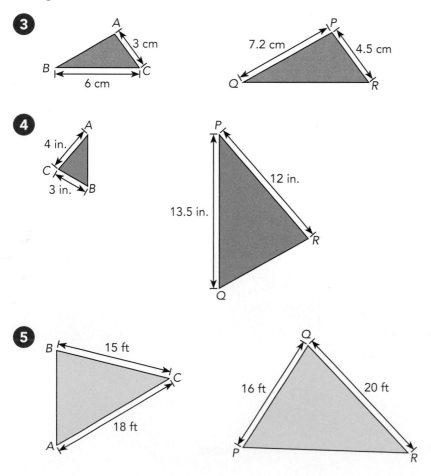

3 A, 3 cm, B, 6 cm, C ; 7.2 cm, P, 4.5 cm, Q, R

4 A, 4 in., C, 3 in., B ; P, 12 in., 13.5 in., R, Q

5 B, 15 ft, C, 18 ft, A ; Q, 16 ft, 20 ft, P, R

Each pair of figures are similar. Find the value of each variable.

6 $ABCD \sim EFGH$

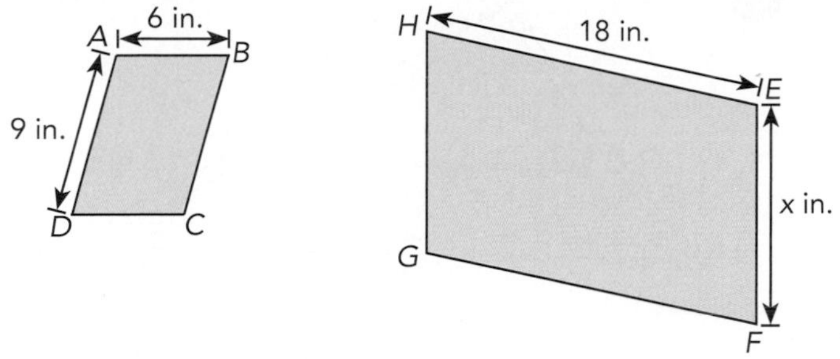

7 $\triangle ABC \sim \triangle DEF$

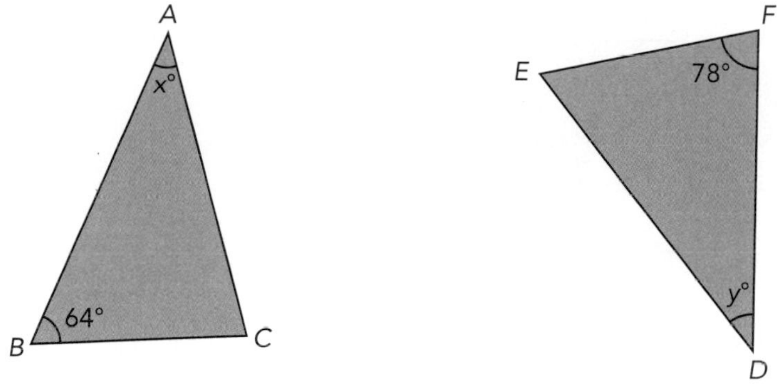

8 $ABCD \sim EFGH$

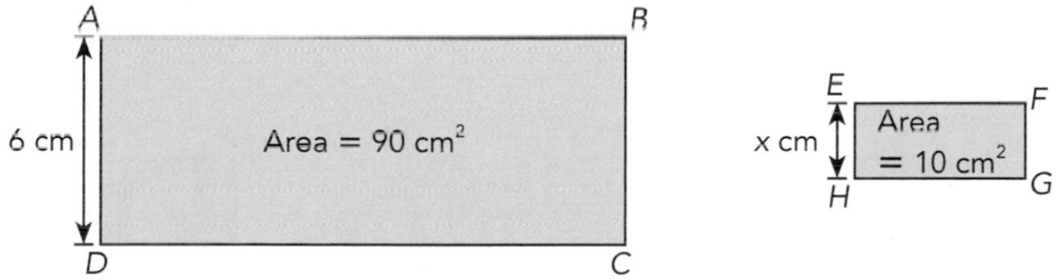

9 $\triangle ABC \sim \triangle DEF$

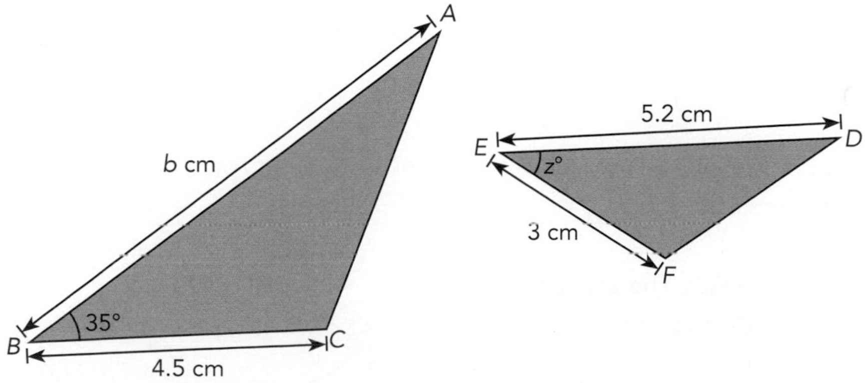

Explain, with a test, why the two triangles in each figure are similar. Find the unknown lengths.

10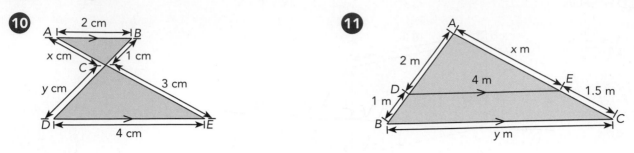

11

Solve. Show your work.

12 Mia made some copies of a drawing using a photocopier. The drawing was either enlarged or reduced. Find the value of x.

a)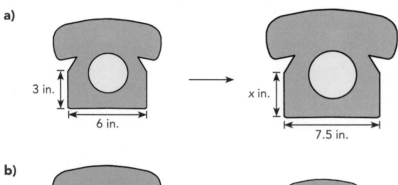

3 in.

6 in.

x in.

7.5 in.

b)

x in.

3 in.

2.25 in.

2.4 in.

13 The slope of a wheelchair ramp is $\frac{1}{15}$.

a) Suppose a wheelchair ramp has to rise 3 feet. Find the horizontal distance it covers.

b) Suppose there is space for a wheelchair ramp to cover at most 30 feet horizontally. How high can it rise then?

Rise

Horizontal distance

14 A circle has 9 times the area of another circle. If the radius of the larger circle is 27 meters, find the radius of the smaller circle.

15 The two ellipses shown on the right are similar. The area of the inner ellipse is 18 square inches and the shaded area is 32 square inches. Find the values for x and y.

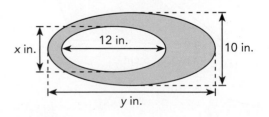

x in.

12 in.

10 in.

y in.

16 Two trees on a street have heights 10 feet and 28 feet. At a certain time of a day, the shorter tree casts a shadow of length 15 feet on the ground. How far apart are the trees?

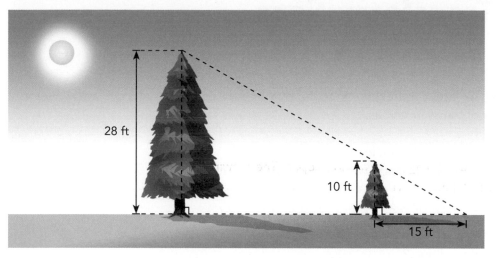

17 A bag in the shape of two regular pentagons is shown on the right. The ratio of the shaded area to the area of the larger pentagon is 27 : 36. If the larger pentagon has sides of length 4 inches, find the length of the sides of the smaller pentagon.

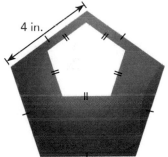

4 in.

18 A cable car travels from a village up to a resort on the top of a mountain. When the cable car has traveled 150 feet along the cable, it is 100 feet above the ground. The total distance the cable car must travel to reach the resort is 12,000 feet. How high is the mountain?

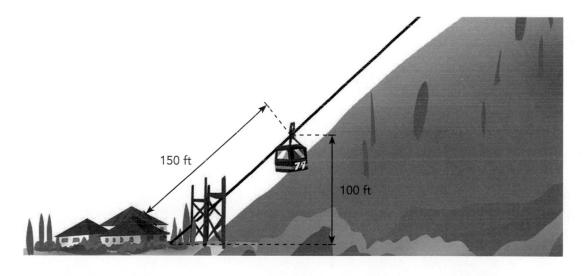

150 ft

100 ft

19 *Math Journal* Are similar figures ever congruent? If so, under which conditions are they congruent? Use two congruent triangles and two similar triangles in your explanation.

20 *Math Journal* Do you know all circles are similar? What other geometric shapes are similar?

Relating Congruent and Similar Figures to Geometric Transformations

Lesson Objectives

- Relate congruent or similar figures using geometric transformations.
- Understand a sequence of transformations.

Relate Congruent Figures Using Geometric Transformations.

In the previous chapter, you studied four types of geometric transformations: translations, reflections, rotations, and dilations. Can you recall the transformations that preserve the size of the figure?

Consider a triangle P and its image Q, R, and S under the following transformations:

a) P is translated 6 units to the right and 2 units down to form triangle Q.

b) P is reflected in the x-axis to form triangle R.

c) P is rotated 90° clockwise about the origin, O, to form triangle S.

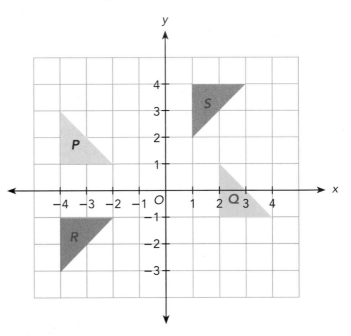

What do you notice about the shape and size of triangles P, Q, R, and S?

Triangles P, Q, R, and S are congruent triangles since their shapes and sizes are the same.

> Translations, reflections, and rotations of a figure result in an image congruent to the figure. Conversely, if two figures are congruent, there is always a series of translations, reflections, and/or rotations that will map one onto the other.

Think Math

Do dilations result in a congruent image? Explain.

Example 9 **Relate congruent figures using geometric transformations.**

Triangles *U* and *V* are congruent triangles. Describe a transformation that maps triangle *U* onto triangle *V*.

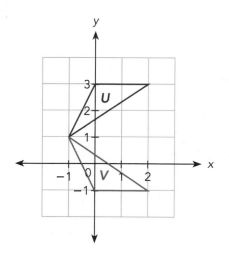

Congruent triangles are related by isometries: translations, reflections, or rotations.

Solution

Triangle *U* is mapped onto triangle *V* by a reflection in the line $y = 1$.

Guided Practice

Solve.

1. $\triangle ABC$ and $\triangle A'B'C'$ are congruent isosceles triangles. Describe a rotation that maps $\triangle ABC$ onto $\triangle A'B'C'$.

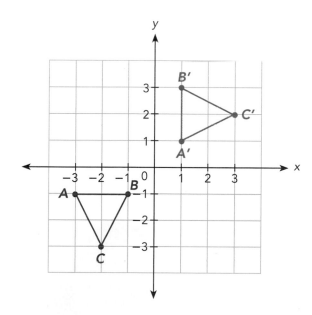

Relate Similar Figures Using Geometric Transformations.

You know that the shape of a figure is preserved after it is dilated. The size, however, is scaled up or down when the scale factor is not 1 or −1. When you photocopy a drawing to get an enlarged or reduced copy, you use a dilation. When an architect draws the blueprint for a building, he or she will reduce the footprint of the building using a dilation to produce a plan similar to that of the building.

Josh is looking at a photo *OABC* on his computer screen and wants to enlarge it to the size of *O′A′B′C′* for a newsletter. The scale factor of the dilation is 1.5 and the center of the dilation is the origin.

Rectangles *OABC* and *OA′B′C′* are similar figures, since their shapes are the same and their corresponding lengths are proportional.

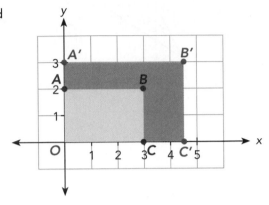

$$\frac{A'B'}{AB} = \frac{4.5}{3}$$
$$= 1.5$$

$$\frac{B'C'}{BC} = \frac{3}{2}$$
$$= 1.5$$

> A dilation of a figure results in an image similar to the figure.

Example 10 Relate similar figures using geometric transformations.

A snowball of diameter 3 inches rolled down a slope to become a similar snowball of diameter 3 feet.

a) Explain why the geometric transformation that resulted in the similar snowball is a dilation.

b) What is the scale factor of the dilation?

Solution

a) The two snowballs have the same shape but their sizes are different.

b) Scale factor of dilation $= \dfrac{3 \text{ ft}}{3 \text{ in.}}$

$$= \frac{3 \cdot 12 \text{ in.}}{3 \text{ in.}}$$

$$= 12$$

Remember to use the same units when you find the scale factor of a dilation.

Guided Practice

Complete each __?__ with a value or word and each (?) with +, −, ×, or ÷.

2 △JKL is dilated by a scale factor of 1.2 to form △J′K′L′.

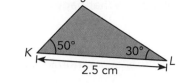

a) Find m∠J′.

△JKL and △J′K′L′ are __?__ triangles.

So, m∠J′ = m∠__?__.

__?__ − 50° − 30° = __?__   ∠ sum of triangle

m∠J′ is __?__.

b) Find the length of $\overline{K'L'}$.

K′L′ = 2.5 (?) 1.2

= __?__ cm

3 △UVW undergoes a geometric transformation to form △XYZ.

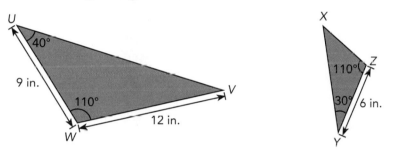

a) Identify whether △UVW ~ △XYZ.

m∠V = 180° − __?__ − __?__   ∠ sum of triangle

= __?__

Since m∠W = m∠Z and m∠V = m∠__?__, two pairs of corresponding angles have equal measures. So, △UVW is __?__ to △XYZ.

b) If △UVW ~ △XYZ, what is the geometric transformation and scale factor?

Scale factor = $\dfrac{YZ}{?}$

= $\dfrac{6}{?}$

= __?__

△UVW undergoes a __?__ by a scale factor __?__ to form △XYZ.

Describe a Sequence of Transformations.

You have seen four types of geometric transformations: translations, reflections, rotations, and dilations. What happens when a figure undergoes a sequence of transformations?

William walks to school every morning. He usually buys a granola bar at the convenience store along his route from home to school, as shown on the map.

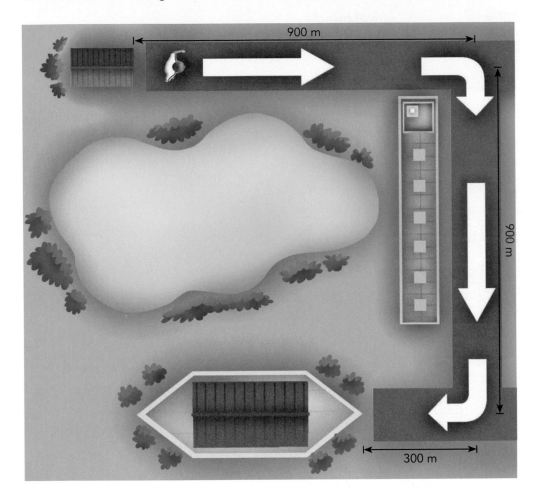

William walks 900 meters east to reach the convenience store. He then turns 90° clockwise and walks another 900 meters south. After that, he turns 90° clockwise and walks 300 meters west to get to school.

Can you describe William's path using a series of geometric transformations?

William's path follows a translation of 900 meters to the right, a clockwise rotation of 90°, followed by a translation 900 meters down, a clockwise rotation of 90°, and then a translation of 300 meters to the left.

You can also describe William's change in position using a single transformation: a translation of 600 meters to the right and 900 meters down.

Example 11 **Describe a sequence of transformations.**

Two pitchers of milk A and B are placed on a dining table. The table is covered with a checkered print table cloth. Describe a sequence of a reflection followed by a translation that maps pitcher A onto pitcher B.

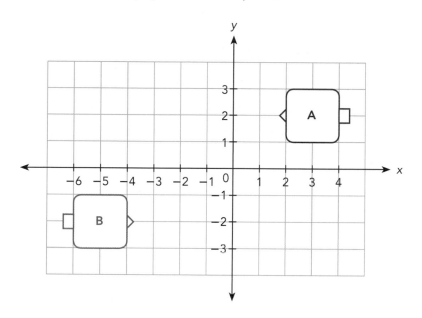

Solution

Pitcher A is mapped onto pitcher B by a reflection in the line $x = -1$ and a translation of 4 units down.

Think Math

Can pitcher A be mapped onto pitcher B by other sequences of two transformations? By a single transformation? If so, what are they?

Guided Practice

Copy and complete.

4 An engineer designs a manufacturing machine to transfer a food package *GHIJ* onto *G'H'I'J'*. Describe a sequence of two transformations that maps *GHIJ* onto *G'H'I'J'*.

GHIJ is mapped onto *G'H'I'J'* by a translation of 2 units up and a reflection in the line ___?___.

Think Math

Does the order in which you do the transformations affect the image in Example 11? in **4** ?

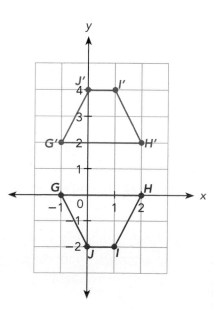

Technology Activity

Materials:
• geometry software

EXPLORE SEQUENCES OF TRANSFORMATIONS

STEP 1 Draw a triangle on a coordinate system using a geometry software. Record the position of each vertex.

STEP 2 Translate the triangle 1 unit down. Then reflect it in the x-axis. Select the *Translate* function and *Reflect* function, within the *Transform* menus. Record the position of each vertex of the image triangle.

STEP 3 Change the order of transformations in **STEP 2**. Record the position of each vertex of this image triangle.

STEP 4 Draw another triangle on a coordinate system using a geometry software. Record the position of each vertex.

STEP 5 Translate the triangle 1 unit to the right. Then dilate it with the center at the origin and scale factor 2. Select the *Translate* function and *Dilate* function, within the *Transform* menus. Record the position of each vertex of the image triangle.

STEP 6 Change the order of transformations in **STEP 5**. Record the position of each vertex of this image triangle.

Math Journal Compare the positions of the original and transformed triangles. Does the order in which you perform two transformations make a difference in the position of the image triangle? Explain.

Relate Congruent and Similar Figures Using a Sequence of Transformations.

A single translation, reflection, or rotation results in an image that is congruent to the original figure. A sequence of these transformations also preserves congruence.

A dilation results in an image that is similar to the original figure. A sequence of transformations that includes a dilation produces a similar image with the same scale factor as the single dilation.

When combining transformations, the order in which the transformations are performed is important. If the order is reversed, the two images may not be in the same position.

△*ABC* is mapped onto △*A'B'C'* under a transformation. △*A"B"C"* is the image of △*A'B'C'* under another transformation.

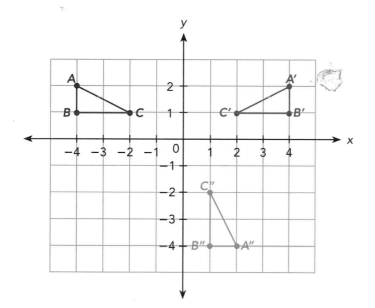

a)   Describe the sequence of transformations that maps △*ABC* onto △*A"B"C"*. Then describe a single transformation equivalent to the combined transformations.

Solution

One sequence is a reflection of △*ABC* in the y-axis and then a rotation of △*A'B'C'* 90° clockwise about the origin. A single transformation is a reflection in the line $y = x$.

b)   If the order of transformations is reversed, draw △*ABC*, △*A'B'C'*, and △*A"B"C"* on a coordinate plane. Does the order of transformations affect the position of △*A"B"C"*?

Solution

△*ABC* is mapped onto △*A'B'C'* by using a rotation of 90° clockwise about the origin. △*A'B'C'* is mapped onto △*A"B"C"* by using a reflection in the y-axis.

In this case, the order of transformations affects the position of the image △*A"B"C"*.

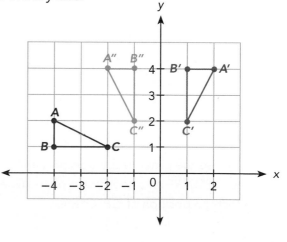

Guided Practice

Copy and complete on a graph paper.

5 *DEFG* is mapped onto *D'E'F'G'* under a transformation. *D"E"F"G"* is the image of *D'E'F'G'* under another transformation.

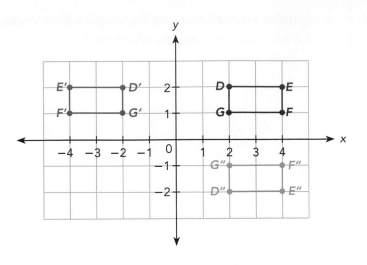

a) Describe the transformations that map *DEFG* onto *D'E'F'G'* and *D'E'F'G'* onto *D"E"F"G"*. Then describe a single transformation that maps *DEFG* onto *D"E"F"G"*.

DEFG is mapped onto *D'E'F'G'* by using a reflection in the ___?___. *D'E'F'G'* is mapped onto *D"E"F"G"* by using a rotation of ___?___ about the origin. *DEFG* is mapped onto *D"E"F"G"* by using a single transformation, which is ___?___.

b) Suppose the order of the transformations is reversed. Draw *DEFG*, *D'E'F'G'*, and *D"E"F"G"* on a coordinate plane. Does the order of the transformations affect the position of *D"E"F"G"*?

6 △*PQR* is mapped onto △*P'Q'R'* under a transformation. △*P"Q"R"* is the image of △*P'Q'R'* under another transformation.

a) Describe the transformation that maps △*PQR* onto △*P'Q'R'* and △*P'Q'R'* onto △*P"Q"R"*.

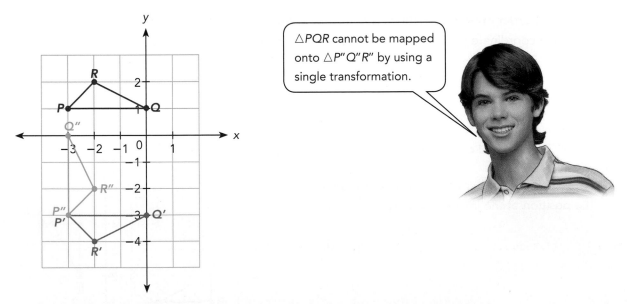

△*PQR* cannot be mapped onto △*P"Q"R"* by using a single transformation.

b) Suppose the order of the transformations is reversed. Draw △*PQR*, △*P'Q'R'*, and △*P"Q"R"* on a coordinate plane. Does the order of the transformations affect the position of △*P"Q"R"*?

Example 13

Relate similar figures using a sequence of transformations.

$\triangle ABC$ is mapped onto $\triangle A'B'C'$ under a transformation. $\triangle A''B''C''$ is the image of $\triangle A'B'C'$ under another transformation. Describe the sequence of transformations from $\triangle ABC$ to $\triangle A''B''C''$.

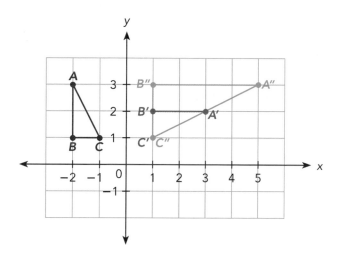

Solution

First rotate $\triangle ABC$ 90° clockwise about the origin. Then dilate the image $\triangle A'B'C'$ by a scale factor 2 and with center (1, 1).

Guided Practice

Copy and complete on a graph paper.

7 $\triangle PQR$ is mapped onto $\triangle P'Q'R'$ under a transformation. $\triangle P''Q''R''$ is the image of $\triangle P'Q'R'$ under another transformation.

a) Describe the transformations that map $\triangle PQR$ onto $\triangle P'Q'R'$ and $\triangle P'Q'R'$ onto $\triangle P''Q''R''$. Then describe a single transformation that maps $\triangle PQR$ onto $\triangle P''Q''R''$.

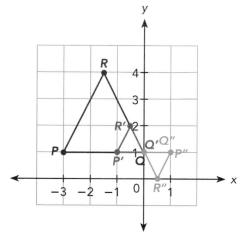

$\triangle PQR$ is mapped onto $\triangle P'Q'R'$ by using a dilation with center (__?__, __?__) and scale factor __?__. $\triangle P'Q'R'$ is mapped onto $\triangle P''Q''R''$ by using a rotation of __?__ about the point (__?__, __?__). $\triangle PQR$ can be mapped onto $\triangle P''Q''R''$ by a single dilation with center (__?__, __?__) and scale factor __?__.

b) If the order of transformations is reversed, draw $\triangle PQR$, $\triangle P'Q'R'$, and $\triangle P''Q''R''$ on a coordinate plane.

State whether the figure and image are congruent or similar.

1 A triangle is rotated 180° about the origin.

2 A pentagon is translated 1 unit to the left and 5 units up.

3 A projector dilates a picture by a scale factor of 10, and projects the image on a screen.

4 A parallelogram is dilated with center (−2, 4) and scale factor 3.5, and rotated 90° clockwise.

5 A cartoon character is reflected in the y-axis and translated to the right.

Solve on a coordinate grid.

6 △ABC undergoes two transformations.

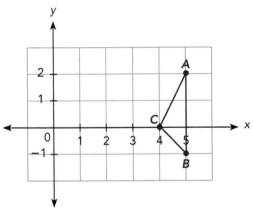

a) What would be the coordinates of △A″B″C″ if △ABC is first translated 2 units up and 3 units left, and then reflected in the line x = 1?

b) What would be the coordinates of △A″B″C″ if △ABC is first reflected in the line x = 1, and then translated 2 units up and 3 units left?

c) Do the two triangles △A″B″C″ have the same coordinates? Are they congruent? Explain.

Solve.

 $\triangle PQR$ is mapped onto triangle $\triangle P'Q'R'$ by using a transformation. $\triangle P''Q''R''$ is the image of $\triangle P'Q'R'$ by using another transformation. Describe the sequence of transformations from $\triangle PQR$ to $\triangle P''Q''R''$.

a)

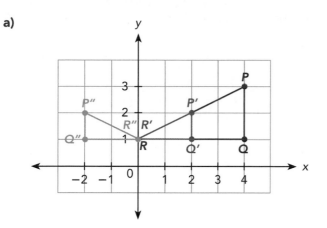

b)

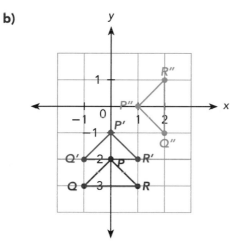

c)

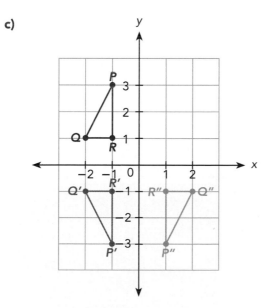

8 △ABC is mapped onto △A'B'C', which is then mapped onto △A"B"C". △ABC and △A"B"C" are shown in each diagram. Describe the sequence of transformations from △ABC to △A"B"C". Then describe a single transformation from △ABC to △A"B"C", if any.

a) △ABC is mapped onto △A'B'C' by a rotation of 180° about (0, 0).

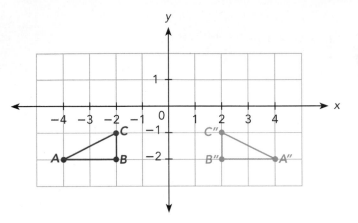

b) △ABC is mapped onto △A'B'C' by a reflection in the line y = 1.

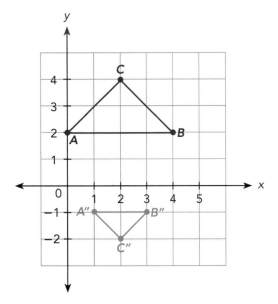

Solve. Show your work.

9 Tom is at position A of a hall whose floor is a square with a bay of window across the front of the room. The length of the square is 30 meters. Describe how he gets to position C by a translation followed by a rotation about the center of the square.

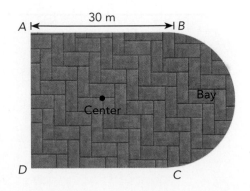

156   **Chapter 9** Congruence and Similarity

10 The figure *PQRST* is dilated with center *P* and a scale factor 1.2. *PQRST* is mapped onto *UVWXY*. The area of *PQRST* is 24 square inches.

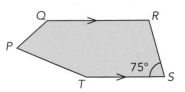

a) Find m∠*VWX*.

b) Find the area of *UVWXY*.

 11 Jack walks into a dark room. The area of the pupils of his eyes dilates to 3 times their normal area to allow more light into his eyes. By what scale factor is the diameter of his pupils enlarged?

12 Two similar cups are filled with water. The volume of water in the big cup is 80 cubic centimeters and the volume of water in the small cup is 10 cubic centimeters. If the height of the big cup is 8 centimeters, what is the height of the small cup?

13 Edward was blowing a circular bubble whose volume grew to 27 times its original size. It then drifted 8 units to the right and 11 units up before it burst.

a) Describe the sequence of transformations that the bubble went through.

b) The original radius of the bubble was 2 centimeters. Find the final radius of the bubble.

14 An airplane at an airport terminal is cleared to take off by the control station after it moves from *P* to *Q*. The airplane's path is marked by the thick arrows in the diagram. Describe the sequence of transformations that the airplane undergoes from *P* to *Q*.

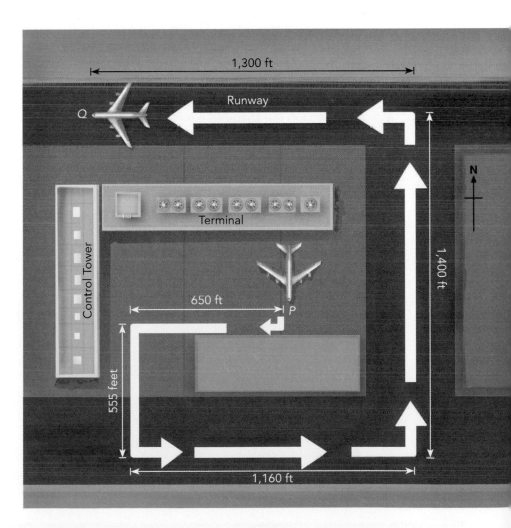

Brain @ Work

1. A bridge is strung between two big trees on opposite sides of a river at *P* and *Q*. The bridge is to be removed and a new bridge is to be built across the river. The new bridge starts at *P* and spans the shortest distance across the river. Briefly describe how you would find the length of the new bridge using congruent triangles.

2. A souvenir in the shape of a rectangular prism is 20 centimeters by 15.5 centimeters by 13 centimeters. A pattern for a rectangular box, 29.2 centimeters by 18.6 centimeters by 16.9 centimeters, needs to be scaled down to fit the souvenir better. What is the minimum size of the box? Recommend a suitable set of measurements to the nearest 0.1 centimeter.

Chapter Wrap Up

Concept Map

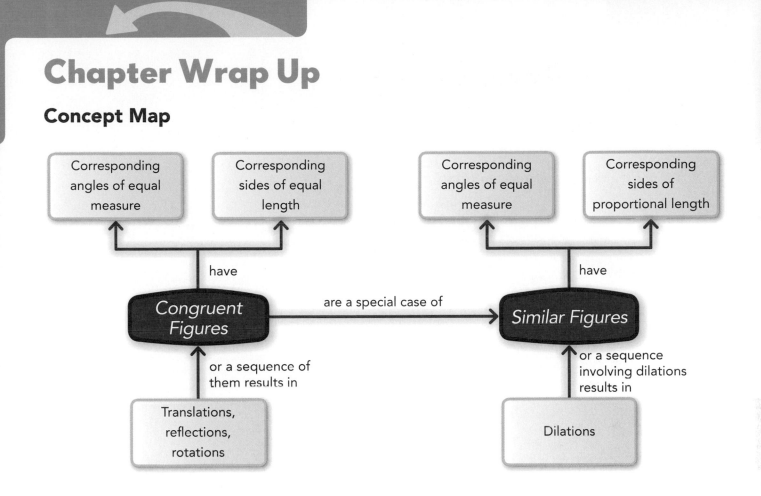

Key Concepts

▶ Congruent figures have the same shape and size.

▶ Similar figures have the same shape and may have different sizes.

▶ When you write a statement of congruence or similarity for two figures, the corresponding vertices must be matched in the same order.

▶ Congruent figures have corresponding angles of the same measure and corresponding sides of the same length.

▶ Similar figures have corresponding angles of the same measure and corresponding sides of proportional lengths.

▶ For any two congruent figures, there is a translation, rotation, reflection, or a sequence of these transformations that maps one figure onto the other.

▶ For any two similar figures, there is a dilation or a sequence involving dilations that maps one figure onto the other.

Chapter Review/Test

Concepts and Skills

Solve.

1 Name the triangle congruent to △ABC.

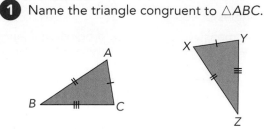

2 ABCDEF is a regular hexagon. Name a quadrilateral congruent to ADCB.

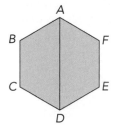

3 $\overline{SQ}$ and $\overline{TP}$ are straight lines. Name the triangle similar to △PQR.

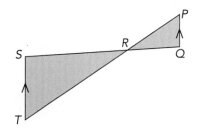

Solve. Show your work.

4 The two figures are congruent. Find the value of each variable.

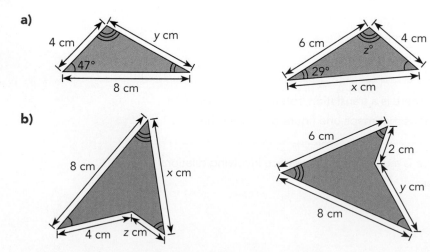

5 The two figures are similar. Find the value of each variable.

a)

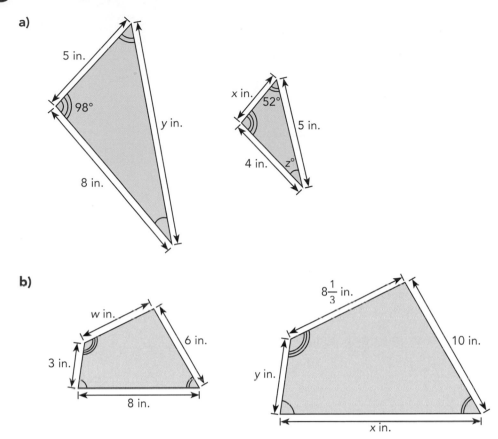

b)

6 State whether the triangles are congruent. If they are congruent, write the statement of congruence and state the test used.

a)

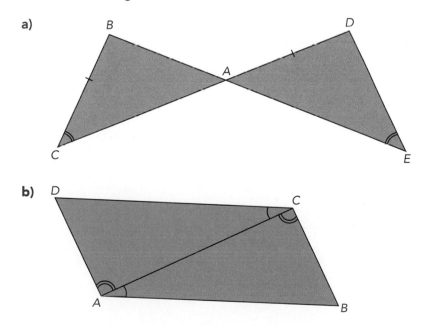

b)

7 State whether the triangles are similar. Explain with a test for similar triangles.

a)

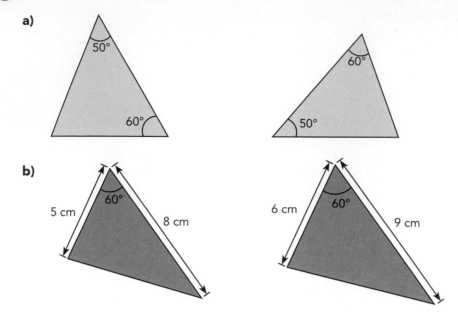

b)

8 △ABC undergoes two reflections to be mapped onto △A″B″C″.

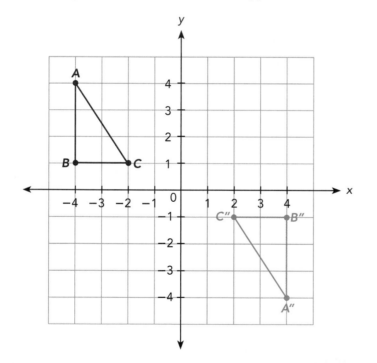

a) Describe one such pair of reflections.

b) Describe a single transformation that would also map △ABC onto △A″B″C″.

Describe the single transformations that maps △ABC onto △A'B'C', △A'B'C' onto △A"B"C", and △ABC onto △A"B"C".

9

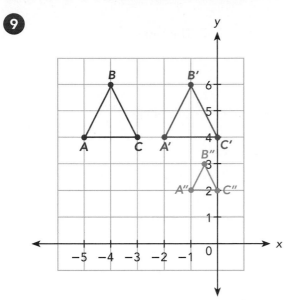

10

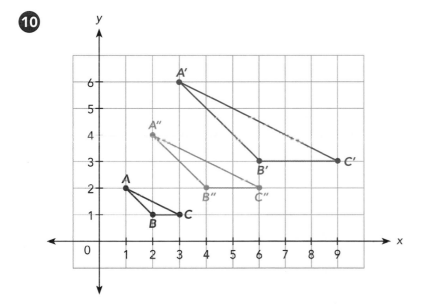

11

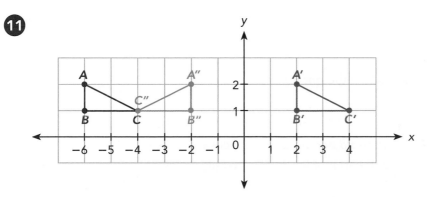

Problem Solving

Solve. Show your work.

12 Two geometrically similar buckets have bases with radii in the ratio 2 : 5. The top of the small bucket has radius 7 inches.

    a) Find the radius of the top of the big bucket.

    b) Write the ratio of the height of the small bucket to the height of the big bucket.

13 A 5-foot tall vertical rod and a 25-foot tall vertical flagpole stand on horizontal ground. At a certain time of the day, the flagpole casts a shadow 30 feet long.

    a) Write a ratio comparing the height of the rod to the height of the flagpole.

    b) Calculate the length of the shadow cast by the rod.

14 Two barrels are geometrically similar. Their heights are 16 inches and 20 inches. The diameter of the base of the larger barrel is 8 inches. Calculate the diameter of the base of the smaller barrel.

15 A photograph is 4 inches wide and 6 inches long. It is enlarged to a width 6 inches.

    a) What is the length of the enlarged photo?

    b) If the original photo is enlarged to a length 12 inches, find the new width.

16 Anthony made an exact copy of the shape *ABCDE* using a photocopier.

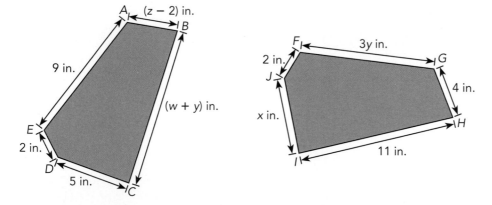

    a) Name the shape congruent to *ABCDE* on the photocopy.

    b) Find the values for *w, x, y,* and *z.*

17 A framed poster has a length of 28 inches and a perimeter of 88 inches. A similar poster has a perimeter of 66 inches. Find the area of the similar poster.

18 A robotic arm with two circular ends moves through a sequence of translations and rotations. The diagram shows two positions of the arm. All dimensions are in centimeters.

a) Find the values of x and y.

b) 🖩 Calculate the area of the robotic arm. Use $\frac{22}{7}$ as an approximation for π.

19 A table, which is in front of a mirror, has the side view $ABCDEFGH$ shown below (all dimensions are in inches). $ABCH$ and $DEFG$ are rectangles. The side view is reflected in the mirror to form the congruent image $STUVWXYZ$.

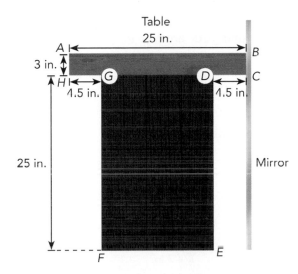

a) State the corresponding angle of $\angle CDE$ and $\angle AHG$.

b) Write the length of $\overline{TU}$, $\overline{WX}$, and $\overline{YZ}$.

c) Find the perimeter of the image.

20 Gisele reduced the size of $\triangle PQR$ with area 14.4 square centimeters using a photocopier. $\triangle PQR \sim \triangle STU$.

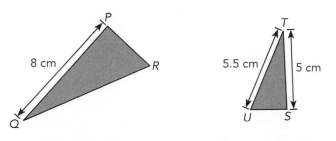

a) What is the scale factor of dilation? Express your answer as a percent.

b) Find the area of $\triangle STU$.

Cumulative Review Chapters 7–9

Concepts and Skills

Find the value of each variable. (Lesson 7.1)

1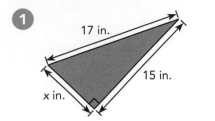
17 in. · 15 in. · x in.

2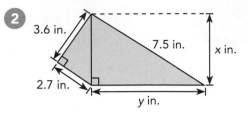
3.6 in. · 7.5 in. · x in. · 2.7 in. · y in.

The side lengths of a triangle are given. Decide whether each triangle is a right triangle. (Lesson 7.1)

3 6 cm, 8 cm, 12 cm

4 9 in., 7.2 in., 5.4 in.

Find the distance between each pair of points. If necessary, round your answer to the nearest tenth of a unit. (Lesson 7.2)

5 P (2, 5), Q (4, 13)

6 X (3, −1), Y (4, 2)

For each solid, find the unknown dimension. If necessary, round your answer to the nearest tenth of a unit. (Lesson 7.3)

7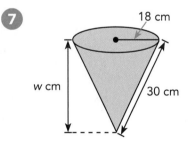
18 cm · w cm · 30 cm

8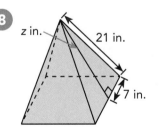
z in. · 21 in. · 7 in.

Find the volume of each composite solid. Use 3.14 as an approximation for π. If necessary, round your answer to the nearest tenth. (Lesson 7.4)

9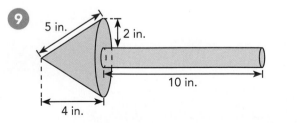
5 in. · 2 in. · 10 in. · 4 in.

10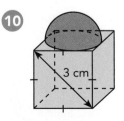
3 cm

Find the coordinates of the image under each translation. (Lesson 8.1)

11 A (3, −2) is translated 1 unit to the right and 8 units up.

12 B (−1, −6) is translated 5 units to the left and 3 units down.

Copy each diagram on graph paper and draw the image under each translation.
(Lesson 8.1)

13 $\overline{XY}$ is translated 3 units to the left and 1 unit up.

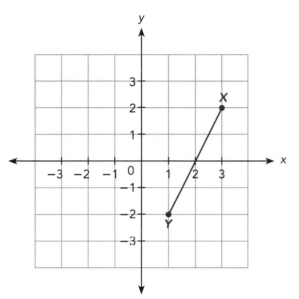

14 Square $ABCD$ is translated 2 units to the right and 2 units down.

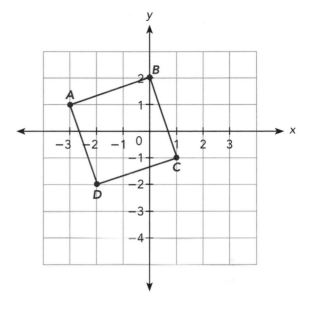

Solve. Show your work.

15 On a coordinate plane, the coordinates of two points are A (3, 4) and B (3, 0). Point A' is the image of point A and point B' is the image of point B under a reflection in the y-axis. (Lesson 8.2)

a)   Find the coordinates of A' and B'.

b)   Draw the image of the line segment OA, where O is the origin, under a reflection in the x-axis. Use 1 grid square on both axes to represent 1 unit for the interval from −4 to 4.

16 Triangle ABC and trapezoid $STUV$ are shown on the coordinate plane. On a copy of the graph, draw the images of triangle ABC under a reflection in the y-axis. Then draw the image of trapezoid $STUV$ under a reflection in the x-axis. (Lesson 8.2)

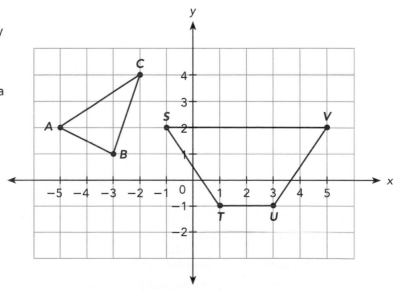

17 A rotation of point A about the origin maps the point onto A'. State the angle and direction of rotation. (Lesson 8.3)

a)

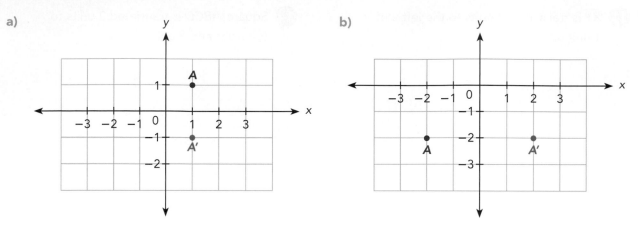

b)

Solve. Show your work.

18 Triangle *ABC* has vertices *A* (2, 3), *B* (3, 1) and *C* (4, 2). Draw the triangle *ABC* and its image under a rotation of 180° about the origin. Use 1 grid square on both axes to represent 1 unit for the interval from −4 to 4. (Lesson 8.3)

Tell whether each transformation is a dilation. Explain. (Lesson 8.4)

19

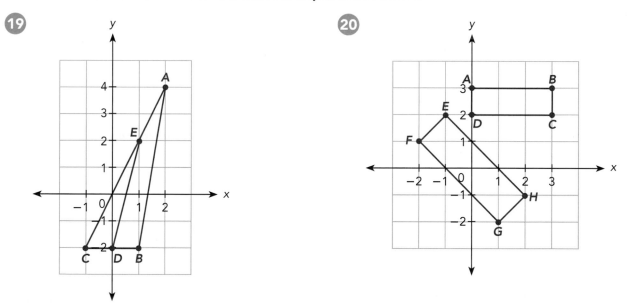

20

Solve. Show your work.

21 The figure described is mapped onto its image by a dilation with its center at the origin, O. Draw each figure and its image on a coordinate plane. (Lesson 8.4)

a) The vertices of triangle *DEF* are *D* (−3, −1), *E* (−3, −4), and *F* (−1, −3). Triangle *DEF* is mapped onto triangle *D'E'F'* with scale factor −2.

b) The vertices of trapezoid *ABCD* are *A* (−2, −2), *B* (−2, −4), *C* (4, −4) and *D* (2, −2). Trapezoid *ABCD* is mapped onto trapezoid *A'B'C'D'* with scale factor $\frac{1}{2}$.

22 The side lengths of a triangle are 3 inches, 6 inches, and 8 inches. The triangle undergoes a dilation. Find the side lengths of the image of the triangle for each of the scale factors in **a)** to **d)**. Tell whether each dilation is an enlargement or a reduction of the original triangle. (Lesson 8.4)

a) 2

b) $\dfrac{1}{4}$

c) 120%

d) 1.6

23 Triangle A with vertices $(-1, 3)$, $(-1, 4)$ and $(-3, 3)$ is mapped onto triangle B. Then triangle B is mapped onto triangle C as shown on the coordinate plane. (Lesson 8.5)

a) Describe the transformation that maps triangle A onto triangle B.

b) Describe the transformation that maps triangle B onto triangle C.

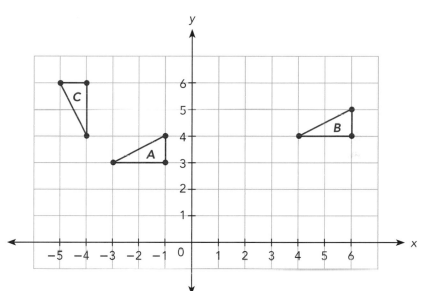

Solve. Show your work.

24 State whether the triangles are congruent. If they are congruent, write the statement of congruence and state the test used. (Lesson 9.1)

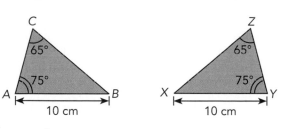

25 $\triangle AMS$ is congruent to $\triangle ERN$. Find the values of x and y. (Lesson 9.1)

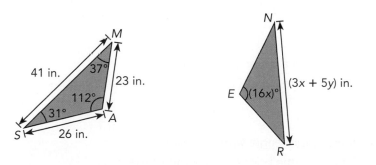

Triangle _ABC_ is similar to triangle _PQR_. Find the value of _a_. (Lesson 9.2)

29

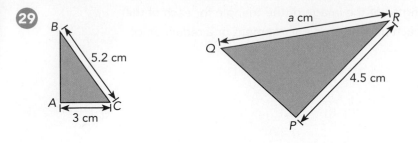

Name the test you can use to determine whether the two triangles are similar. Then find the value of _x_. (Lesson 9.2)

27

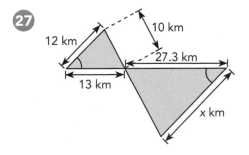

Solve on a coordinate grid. (Lesson 9.3)

28 △_ABC_ undergoes two transformations to form the image △_A″B″C″_.

a) What are the coordinates of △_A″B″C″_ if △_ABC_ is first translated 2 units to the right and 3 units down, and then reflected in the line _x_ = 2?

b) What are the coordinates of △_A″B″C″_ if △_ABC_ is first reflected in the line _x_ = 2, and then translated 2 units to the right and 3 units down?

c) Do the two triangles △_A″B″C″_ described in a) and b) have the same coordinates? Are they congruent? Explain.

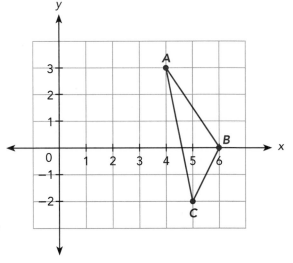

Problem Solving

Solve. Show your work.

29 A pool table has a width of 5.5 inches. A ball travels a distance of 12.3 inches diagonally from one corner to the other corner of the table. Find the length of the pool table, rounded to the nearest tenth. (Chapter 7)

30 When a drawbridge is open, the bridge forms a right angle with the doorway it leads to. A straight chain connects the far end of the bridge to the top of the doorway. If the doorway is 2 meters high and the chain is 2.5 meters long, find the length of the bridge, rounded to the nearest tenth. (Chapter 7)

31 Gabriel photocopied an exact copy of the shape *ABCDE*. The photocopied shape is shown on the right. (Chapter 9)

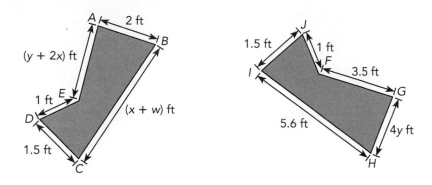

a) Name the shape congruent to *ABCDE*.

b) Find the values of *w*, *x*, and *y*.

Solve. Show your work. (Chapters 7, 9)

32 Mary wants to pour 130 cm³ of water into the conical cup shown.

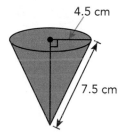

a) 🖩 Find the volume of the conical cup. Use 3.14 as an approximation for π. Round your answer to the nearest tenth.

b) Will the water overflow? Explain.

33 Two cones are similar in shape. The ratio of the diameters of their bases is 2 : 7. The radius of the smaller cone is 4.5 inches.

a) Find the radius of the larger cone.

b) Write the ratio of the height of the smaller cone to the height of the larger cone.

Solve. Show your work. (Chapters 8, 9)

34 A car is 25 feet long and 6 feet wide. A model of the same car is 9 inches long. What is the width of the model of the car if the model is a dilation of the car?

35 Figure *PQRST* is dilated with center *P* and a scale factor of 1.45. Under this dilation, it is mapped onto figure *UVWXY*. Figure *UVWXY* is then mapped onto *ABCDE* by a reflection about segment *UV*.

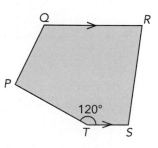

a) Tell whether *PQRST* and *ABCDE* are congruent or similar figures. Explain.

b) Find m∠*UYX*.

c) The area of *PQRST* is 20 square inches. Find the area of *ABCDE*.

CHAPTER

10

10.1 Scatter Plots

10.2 Modeling Linear Associations

10.3 Two-Way Tables

Statistics

Have you ever been in a bike race?

Two things that a cyclist has to think about in a bike race are cadence and speed. The cyclist's cadence is the rate at which he or she turns the pedals. The cyclist can try to maintain a steady cadence by adjusting gears as he or she travels up or down hills.

The cyclist's speed, or the distance he or she travels over time, is related to his or her cadence. For a given gear setting, an increase in cadence leads to an increase in speed.

Cadence and speed are an example of bivariate data. In this chapter, you will learn to use scatter plots and draw lines of fit for sets of bivariate data.

BIG IDEA

▶ A line of best fit can be used to model the linear association of bivariate quantitative data. A two-way table displays the relative frequencies of categorical data.

Recall Prior Knowledge

Finding relative frequencies

The table shows the numbers of items ordered by 90 customers at a snack bar during a noontime rush hour. It also shows the relative frequency of each item.

Item	Number Ordered	Relative Frequency
Hot dogs	18	$\frac{18}{90} = 0.2$
Nachos	9	$\frac{9}{90} = 0.1$
Hamburgers	36	$\frac{36}{90} = 0.4$
Grilled cheese sandwiches	18	$\frac{18}{90} = 0.2$
Popcorn buckets	9	$\frac{9}{90} = 0.1$

The sum of the relative frequencies is 1.

Quick Check

Solve.

1. The table shows the numbers of students involved in four sports at a high school. Find the relative frequency for each sport.

Sport	Number of Students	Relative Frequency
Baseball	35	$\frac{?}{?} = ?$
Tennis	42	$\frac{?}{?} = ?$
Soccer	56	$\frac{?}{?} = ?$
Swimming	7	$\frac{?}{?} = ?$

Scatter Plots

Lesson Objectives

- Construct a scatter plot given two sets of quantitative data.
- Identify patterns of association between two sets of quantitative data.
- Identify outliers in a scatter plot.

Vocabulary

scatter plot	quantitative data
association	bivariate data
clustering	

Construct a **Scatter Plot** Given Two Sets of **Quantitative Data.**

Quantitative data is a set of data that is used to describe a type of information that can be counted or expressed numerically.

Suppose you are exploring whether the steepness of the slope affects the speed of a cyclist cycling up the slope.

Cyclists from Team Blue were timed as they rode a hilly course. Their speeds, y miles per hour, climbing various inclines, x, are shown in the table.

Angle of Incline	6	12	4	10	9	6	7	11	0
Speed (mi/h)	4.6	2	5	1.6	3	4	3.4	3	6.2

Angle of Incline	14	2	9	2	3	10	12	3	5
Speed (mi/h)	2	6	4	5.4	6	2.6	3	5	4

The data recorded in the table is quantitative data. That is, all the data is numeric.

A scatter plot is a graph made by plotting ordered pairs in a coordinate plane. The points show the **association** between two sets of quantitative data or **bivariate data**. You can make a scatter plot to find the association between the angle of incline and the speed of the cyclists.

A scatter plot is created in a coordinate plane. Let one of the variables be represented by the horizontal axis and the other variable by the vertical axis. Then plot the data as points determined by the ordered pairs of corresponding values.

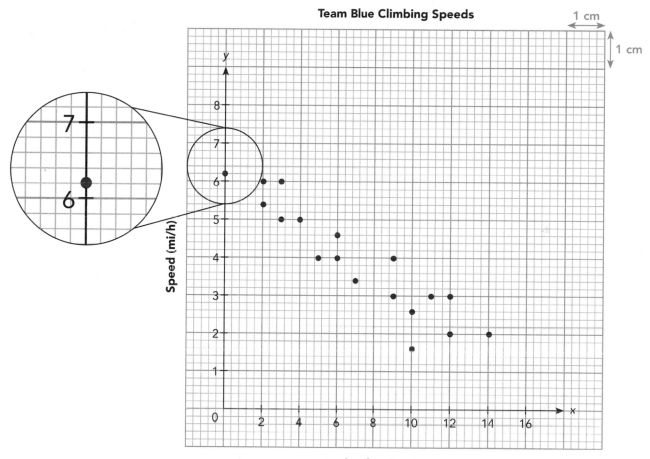

Team Blue Climbing Speeds

Speed (mi/h)

Angle of Incline (°)

The scale for the vertical axis is using 1 cm = 1 mi/h. So, to plot the point (0, 6.2) on the vertical axis, find the value represented by each tick mark between whole numbers. Because there are 5 intervals within 1 unit, each tick mark represents 1 ÷ 5 = 0.2 unit, or 0.2 mi/h.

So, 6.2 mi/h is located at the first mark above 6.

Example 1 **Draw a scatter plot given a table of bivariate data.**

The table shows the results of an experiment to determine the length, y centimeters, that a spring stretches with mass, x grams.

Mass (g)	100	200	300	200	400	500	100	600	200
Length of spring (cm)	13.5	17.5	20.0	19.5	22.0	25.5	15.0	28.0	18.0

Mass (g)	300	400	100	400	200	100	600	300	500
Length of spring (cm)	20.5	21.5	16.0	22.5	18.5	15.5	27.0	21.0	25.0

Use 2 centimeters on the horizontal axis to represent 100 grams. Use 2 centimeters on the vertical axis to represent 5 centimeters. Construct a scatter plot of this data.

100 g

Solution

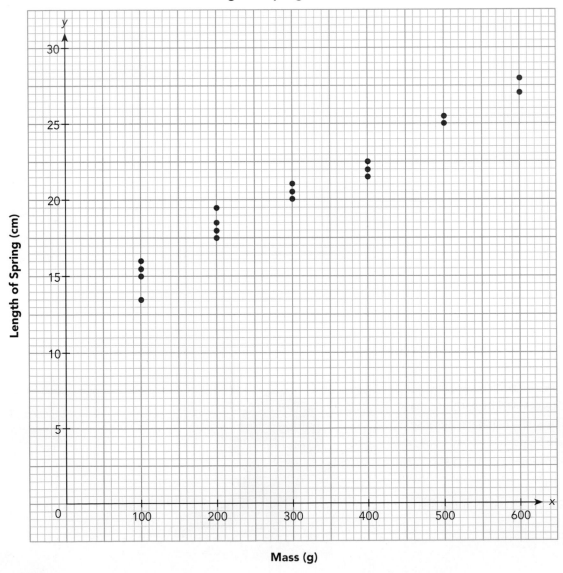

Length of Spring When Stretched

Guided Practice

Use graph paper. Solve.

 The table shows some monetary exchanges between U.S. dollars, x dollars, and Japanese yen, y yen, over a time period of 4 months at a major airport.

U.S. Dollar	10	20	28	42	54	60	12	18	34
Japanese Yen (1,000s)	0.8	1.7	2.3	3.4	4.6	4.9	1.0	1.5	2.7

U.S. Dollar	36	48	54	34	52	18	12	26	44
Japanese Yen (1,000s)	3.1	3.8	4.5	2.9	4.2	1.4	0.9	2.0	3.6

Construct a scatter plot for this data. Use 2 centimeters on the horizontal axis to represent $10. Use 2 centimeters on the vertical axis to represent 500 yen.

Identify Patterns of Association Between Two Sets of Quantitative Data.

You can use scatter plots to identify and study association between any bivariate data. A scatter plot can show whether there is an association or no association between the two sets of data. If there is an association, it can be strong or weak, linear or nonlinear, positive or negative.

Association between data sets

Two data sets can have a strong association, a weak association, or no association, depending on the **clustering** of data points in the coordinate plane.

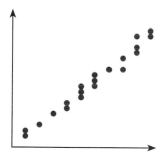

Strong Association

The data points cluster in a predictable pattern.

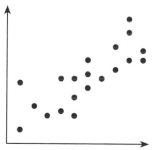

Weak Association

The data points cluster loosely in a pattern that is less predictable.

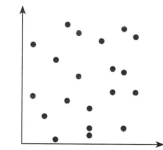

No Association

The data points show no apparent trend at all. A pattern cannot be found.

1. Strong Association

If the data sets have a strong enough association, you can probably determine whether the pattern is positive or negative and linear or nonlinear.

Continue on next page

a) Data sets with positive or negative association

When two data sets have a positive association, an increase in one data set corresponds to an increase in the other data set. When they have a negative association, an increase in one data set corresponds to a decrease in the other data set.

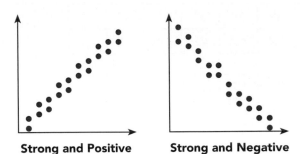

Strong and Positive   **Strong and Negative**

b) Data sets with linear or nonlinear association

When two data sets have linear association, the points tend to cluster along a line. When they have nonlinear association, the points tend to cluster along a nonlinear pattern.

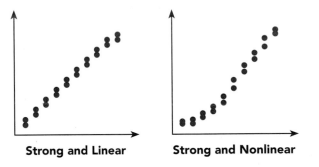

Strong and Linear   **Strong and Nonlinear**

2. Weak Association

If the data sets have a weak association, it is harder to tell whether there is any pattern between the bivariate data.

Sometimes bivariate data that have an association can appear to have a weak association due to insufficient data points.

3. No Association

If the data sets have no association, you can conclude that the bivariate data do not vary with each other.

Example 2 **Identify association between bivariate data.**

Describe the association between the bivariate data shown in each scatter plot.

Solution

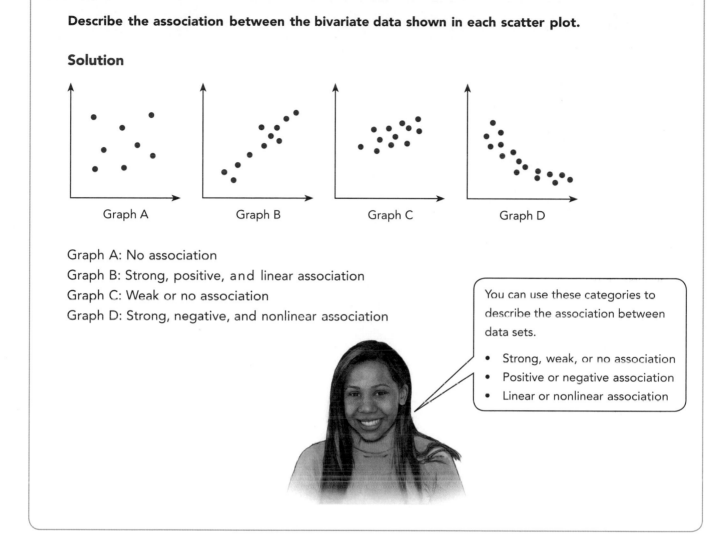

Graph A | Graph B | Graph C | Graph D

Graph A: No association

Graph B: Strong, positive, and linear association

Graph C: Weak or no association

Graph D: Strong, negative, and nonlinear association

You can use these categories to describe the association between data sets.

- Strong, weak, or no association
- Positive or negative association
- Linear or nonlinear association

Guided Practice

Complete.

2 Describe the association between the bivariate data shown in each scatter plot.

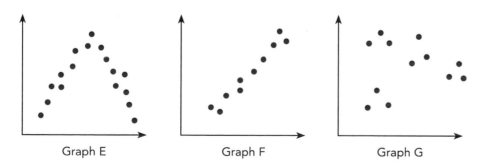

Graph E | Graph F | Graph G

Graph E: __?__ and __?__ association

Graph F: __?__, __?__, and __?__ association

Graph G: __?__ association

Identify Outliers in a Scatter Plot.

An outlier is a data point that is very different from the rest of the data points in the data set.

Suppose the number of vehicles, y, passing through an intersection, x minutes past 7:00 A.M. in a business district is recorded for three days. The data is shown below.

Time Past 7:00 A.M. (min)	0	60	30	45	60	15	90	30
Vehicles	7	27	17	22	26	10	15	18

Time Past 7:00 A.M. (min)	75	15	30	75	45	45	15	60
Vehicles	32	13	15	33	25	24	12	24

Traffic Patterns at Intersection

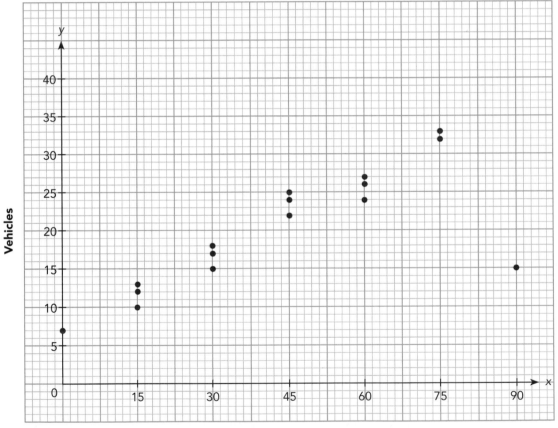

Time Past 7.00 A.M. (min)

The scatter plot shows a strong, positive, and linear association. However, the point at 90 minutes past 7:00 A.M. is very different from the pattern seen in the other data points. This point is called an outlier. The outlier could indicate that the busiest commuting time is ending.

Example 3 **Identify outliers in a scatter plot.**

The scatter plot displays bivariate data on the time, x hours, students spend studying for a history exam and the corresponding scores, y, earned on the exam.

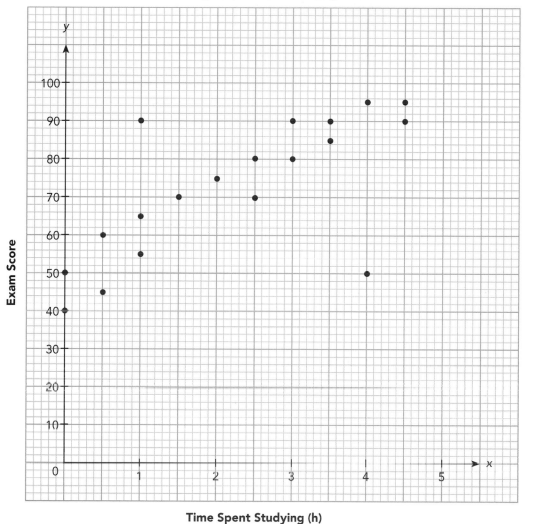

Study and Scores on History Exam

a) Identify any outlier(s).

Solution

Outliers appear to be located at (1, 90) and (4, 50).

b) Explain what the outlier(s) likely represent(s) in this context.

Solution

The data point (1, 90) represents a score of 90 earned by a student who studied only 1 hour for the exam. The data point (4, 50) represents a score of 50 earned by a student who studied 4 hours for the exam.

Continue on next page

c) Describe the meaning in context of the association between the two data sets. Validate the outliers as being very different from the rest of the data points.

Solution

The strong, positive, and linear association indicates that students who studied more for the history exam earned higher scores. The general trend shows that students who studied only 1 hour earned a score between 50 and 70. However, one student, represented by the outlier, scored a 90 with only 1 hour of study. The general trend shows that students who studied as much as 4 or more hours tended to earn a score of 90 or above. One outlier represents a student's score of 50 after 4 hours of study.

Guided Practice

Use graph paper. Solve.

3 Dan is investigating the effect of the amount of water, x, given to tomato seedlings on their growth. He waters each of the 22 plants with a given amount of water daily. He records their height, y, at the end of two weeks. His data is shown below.

Water (fl oz)	4	24	20	12	16	4	20	8	20	28	12
Height (in.)	2.2	11.2	8.8	5.4	8.8	2.4	9.6	3.0	9.2	4.8	6.2

Water (fl oz)	8	4	12	12	28	24	24	8	16	16	28
Height (in.)	4.0	1.6	5.0	4.8	12.4	9.6	10.4	3.2	7.8	8.0	13.2

a) Construct a scatter plot for this data. Use 1 centimeter on the horizontal axis to represent 4 fluid ounce. Use 1 centimeter on the vertical axis to represent 1 inch. Identify any outlier(s).

An outlier appears to be located at (__?__ , __?__).

b) Explain what the outlier(s) likely represent(s) in this context.

The outlier represents __?__ and __?__ after two weeks.

c) Describe the meaning in context of the association between the two data sets. Validate the outliers as being very different from the rest of the data points.

The __?__ , __?__ , and __?__ association indicates that tomato seedlings that are given more water daily experience __?__ growth over the two weeks. The general trend shows that seedlings that are given 28 fluid ounces of water daily generally grew about __?__ inches, but the outlier represents a seedling that grew only __?__ inches with __?__ fluid ounces of water daily.

Practice 10.1

Draw scatter plot for each of the given table of bivariate data.

1 Use 1 centimeter on the horizontal axis to represent 10 units. Use 1 centimeter on the vertical axis to represent 20 units.

x	10	20	30	70	50	40	50
y	36	60	100	212	156	124	144

x	30	20	30	10	60	60	70
y	96	64	92	40	184	180	216

2 Use 1 centimeter on the horizontal axis to represent 5,000 people. Use 2 centimeters on the vertical axis to represent 5,000 cars.

Population (x in 1,000s)	10	20	20	35	30	10	40
Cars (y in 1,000s)	1	2	3	15	9	2	32

Population (x in 1,000s)	25	15	15	25	40	35	20
Cars (y in 1,000s)	4	1	2	5	30	16	5

3 Use 1 centimeter on the horizontal axis to represent 1 hour. Use 1 centimeter on the vertical axis to represent a score of 10.

Study Time (x hours)	2	3	5	6	7	4	9
Test Score (y)	22	32	48	62	76	40	90

Study Time (x hours)	8	5	6	4	7	9	3
Test Score (y)	84	52	60	42	72	86	36

Describe the association between the bivariate data shown in each scatter plot.

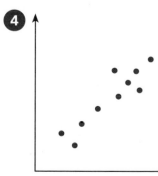

Describe the association between the bivariate data shown in each scatter plot.

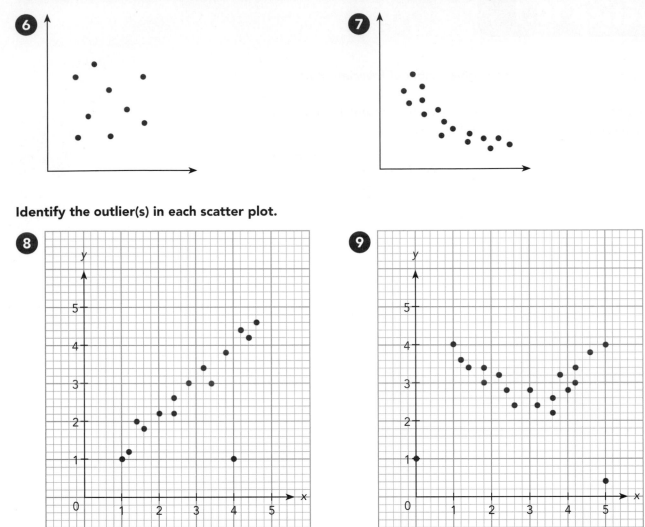

6

7

Identify the outlier(s) in each scatter plot.

8

9

Use the table of bivariate data below to answer questions 10 to 13.

A retailer wanted to know the association between the number of items sold, *y*, and the number of salespeople, *x*, in a store. So she recorded the number of salesperson and items sold over 16 days in the table below.

Salespeople	46	48	43	52	52	51	43	47
Items Sold	208	200	192	200	184	212	208	200

Salespeople	48	44	45	51	46	50	49	50
Items Sold	188	200	204	196	192	52	184	200

10 Use graph paper to construct the scatter plot. Use 1 centimeter on the horizontal axis to represent 1 salesperson for the *x* interval from 43 to 52. Use 1 centimeter on the vertical axis to represent 20 items.

11 Identify the outlier. Give a likely explanation for the occurrence of the outlier.

12 Describe the association between the number of items sold and the number of salespeople in the store. Explain your answer.

13 *Math Journal* If the data collected for the number of salespeople ranged from 0 to 100, do you think the answer to **12** would be different? Explain why a wide range of sampling values might be important when investigating the association between bivariate data.

Use the table of data below to answer questions 14 to 17.

To investigate the benefits of warming up before playing a baseball game, 14 amateur baseball players were surveyed. The number of game injuries, *x*, in a year and the time the player spent warming up for each game, *y* minutes, are recorded below.

Warm-up Time (min)	4.5	1.5	1	2.5	3	5	0
Game Injuries	11	27	32	23	18	10	39

Warm-up Time (min)	4	2	3.5	0.5	1	2	4.5
Game Injuries	10	24	11	36	30	23	10

14 Use graph paper to construct the scatter plot. Use 2 centimeters on the horizontal axis to represent 1 minute. Use 1 centimeter on the vertical axis to represent 5 game injuries.

15 Identify any outliers.

16 *Math Journal* Is there a linear association between the number of game injuries and the time spent warming up before each game? Explain.

17 *Math Journal* From the results shown, can you recommend minimum warm-up time for baseball players before they start a game? How does analyzing association of data sets help to provide useful information?

10.2 Modeling Linear Associations

Lesson Objectives

- Understand a line of best fit.
- Write a linear equation for a line of best fit.
- Use an equation for a line of best fit.

Vocabulary

line of best fit   interpolate

extrapolate

Hands-On Activity

Materials:
- measuring tape

CONSTRUCT AND INTERPRET SCATTER PLOTS

Work in groups of 5.

Background

A person's height is closely associated with their arm span. In a medical context, this association can be used to estimate realistic lengths for prosthetic limbs. In this activity, you will collect data on the heights and arm spans of classmates.

STEP 1 Measure the arm span of one group member while he or she is standing straight up against a wall with arms stretched out from the body and with all the fingers extended fully. Measure the arm span from the tip of the middle finger of one hand all the way to the other middle finger on the other hand.

STEP 2 While in the same position, use a ruler to mark the member's height on the wall. While holding the ruler, ask the member to step away so you can measure the height.

STEP 3 Repeat **1** and **2** with the other group members.

STEP 4 Organize the data in a table like the one shown below.

Height (x inches)	?	?	?	?	?
Arm Span (y inches)	?	?	?	?	?

STEP 5 Collect data from all the groups. Construct a scatter plot with the collected data.

Math Journal From the scatter plot drawn, describe any association you see between the height and arms span.

Using the collected data, obtain a measure for the arm span of a schoolmate. Use the scatter plot to predict his or her height. Compare your estimations with the actual measurements to find how accurate the estimate is.

Understand Line of Best Fit.

Consider a scatter plot with a strong linear association between a set of bivariate data. In order to describe the association quantitatively for a set of bivariate data, you can estimate a line of best fit for the scatter plot. A line of best fit closely follows the linear pattern of the data points.

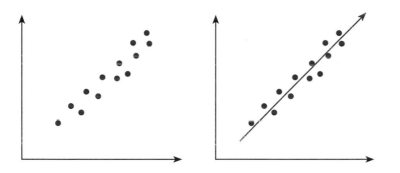

One method for constructing a line of best fit is:

STEP 1 Plot the points.

STEP 2 Use a ruler to divide the points equally on both sides. Ignoring outliers, about half of the data points should be above the line and about half of the data points should be below the line. It is possible to have some points lying on the ruler line.

STEP 3 Select two points that your line of best fit would go through, and use them to sketch a line through the data points.

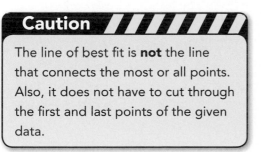

Caution ////////

The line of best fit is **not** the line that connects the most or all points. Also, it does not have to cut through the first and last points of the given data.

Example 4 **Graph a line of best fit given bivariate data with a linear association.**

Data from a study of the association between the amount of rainfall, x inches, and the number of car accidents, y, along a particular stretch of highway are shown below.

Rainfall (in.)	2	3	4	6	6	5	4	7	8
Accidents	3	8	9	12	11	9	7	14	16

Rainfall (in.)	6	7	2	8	5	3	4	8	7
Accidents	1	15	6	17	10	6	8	14	13

a) Construct the scatter plot and sketch a line of best fit to represent the data. Use 1 centimeter on the horizontal axis to represent 1 inch. Use 1 centimeter on the vertical axis to represent 2 car accidents.

Solution

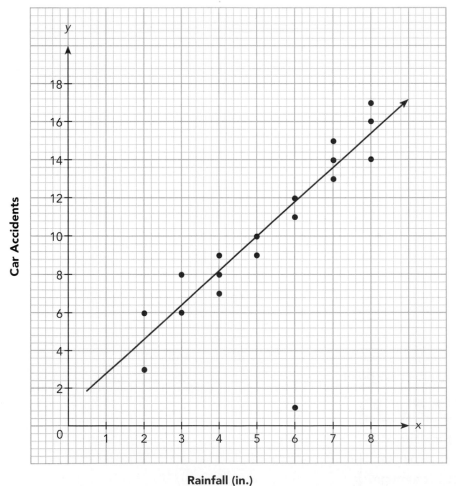

Car Accidents in the Rain

Use a ruler to draw a line of best fit that has about half of the data points above and half of the points below the line. Ignore any outliers when sketching a line of best fit.

b) Identify the association and describe the meaning of the association in context.

Solution

There is a strong, positive, and linear association between the number of car accidents and the amount of rainfall. In other words, more rainfall is associated with more car accidents.

c) Identify the outlier and describe the meaning of the outlier in context.

Solution

The data point (6, 1) is an outlier representing only 1 accident when there is 6 inches of rain.

> **Think Math**
>
> What are some possible reasons that could cause the outlier?

Guided Practice

Use graph paper. Solve.

1 A city collected data over the course of a week to find the association between the number of waste bins per acre, x, in their parks and the pounds of litter collected, y pounds, in each bin. The data is shown below.

Waste Bins Per Acre	12	24	16	10	18	20	26	16
Litter (lb/bin)	70	18	50	66	42	32	12	44

Waste Bins Per Acre	22	16	14	22	10	20	12	18
Litter (lb/bin)	26	58	62	30	74	40	62	4

a) Construct a scatter plot for this data. Use 1 centimeter on the horizontal axis to represent 2 waste bins per acre for x interval from 8 to 26. Use 1 centimeter on the vertical axis to represent 5 pounds of litter per week. Sketch a line of best fit for the given table of data.

b) Identify the association and describe the meaning of the association in context.

There is a __?__, __?__, and __?__ association between the number of waste bins per acre and the pounds of litter collected per bin.

c) Identify the outlier and describe the outlier in context.

The data point (__?__, __?__) is an outlier representing only __?__ pounds of litter collected per bin when there are __?__ waste bins per acre in the park.

Write a Linear Equation for a Line of Best Fit.

Recall that a line can be represented in the form $y = mx + b$. So, the line of best fit can be represented as a linear equation where the values of m and b can be determined from the scatter plot.

Example 5 **Write a linear equation for a line of best fit.**

The table below gives the percent of adults, y percent, that get their news from newspapers compared to television or online during x years since 1990.

Years Since 1990	0	2	4	6	8	10	12	14	16
Percent of Adults	64.8	66.4	64.0	61.2	62.4	60.4	60.0	59.6	54.8

a) Construct the scatter plot for the given table of bivariate data. Use 1 centimeter on the horizontal axis to represent 2 years. Use 1 centimeter on the vertical axis from 54 to 68 to represent 2%. Sketch a line of best fit and write its equation.

Solution

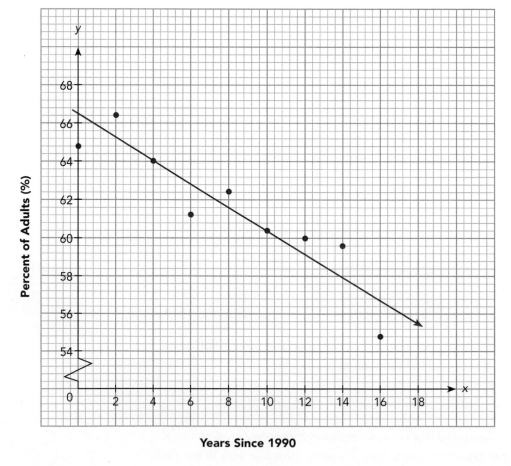

First find the slope of the line of best fit that passes through the points (4, 64) and (14, 58).

$$m = \frac{58 - 64}{14 - 4} = \frac{-6}{10} = -0.6$$

Math Note

You can pick any two points on the line of best fit to calculate the value of m. Only use data values if they happen to lie on the line.

Next find the y-intercept using the equation in slope-intercept form.

$y = mx + b$	Use slope-intercept form.
$64 = -0.6(4) + b$	Substitute for m, x, and y.
$64 = -2.4 + b$	Multiply.
$64 + 2.4 = -2.4 + b + 2.4$	Add 2.4 to both sides.
$66.4 = b$	Simplify.

Finally, write an equation.

$y = mx + b$

$y = -0.6x + 66.4$ Substitute -0.6 for m and 66.4 for b.

The equation of the line of best fit is $y = -0.6x + 66.4$.

b) Interpret the meaning of the slope and the y-intercept in context.

Solution

The slope m represents the decreasing percent of adults that acquire their news from newspapers. Specifically, the data show an average decrease by 0.6% per year.

The intercept b represents the percent of adults that get their news from newspapers at the beginning of the study in 1990. Specifically, the data show that about 66.4% of adults got their news from newspaper in 1990.

Guided Practice

Use graph paper. Solve.

2 A city collected data to find the association between the daily high temperature, x °F, and the number of pool visitors, y, that day. The data is shown below.

Daily High Temperature (°F)	96	92	86	90	98	88	94	96
Daily Pool Visitors	312	304	256	284	352	272	320	336

Daily High Temperature (°F)	90	98	86	92	98	92	94	98
Daily Pool Visitors	276	340	248	296	360	324	300	316

Construct a scatter plot for this data. Use 1 centimeter on the horizontal axis to represent 2°F on the x interval from 84 to 98. Use 1 centimeter on the vertical axis to represent 10 pool visitors on the y interval from 220 to 360. Sketch a line that appears to best fit the data and write its equation.

Use an Equation for a Line of Best Fit.

You can use an equation of a line of best fit to make estimates or predictions. When you use a line of best fit or its equation to predict a value between data points that you already know, you **interpolate** the predicted value. When you make a prediction that is outside of the range of the data, you **extrapolate** the predicted value.

Example 6 **Use a line of best fit to estimate data.**

The diagram below shows the scatter plot of data in **Example 5**.

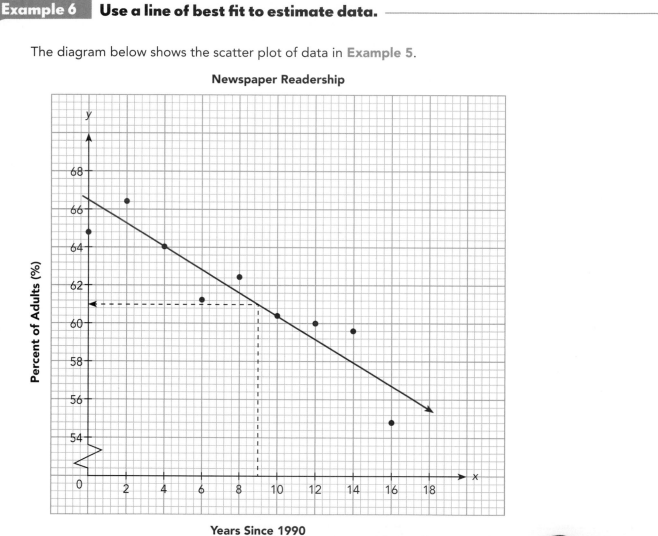

Newspaper Readership

Years Since 1990

a) Estimate the percent of adults that got their news from newspaper in the year 1999.

Solution

1999 is 9 years after 1990, so find the point on the line of best fit that has an x-value of 9.

The estimate is reasonable because the linear trend followed through the year 1999. Usually, interpolating data is more accurate than extrapolating data.

The point is approximately (9, 61), so the percent of adults that got their news from newspapers in 1999 is about 61%.

b) Estimate the percent of adults that got their news from newspapers in the year 2010.

Solution

The data includes up to year 2006. You can use the equation of the line to extrapolate an estimate for the year 2010.

Using $y = -0.6x + 66.4$, substitute 20 for x.
$y = -0.6(20) + 66.4 = 54.4\%$

According to the trend observed in previous years, about 54.4% of adults got their news from newspapers in year 2010.

Caution ////////

Be careful when you extrapolate estimates or predictions because you need to assume that the linear trend continues outside the range of the data collected. The farther out from the data you estimate, the less reliable your estimate will be.

Guided Practice

Use graph paper. Solve.

3 The scatter plot below shows the number of eggs hatched, y, per 100 eggs in an incubator with varying temperatures, $x°F$.

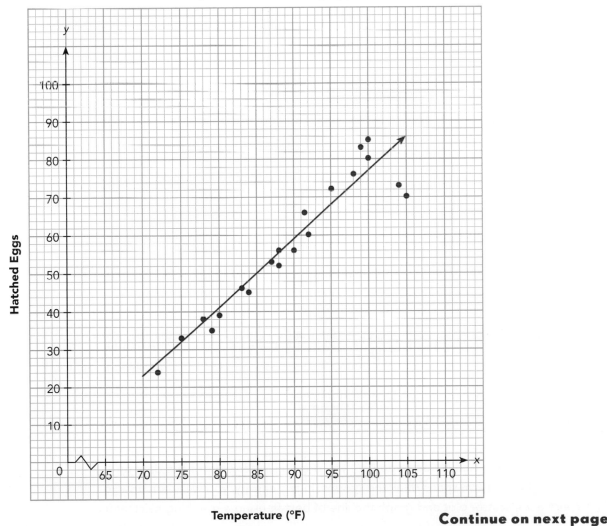

Temperature and Hatching Eggs

Continue on next page

a) Given that the line of best fit passes through (80, 41) and (95, 68), find the equation of the line of best fit.

First find the slope of the line of best fit that passes through the points (80, 41) and (95, 68).

$$m = \frac{?-?}{?-?} = \frac{?}{?} = \underline{\quad?\quad}$$

Next find the *y*-intercept using the equation in slope-intercept form.

$y = mx + b$	Use slope-intercept form.
$\underline{\;?\;} = \underline{\;?\;}(\underline{\;?\;}) + b$	Substitute for *m*, *x*, and *y*.
$\underline{\;?\;} = \underline{\;?\;} + b$	Multiply.
$\underline{\;?\;} - \underline{\;?\;} = \underline{\;?\;} + b - \underline{\;?\;}$	Subtract $\underline{\;?\;}$ from both sides.
$\underline{\;?\;} = b$	Simplify.

Finally, write an equation.

$y = mx + b$

$y = \underline{\;?\;}x + \underline{\;?\;}$ Substitute $\underline{\;?\;}$ for *m* and $\underline{\;?\;}$ for *b*.

The equation of the line of best fit is $\underline{\;?\;}$.

b) Use the graph to estimate the number of eggs that would hatch per 100 eggs if the temperature of the incubator is kept at 86°F.

About $\underline{\;?\;}$ eggs could be predicated to hatch if the incubator is kept at a temperature of $\underline{\;?\;}$.

c) Use the equation to estimate the number of eggs that would hatch per 100 eggs if the temperature of the incubator is kept at 65°F.

Using the equation $\underline{\;?\;}$, substitute $\underline{\;?\;}$ for *x*.

$y = \underline{\;?\;} \cdot \underline{\;?\;} - \underline{\;?\;} = \underline{\;?\;}$

About $\underline{\;?\;}$ eggs could be expeced to hatch when the temperature of the incubator is kept at 65°F.

Technology Activity

Materials:
• graphing calculator

USE A GRAPHING CALCULATOR TO GRAPH A LINE OF BEST FIT FOR A SCATTER PLOT

Background

In the Hands-On Activity on page 186, you drew a scatter plot for the data on the heights and arm spans of all the groups. In this activity, you will learn how to construct a scatter plot and graph the line of best fit using a graphing calculator.

STEP 1 Press **STAT** and select 1:Edit to choose the edit function. Input the data for arm spans in column L1 and the data for heights in column L2. You should have at least 20 data points to interpret the data accurately.

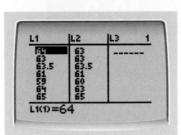

STEP 2 Press **2ND** **Y=** and select 1 to go to the scatter plot setting screen. Under Type, select the scatter plot options as shown.

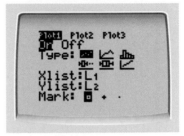

STEP 3 Press **GRAPH** to see the scatter plot.

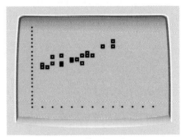

STEP 4 Press **STAT** and select CALC, 4: LinReg(ax+b). Press **2ND** **1** **,** **2ND** **2** **,** **VARS** and select Y VARS, 1:Function and 1:Y1. Press **ENTER**. This step is to find the values of m and b for the line of best fit. In the graphing calculator, the value of m is denoted by a.

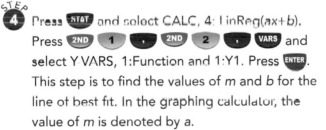

STEP 5 Press **GRAPH** to see the scatter plot and the line of best fit. Press **ZOOM** and select 9:ZoomStat to zoom in the graph.

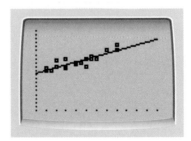

Math Journal Compare the hand drawn scatter plot and the one drawn using graphing calculator. Is there any difference between the line of best fit drawn by hand and by the graphing calculator? Compare both sets of m and b values. Discuss how you can plot a better line of best fit based on the m and b values obtained using the graphing calculator.

Practice 10.2

State the line that represents the line of best fit for each scatter plot.

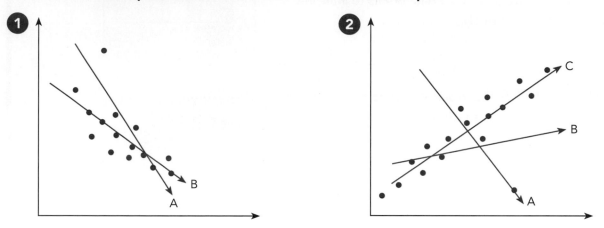

Construct each scatter plot and draw a line of best fit for each table of bivariate data.

3 Use 1 centimeter on the horizontal axis to represent 1 unit. Use 1 centimeter on the vertical axis to represent 20 units.

x	4	1	2	3	5	6	3	6	2	7
y	72	12	32	164	88	112	52	88	40	136

4 Use 1 centimeter on the horizontal axis to represent 1 unit for the x interval from 80 to 87. Use 1 centimeter on the vertical axis to represent 10 units for the y interval from 200 to 300.

x	80	84	81	87	81	86	82
y	220	236	214	256	200	250	292

x	83	83	84	85	85	83	82
y	220	240	238	240	244	232	222

5 Use 1 centimeter on the horizontal axis to represent 0.1 unit. Use 1 centimeter on the vertical axis to represent 5 units for the y interval from 20 to 70.

x	0.1	0.9	0.3	0.4	0.4	1.1	1.0
y	69	59	66	65	64	58	61

x	0.8	0.5	0.7	0.7	0.6	0.2	0.5
y	59	65	63	60	30	68	62

Construct a scatter plot and draw a line of best fit for each table of bivariate data. Find an equation of the line of best fit.

6 Use 2 centimeters on the horizontal axis to represent 1 tree for the *x* interval from 13 to 18. Use 1 centimeter on the vertical axis to represent 20 squirrels for the *y* interval from 260 to 480.

Trees (x)	13	15	13	17	18	16	17
Squirrels Population (y)	344	408	356	388	468	420	476

Trees (x)	14	14	16	16	18	15	15
Squirrels Population (y)	264	368	440	400	476	400	392

7 Use 1 centimeter on the horizontal axis to represent 5 kilometers. Use 1 centimeter on the vertical axis to represent 1 liter for the *y* interval from 5 to 16.

Distance (x kilometers)	15	23	56	32	53	23	48
Gasoline Used (y liters)	5.8	6.6	10.2	7.4	16.0	6.8	9.4

Distance (x kilometers)	53	20	43	28	37	31	16
Gasoline Used (y liters)	9.6	6.2	8.8	7.2	8.0	7.4	5.8

Use the scatter plot below to answer questions 8 to 13.

Snow density is an important factor affecting the speed and control in snow boarding. To understand the relationship between snow density, y grams per cubic centimeters, and air temperature, x°C, data are collected and shown below.

Air Temperature (°C)	−17	−16	−15	−14	−13	−12	−11	−10
Snow Density (g/cm³)	0.036	0.060	0.050	0.060	0.054	0.070	0.086	0.090

8 Use graph paper to construct the scatter plot. Use 1 centimeter on the horizontal axis to represent 1°C for the *x* interval from −17 to −9. Use 1 centimeter on the vertical axis to represent 0.010 grams per cubic centimeter.

9 Describe the association between air temperature and snow density.

10 Sketch a line of best fit.

11 Find an equation for the line of best fit.

12 Predict the density when the temperature is at −14.5°C.

13 Predict the density when the temperature is at −9°C.

10.3 Two-Way Tables

Lesson Objectives

- Read data from a two-way table.
- Construct and interpret a two-way table.
- Convert data to relative frequencies in a two-way table.

Read Data from a Two-Way Table.

A scatter plot represents two sets of quantitative data, such as distance, time, height, or area, which are expressed with numerical measurements. A two-way table represents frequencies for two sets of **categorical data** or **qualitative data**, such as gender, sport, flavor, color, or shape. The rows indicate one category and the columns indicate another.

Consider a class of 40 students. There are 15 boys and 25 girls. 8 boys wear glasses and 9 girls wear glasses. The frequencies can be represented neatly using a two-way table.

Number of boys who do not wear glasses = 15 − 8 = 7
Number of girls who do not wear glasses = 25 − 9 = 16

> The number **7** in the two-way table is placed in the **Boy** row and under the **No** column. This is read as there are 7 boys who do not wear glasses.

Glasses

Gender		Yes	No	Total
	Boy	8	7	15
	Girl	9	16	25
	Total	17	23	40

Notice that the totals, or cumulative frequencies, allow you to see how the class is distributed among the two categories, **Gender** variables and **Glasses** variables. There are 10 more girls in the class than boys in the class.

You can also use relative frequencies to summarize relationships in the data.

Example 7　Read a two-way table.

The results of a poll of 100 adults about their favorite sport are shown in the two-way table below. Some information is missing from the table.

Favorite Sport

		Basketball	Baseball	Tennis	Swimming	Total
Gender	**Men**	16	27	5	12	60
	Women	2	6	16	?	?
	Total	?	?	?	?	?

a) Find the total number of women.

Solution

Total number of women = 100 − 60 = 40

There are 40 women in total.

b) Find the number of women who chose swimming as their favorite sport.

Solution

Number of women who chose swimming
= Total number of women − Number of women who chose other sports
= 40 − 2 − 6 − 16
= 16

16 women chose swimming as their favorite sport.

c) Complete the table with the total number of men and women who chose each sport.

Solution

Total number of people who chose basketball = 16 + 2 = 18
Total number of people who chose baseball = 27 + 6 = 33
Total number of people who chose tennis = 5 + 16 = 21
Total number of people who chose swimming = 12 + 16 = 28

Favorite Sport

		Basketball	Baseball	Tennis	Swimming	Total
Gender	**Men**	16	27	5	12	60
	Women	2	6	16	16	40
	Total	18	33	21	28	100

Guided Practice

Solve.

1 A survey asked 1,000 gym members what type of exercises they do when they visit the gym. The results are recorded in a two-way table as shown.

Exercise Type

<table>
<thead>
<tr><th rowspan="2">Gender</th><th></th><th>Cardio</th><th>Weights</th><th>Both</th><th>Total</th></tr>
</thead>
<tbody>
<tr><td>**Male**</td><td>125</td><td>279</td><td>?</td><td>?</td></tr>
<tr><td>**Female**</td><td>295</td><td>68</td><td>118</td><td>481</td></tr>
<tr><td>Total</td><td>?</td><td>347</td><td>233</td><td>1,000</td></tr>
</tbody>
</table>

a) Find the total number of male gym members surveyed.

Total number of males = Total surveyed − Total number of females

$$= \underline{\quad?\quad} - \underline{\quad?\quad}$$

$$= \underline{\quad?\quad}$$

The total number of male gym members surveyed is __?__.

b) Find the number of male gym members who chose both types of exercises.

Number of males who chose both
= Total number of males − Number of males who chose cardios − Number of males who chose weights

$$= \underline{\quad?\quad} - \underline{\quad?\quad} - \underline{\quad?\quad}$$

$$= \underline{\quad?\quad}$$

The number of male gym members who chose both types of exercises is __?__.

c) Find the total number of gym members who chose cardio exercises.

Total number of members who chose cardios
= Number of males who chose cardios + Number of female who chose cardios

$$= \underline{\quad?\quad} + \underline{\quad?\quad}$$

$$= \underline{\quad?\quad}$$

The total number of gym members who chose cardio exercises is __?__.

Construct and Interpret a Two-Way Table

Look at the cards shown below.

A two-way table can be constructed to display the frequencies of categories in the cards shown. Follow these steps:

STEP 1 Look for categories for the given cards. For this example, you can see that there are 3 colors (blue, red, and green), and 3 shapes (circle, triangle, and square).

STEP 2 Create columns for one category and rows for the other category. For this example, create columns for the shapes and rows for the colors.

STEP 3 Complete the table with the frequencies for each pair of categories, such as blue card with circles, blue card with triangles, blue card with squares, and so on.

STEP 4 Add a Total column and Total row to record the sums.

The constructed two-way table will be as follows:

		Shape			
		Circle	**Triangle**	**Square**	Total
Color	**Blue**	1	2	0	3
	Red	2	3	1	6
	Green	0	2	1	3
	Total	3	7	2	12

Example 8 **Construct and interpret a two-way table.**

A survey of 20 students was conducted regarding their study preferences and sports preferences.

Study	S	S	G	S	G	S	S	G	G	S
Sport	I	I	I	T	T	I	I	T	T	T

Study	G	S	G	G	G	S	S	G	G	S
Sport	I	T	T	I	T	I	I	T	T	T

S represents self study
G represents group study
I represents individual sport
T represents team sport

a) Construct a two-way table to display the data.

Solution

Sport

		Individual	Team	Total
Study	**Self**	6	4	10
	Group	3	7	10
	Total	9	11	20

Math Note

Always check that column totals and row totals have equal sums. In this table, both sums are 20.

b) Describe what you can see in the data from the totals row and column.

Solution

From the table, it appears that the preferences for self study and group study is equally divided. The team or individual sports preferences also appear to be divided equally.

c) Is there any association between student study preferences and the type of sports they prefer?

Solution

From the table, it appears that those who prefer self study also prefer individual sports. Also, those who prefer group study prefer team sports.

Guided Practice

Solve.

2 An athletic club owner wants to know which cardio exercise is most popular: cycling, running, or swimming. The owner is also interested in whether athletic club members read sports magazines. He surveys 20 randomly selected athletic club members. Results are shown below.

Favorite Cardio Exercise	S	R	S	C	C	R	C	R	S	R
Sports Magazines	N	N	Y	Y	Y	N	N	N	N	Y

Favorite Cardio Exercise	R	C	C	R	R	R	R	S	S	C
Sports Magazines	N	Y	Y	N	N	Y	N	Y	Y	Y

C represents cycling
R represents running
S represents swimming
Y represents read sports magazines
N represents do not read sports magazines

a) Summarize the data into a two-way table.

b) Which cardio exercise do club members prefer?

The total number of members who chose cycling, running, and swimming is
__?__, __?__, and __?__ respectively. So members prefer __?__.

c) What percent of club members read sports magazines?

The total number of club members surveyed is __?__.

The number of people that read sports magazines is __?__.

Percent of participants that read sports magazines is __?__.

d) Describe any association between the type of cardio exercise that the club members prefer and whether the members read sports magazines.

The number of cyclists, runners, and swimmers that read sports magazines is
__?__, __?__, and __?__. So, more __?__ prefer to read sports magazines.

There is __?__ association between the type of cardio exercise that the club members prefer and whether the members read sports magazines.

Convert Data to Relative Frequencies in a Two-Way Table.

Data can be converted to relative frequencies in a two-way table so that the result can be easily compared, especially when numbers are large.

Consider a factory of 1,984 workers. The two-way table below shows the number of male and female workers and whether or not they are late for work.

		Late		Total
		Yes	**No**	Total
Gender	**Male**	140	575	715
	Female	183	1,086	1,269
	Total	323	1,661	1,984

There are two ways of converting this data into relative frequencies.

Recall that relative frequency of an item is the number of items divided by the total number of all items. The sum of the relative frequencies is 1.

The relative frequencies in the table below show the distribution of male and female workers among workers who are late for work and the distribution of male and female workers among workers who are not late for work.

		Late	
		Yes	**No**
Gender	**Male**	$\frac{140}{323} \approx 0.43$	$\frac{575}{1,661} \approx 0.35$
	Female	$\frac{183}{323} \approx 0.57$	$\frac{1,086}{1,661} \approx 0.65$
	Total	1	1

The relative frequencies in the table below show the distribution of the workers who are late or not late by gender.

		Late		Total
		Yes	**No**	Total
Gender	**Male**	$\frac{140}{715} \approx 0.20$	$\frac{575}{715} \approx 0.80$	1
	Female	$\frac{183}{1,269} \approx 0.14$	$\frac{1,086}{1,269} \approx 0.86$	1

Example 9 **Convert data to relative frequencies in a two-way table.**

From **Example 7**, the two-way table below shows the results of a poll of 100 adults about their favorite sport.

Favorite Sport

Gender		Basketball	Baseball	Tennis	Swimming	Total
	Men	16	27	5	12	60
	Women	2	6	16	16	40
	Total	18	33	21	28	100

a) Find the relative frequencies to compare and describe the distribution of the genders among each sport. Round your answer to the nearest hundredth where necessary.

Solution

Favorite Sport

Gender		Basketball	Baseball	Tennis	Swimming
	Men	$\frac{16}{18} \approx 0.89$	$\frac{27}{33} \approx 0.82$	$\frac{5}{21} \approx 0.24$	$\frac{12}{28} \approx 0.43$
	Women	$\frac{2}{18} \approx 0.11$	$\frac{6}{33} \approx 0.18$	$\frac{16}{21} \approx 0.76$	$\frac{16}{28} \approx 0.57$
	Total	1	1	1	1

There are more men than women who prefer basketball and baseball. There are more women than men who prefer tennis and swimming.

b) Find the relative frequencies to compare and describe the distribution of favorite sports among each gender. Round your answer to the nearest hundredth where necessary.

Solution

Favorite Sport

Gender		Basketball	Baseball	Tennis	Swimming	Total
	Men	$\frac{16}{60} \approx 0.27$	$\frac{27}{60} = 0.45$	$\frac{5}{60} \approx 0.08$	$\frac{12}{60} = 0.20$	1
	Women	$\frac{2}{40} = 0.05$	$\frac{6}{40} = 0.15$	$\frac{16}{40} = 0.40$	$\frac{16}{40} = 0.40$	1

Most men chose baseball as their favorite sport and tennis was chosen by the fewest men. Most women chose tennis and swimming as their favorite sports and basketball was chosen by the fewest women.

Guided Practice

Copy the table. Solve. Round your answer to the nearest hundredth where necessary.

3 A survey asked 1,000 gym members what type of exercises they do when they visit the gym. The results are recorded into a two-way table as shown.

Exercise

Gender		Cardio	Weights	Both	Total
	Male	125	279	115	519
	Female	295	68	118	481
	Total	420	347	233	1,000

a) Find the relative frequencies to compare the distribution of genders among each type of exercises.

Exercise

Gender		Cardio	Weights	Both
	Male	$\frac{?}{?} \approx$ ___?___	$\frac{?}{?} \approx$ ___?___	$\frac{?}{?} \approx$ ___?___
	Female	$\frac{?}{?} \approx$ ___?___	$\frac{?}{?} \approx$ ___?___	$\frac{?}{?} \approx$ ___?___
	Total	1	1	1

b) Describe the distribution of male and female gym members for each type of exercises.

More ___?___ members do cardio exercises than ___?___ members.

More ___?___ members do weight exercises than ___?___ members. Among those who do both types of exercises, it is ___?___ distributed between male and female gym members, with slightly more ___?___ members.

c) Find the relative frequencies to compare the distribution of the type of exercises among each gender.

Exercise

Gender		Cardio	Weights	Both	Total
	Male	$\frac{?}{?} =$ ___?___	$\frac{?}{?} =$ ___?___	$\frac{?}{?} =$ ___?___	1
	Female	$\frac{?}{?} =$ ___?___	$\frac{?}{?} =$ ___?___	$\frac{?}{?} =$ ___?___	1

d) Describe the distribution of male and of female gym members for each type of exercises.

Among male members, most do ___?___ exercises and least do ___?___ exercises.

Among female members, most do ___?___ exercises and least do ___?___ exercises.

Identify the categorical data.

1 Temperature, Weight, Color

2 Street name, Number of boxes, Time

Identify whether the given data is categorical or quantitative.

3 Large, medium, small

4 20 mi/h, 40 mi/h, 50 mi/h

Use the two-way table to answer questions 5 to 9.

In some states, all passengers in a vehicle are required to wear a seat belt when the vehicle is on a public road. A poll of 275 randomly selected vehicle passengers was conducted in a state that has the seat belt law to determine the association between passengers who know the seat belt law and passengers who obey this law.

Knows Seat Belt Law

		Yes	No	Total
Wears Seat Belt	Yes	130	?	?
	No	?	15	50
	Total	165	110	275

5 Find the number of passengers who wear seat belts.

6 Find the number of passengers who wear seat belts and do not know the seat belt law.

7 Find the number of passengers who do not wear seat belts and know the seat belt law.

8 Describe what you can see in the data from the row totals and column totals.

9 Is there any association between the passengers who know the seat belt law and passengers who obey the seat belt law?

Use the data below to answer questions ⑩ to ⑫.

A survey of 24 households shows whether they save a portion of their income regularly and whether they have life insurance.

Save Regularly	NS	S	S	S	NS	NS	NS	NS	NS	S	S	S
Have Life Insurance	NL	NL	L	L	L	NL	NL	NL	NL	L	NL	L

Save Regularly	S	NS	NS	NS	S	S	S	S	NS	NS	NS	NS
Have Life Insurance	L	NL	NL	L	NL	L	L	L	NL	L	NL	NL

S represents save regularly
NS represents do not save regularly
L represents have life insurance
NL represents do not have life insurance

⑩ Arrange the above data into a two-way table.

⑪ Do more or fewer households have life insurance than not? Support your answer with the given data.

⑫ Is there any association between households that save regularly and households that have life insurances? Justify your answer from the data.

Use the table to answer questions ⑬ to ⑮.

The table below shows whether the sales target of salesperson are met and whether they are paid on commission.

Sales Target Met

Commission		Yes	No	Total
	Yes	245	85	330
	No	12	64	76
	Total	257	149	406

⑬ Find the relative frequencies among the rows, and interpret their meanings. Round your answer to the nearest hundredth where necessary.

⑭ Find the relative frequencies among the columns, and interpret their meanings. Round your answer to the nearest hundredth where necessary.

⑮ Describe the association between a salesperson meeting the sales target and whether the salesperson is paid on commission.

Brain @ Work

1. Mindy was shown two scatter plots.

   a) The diagram below shows the first scatter plot.

   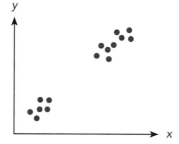

   Mindy concluded that there is a linear association between the bivariate data. But her teacher told her she is wrong. Explain why her teacher says so.

   b) The diagram below shows the second scatter plot.

   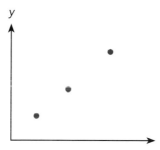

   Mindy concluded that there is a linear association between the bivariate data. Her teacher disagree with her. Explain why.

2. A school principal conducted research to find out about students learning a second language and students learning music. He surveyed 500 students, and the relative frequencies of the data are shown below.

		Learn Second Language	
		Yes	No
Learn Music	Yes	0.9	0.45
	No	0.1	0.55
	Total	1	1

   a) The total number of students who are learning second language is 200. Find the total number of students who are and who are not learning music.

   b) Represent the actual data in a two-way table.

Chapter Wrap Up

Concept Map

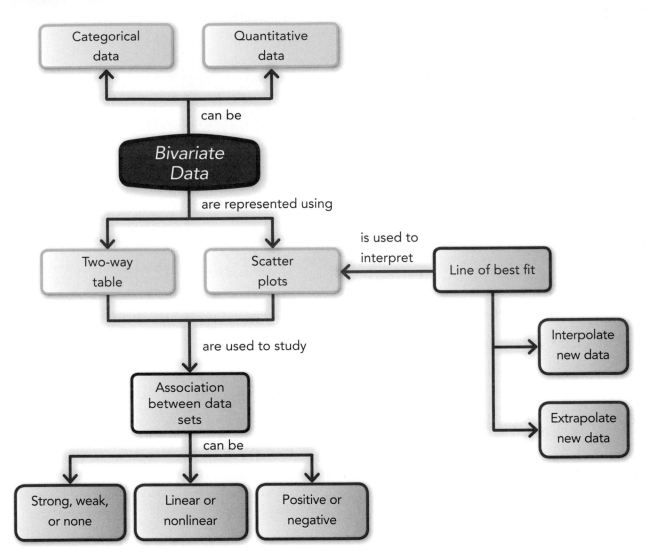

Key Concepts

▶ Scatter plots are used to show and investigate patterns of association between bivariate data.

▶ A line of best fit can be used to interpret the association between bivariate data represented in a scatter plot.

▶ An equation for the line of best fit can help to estimate unknown values in a situation or make predictions.

▶ A two-way table can be used to represent data and study the association between two categorical data sets of a population.

Chapter Review/Test

Concepts and Skills

Draw scatter plot for each of the given table of bivariate data.

1 Use 2 centimeters on the horizontal axis to represent 1 unit. Use 1 centimeter on the vertical axis to represent 5 units for the *y* interval from 50 to 110.

x	3.5	2.3	3.4	1.8	2.5	2.9	3.0
y	93	61	88	53	50	80	81

x	2.4	3.2	2.0	3.8	2.1	3.5	3.9
y	67	85	56	101	58	95	106

2 Use 2 centimeters on the horizontal axis to represent 10 units for the *x* interval from 90 to 120. Use 1 centimeter on the vertical axis to represent 5 units for the *y* interval from 60 to 100.

x	100	96	106	92	118	93	97
y	78	76	61	82	77	83	79

x	103	98	107	99	98	115	100
y	79	80	79	96	79	77	80

Describe the association between the bivariate data shown in each scatter plot.

State the line that represents the line of best fit for each scatter plot.

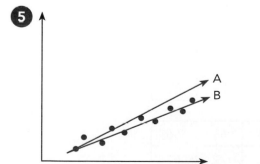

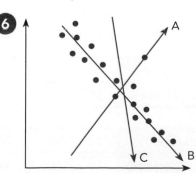

Identify the outlier(s) in each scatter plot.

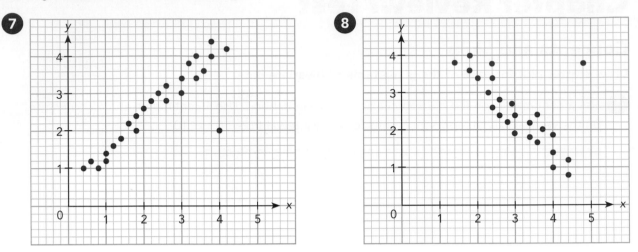

7 **8**

Construct each scatter plot and draw a line of best fit for the given table of bivariate data.

9 Use 1 centimeter on the horizontal axis to represent a score of 10. Use 1 centimeter on the vertical axis to represent a score of 5.

Score for English Test (x)	20	44	32	56	50	68	72
Score for Math Test (y)	18	42	44	52	50	52	66

Score for English Test (x)	68	78	42	58	60	28	48
Score for Math Test (y)	56	60	36	54	62	32	46

10 Use 1 centimeter on the horizontal axis to represent 1,000 products. Use 1 centimeter on the vertical axis to represent $50.

Products Sold (x)	1,000	2,000	2,000	4,000	5,000	8,000	4,000
Commission Earned (y)	120	190	180	330	40	610	340

Products Sold (x)	7,000	6,000	3,000	1,000	5,000	6,000	3,000
Commission Earned (y)	550	470	270	100	400	480	260

11 Use 2 centimeters on the horizontal axis to represent 5 inches. Use 1 centimeter on the vertical axis to represent 5 inches for the y interval from 35 to 90.

Height (x inches)	56	72	70	63	55	56	61
Arm Span (y inches)	58	73	39	67	56	56	89

Height (x inches)	60	65	70	57	64	69	66
Arm Span (y inches)	59	65	69	57	66	72	69

Identify whether the given data is categorical or quantitative.

12 Brown, green, blue

13 $1, $2, $3, $4

14 1 A.M., 2 A.M., 3 A.M.

Use the two-way table to answer questions 15 to 18.

Like Swimming

Like Jogging		Yes	No	Total
	Yes	156	40	_?_
	No	_?_	132	204
	Total	228	_?_	_?_

15 Copy and complete the two-way table.

16 Describe the association between the two categorical data.

17 Find the relative frequencies among the rows, and interpret their meanings. Round your answer to the nearest hundredth where necessary.

18 Find the relative frequencies among the columns, and interpret their meanings. Round your answer to the nearest hundredth where necessary.

19 Construct a two-way table using the data below.

Participated in a Marathon	NM	NM	M	M	NM	NM	NM	NM
Member of a Fitness Club	NF	NF	F	F	F	NF	NF	F

Participated in a Marathon	NM	NM	NM	M	M	NM	NM	M
Member of a Fitness Club	NF	F	NF	F	F	NF	NF	F

M represents participarted in a marathon
NM represents not participarted in a marathon
F represents member of a fitness club
NF represents non-member of a fitness club

Problem Solving

Refer to the scenario below to answer questions 20 to 27.

A bank wants to reduce the number of hours that its tellers work per month. To do this, more Automated Teller Machines (ATMs) are installed in the branch offices. The table below shows the number of ATMs, x, in the branch offices and the corresponding number of hours per month, y, that its tellers work.

ATMs	3	10	4	11	1	12	5
Teller Hours	184	110	176	98	210	88	168

ATMs	6	7	8	8	5	9	7
Teller Hours	154	88	146	150	222	118	156

20 Use graph paper to construct the scatter plot for the above bivariate data. Use 1 centimeter on the horizontal axis to represent 1 ATM. Use 1 centimeter on the vertical axis to represent 10 hours for the y interval from 80 to 230.

21 Describe the association between the number of hours that tellers work and the number of ATMs.

22 Identify the outlier(s).

23 Draw a line of best fit.

24 Write an equation for the line of best fit.

25 Using the equation in **24**, predict the number of teller hours required per month when there are 2 ATMs.

26 Using the equation in **24**, predict the number of teller hours required per month when there are 15 ATMs.

27 *Math Journal* Explain why the equation is **24** cannot be used to predict the number of teller hours required per month for more than 30 ATMs. Discuss the accuracy of the prediction.

Refer to the scenario below to answer questions 28 to 32.

A survey is conducted to find out if providing nutrition information on the menu affects whether patrons recommend the restaurant to others.

Nutritional Information	NP	NP	P	P	NP	NP	NP	P	P	NP
Customer Recommended	R	R	R	NR	R	R	R	R	R	R

Nutritional Information	NP	P	NP	NP	P	NP	NP	P	P	NP
Customer Recommended	NR	R	R	NR	NR	R	NR	R	R	NR

P represents provide nutritional information
NP represents do not provide nutritional information
R represents recommend
NR represents do not recommend

28 Construct a two-way table using the above data.

29 Are there greater or fewer people that are informed of the nutrition of the food they eat?

30 Find the relative frequencies among the rows, and interpret their meanings. Round your answer to the nearest hundredth where necessary.

31 Find the relative frequencies among the columns, and interpret their meanings. Round your answer to the nearest hundredth where necessary.

32 *Math Journal* Would you recommend that restaurant owners provide nutrition information for the menu items to their customers? Explain.

Probability

11.1 Compound Events

11.2 Probability of Compound Events

11.3 Independent Events

11.4 Dependent Events

Have you ever gone fishing?

Imagine that you are fishing in a pond. You know that the pond is stocked with largemouth bass and bluegill. You drop your line in the water and wonder which of these fish you will catch.

Suppose you know that there are 30 bass and 20 bluegill in the pond. You know how to find the probability that the first fish you catch is a bluegill. But you want to know how it likely is that the first three fish you catch will be bluegill.

In this chapter, you will learn how to calculate the probability of this and other compound events.

▶ Compound events consist of simple events that can be dependent or independent. You can use probability of simple events to compute the probability of compound events.

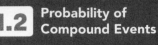

Will our next catch be a  ?

Recall Prior Knowledge

Finding the probability of a simple event

The outcomes of an event are the possible results of an activity or experiment. The collection of all possible outcomes from an activity or experiment is known as the sample space.

Suppose the number of equally likely outcomes in the sample space is n and the number of outcomes favorable to an event E is m.

The probability of event E occurring, $P(E)$, is given by:

$$P(E) = \frac{\text{Number of outcomes favorable to event } E}{\text{Number of equally likely outcomes}} = \frac{m}{n}$$

where $0 \leq P(E) \leq 1$

> Note that $n > m$ because there cannot be more favorable outcomes than there are possible outcomes. So, the probability of an event cannot be greater than 1.

A probability can be expressed as a percent, a decimal, or a fraction from 0 to 1.

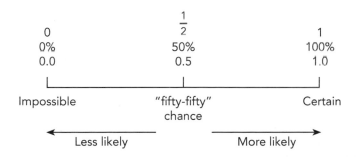

0	$\frac{1}{2}$	1
0%	50%	100%
0.0	0.5	1.0

Impossible   "fifty-fifty" chance   Certain

← Less likely   More likely →

A probability closer to 0 means the chances of the event happening are less likely.
A probability closer to 1 means the chances of the event happening are more likely.

The complement of event E, written as E', is the event that E does not occur.
$P(E') = 1 - P(E)$
The Venn diagram shows the relationship of events E and E' in the sample space S.

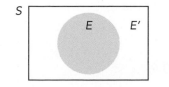

Continue on next page ➡

When two events *A* and *B* cannot occur at the same time, the events are said to be mutually exclusive. This means if event *A* occurs, event *B* cannot occur; and if event *B* occurs, event *A* cannot occur.

So, P(*A* and *B*) = 0 when events *A* and *B* are mutually exclusive.

You observe that the circles representing events *A* and *B* in the Venn diagram do not overlap. This is the characteristic for mutually exclusive events, where the events cannot happen at the same time.

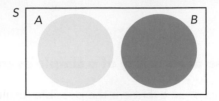

✔ Quick Check

Solve. Show your work.

A box has 2 black balls, 7 red balls, and 3 green balls. A ball is randomly chosen from the box.

1 What is the probability of choosing a green ball?

2 What is the probability of choosing a black ball?

3 What is the probability of choosing a blue ball?

4 What is the probability of choosing a ball that is not red?

5 What is the probability of choosing a red or green ball?

Tell whether the events *X* and *Y* are mutually exclusive events.

6 A fair coin and a fair six-sided number die are tossed. *X* is the event that a head is obtained. *Y* is the event that a six is obtained.

7 A fair six-sided number die is rolled. *X* is the event of obtaining a three. *Y* is the event of obtaining a five.

8 Two fair six-sided number dice are tossed. *X* is the event that the sum of the score is six. *Y* is the event that the sum of the score is 10.

9 *X* is the event consisting of the factors of 24. *Y* is the event consisting of multiples of 6 less than 20.

 **11.1**

Compound Events

Lesson Objectives

- Understand compound events.
- Represent compound events.

Vocabulary

compound event	simple event
possibility diagram	tree diagram

Understand Compound Events.

A compound event consists of two or more **simple events** occurring together or one after another. For example, tossing of a coin or rolling a six-sided number die are both simple events. But tossing a coin and a six-sided number die is a compound event.

Example 1 — Identify events as simple or compound.

Tell whether the outcomes described are from a simple or compound event. If it is a compound event, identify the simple events that form the compound event.

a) Getting a number less than 2 or greater than 4 when spinning the spinner

Solution

This is a simple event. The outcomes are from spinning the spinner one time, so only one outcome can occur.

b) Getting a number less than 2 or greater than 4 when spinning the spinner two times consecutively

Solution

This is a compound event. There are two simple events: spinning a spinner and spinning it a second time.

c) Getting heads and a 3 when a coin and a six-sided number die are tossed

Solution

This is a compound event. There are two simple events: tossing a coin and tossing a six-sided number die.

Guided Practice

Tell whether the outcomes described are from a simple or compound event. If it is a compound event, identify the simple events that form the compound event.

1 Obtaining two heads when two coins are tossed

2 Winning a football game

3 Getting a number less than 4 or getting a number greater than 5 when a fair six-sided number die is rolled

4 Rolling two fair six-sided number dice and obtaining a sum of 10 from the throws

Represent Compound Events.

Suppose you design a game such that a win consists of getting a six on a roll of a fair six-sided number die and heads on a toss of a fair coin.

The simple events that form this compound event are rolling the number die and tossing the coin.

There are six possible outcomes when a number die is rolled. They are {1, 2, 3, 4, 5, 6}.

There are two possible outcomes when a coin is tossed. They are {*H*, *T*}, where *H* denotes the outcome Heads and *T* denotes the outcome Tails.

> The braces { } are used to list the set of possible outcomes, called the sample space, of each simple event.

There are many ways to represent and display all the outcomes of a compound event. An organized list for the outcomes of tossing a number die and a coin is shown here.

Die	1	1	2	2	3	3	4	4	5	5	6	6
Coin	H	T	H	T	H	T	H	T	H	T	H	T
Outcome	1H	1T	2H	2T	3H	3T	4H	4T	5H	5T	6H	6T

A two-way grid or a table is a type of **possibility diagram** that can help you visualize all the possible outcomes of a compound event. You can also circle or mark out the outcomes that you are interested in.

List the outcomes for one simple event on the horizontal axis and the outcomes for the other simple event on the vertical axis. Note that each intersection of grid lines represents a possible outcome of the compound event.

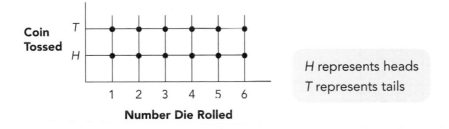

H represents heads
T represents tails

Think Math

Can you think of how the possibility diagram can help you determine the number of possible outcomes in a sample space of a compound event without counting?

Because the two simple events occur together, the order of the events is not important. So, you can use a dot (•) to indicate each possible outcome.

From the diagram, you can see that there are 12 possible outcomes in the sample space for this compound event. Notice that the outcomes in the two-way grid are the same as those in the organized list for this sample space.

Continue on next page

Another diagram that is used to display the outcomes of a compound event is shown.

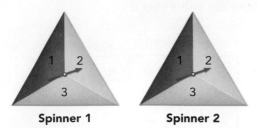

Spinner 1   **Spinner 2**

Suppose there are two spinners, with each spinner divided into three equally-sized areas.

The row labels and column labels of the table list the outcomes of each simple event. Each possible outcome is written in the diagram as an ordered pair: (**first event**, **second event**). You can see that there are 3 · 3 = 9 possible outcomes in the sample space.

Spinner 1

	1	2	3
1	(1, 1)	(2, 1)	(3, 1)
2	(1, 2)	(2, 2)	(3, 2)
3	(1, 3)	(2, 3)	(3, 3)

(left label: **Spinner 2**)

Example 2   **Represent the possible outcomes of a compound event.**

Represent and tell the number of possible outcomes for each compound event described.

a)   The results of rolling two fair six-sided number dice are added.

Solution

1st Toss

+	1	2	3	4	5	6
1	2	3	4	5	6	7
2	3	4	5	6	7	8
3	4	5	6	7	8	9
4	5	6	7	8	9	10
5	6	7	8	9	10	11
6	7	8	9	10	11	12

(left label: **2nd Toss**)

Math Note

You can write the operation of the compound event at the top left cell of the table to indicate that you are finding the sum of the outcomes of two events.

There are 36 possible outcomes.

b) The two spinners shown below are spun.

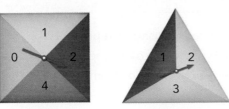

Spinner 1   Spinner 2

Solution

	Spinner 1			
Spinner 2	**0**	**1**	**2**	**4**
1	(0, 1)	(1, 1)	(2, 1)	(4, 1)
2	(0, 2)	(1, 2)	(2, 2)	(4, 2)
3	(0, 3)	(1, 3)	(2, 3)	(4, 3)

There are 12 possible outcomes.

c) One drawer has shirts: 1 blue, 1 yellow, 1 red, and 1 grey. Another drawer has pairs of socks: 1 grey and 1 black. A shirt and a pair of socks are taken from each drawer.

Solution

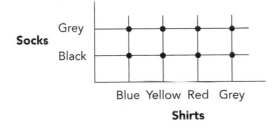

There are 8 possible outcomes.

Guided Practice

Represent and tell the number of possible outcomes for each compound event described.

5 Two fair coins are tossed together.

6 The results of rolling two fair six-sided number dice are multiplied.

7 A fair six-sided number die and a fair four-sided number die labeled 1 to 4 are rolled. The results that face down on both number dice are recorded.

Represent Compound Events Using Tree Diagrams.

A tree diagram is another type of possibility diagram that can be used to represent a compound event. The tree diagram below represents the outcomes of a simple event, tossing a fair coin. The branches from the node represent all possible outcomes.

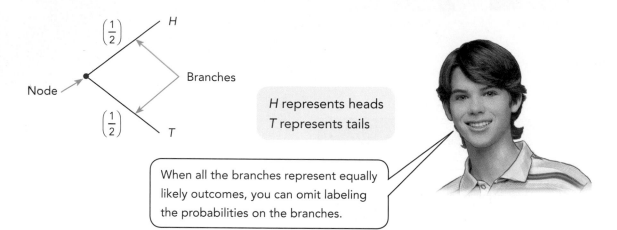

H represents heads
T represents tails

When all the branches represent equally likely outcomes, you can omit labeling the probabilities on the branches.

For drawing any tree diagram, you should take note of the following:
- Each branch starts from the same node.
- The number of branches indicates the number of outcomes the event has.
- The outcome for the event is written at the end of a branch.
- The probability of the outcome of an event is written in parentheses along the branch.
- The probabilities of the branches from each node must add up to 1.

If the coin is tossed twice, one after another, the tree diagram looks like this:

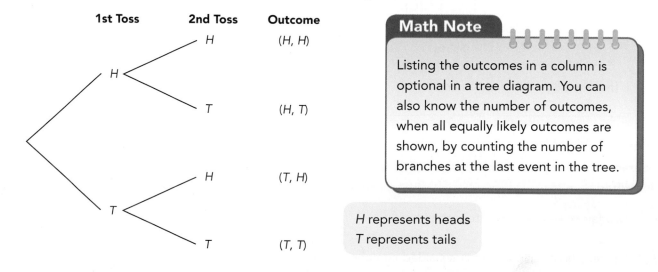

Math Note

Listing the outcomes in a column is optional in a tree diagram. You can also know the number of outcomes, when all equally likely outcomes are shown, by counting the number of branches at the last event in the tree.

H represents heads
T represents tails

You can see from the tree diagram that there are 4 equally likely possible outcomes.

Example 3 **Represent a compound event using a tree diagram.**

a) Robyn has a fair spinner and coin as shown. She first spins the spinner once and then tosses the coin. Draw a tree diagram to represent the possible outcomes. Then tell the number of possible outcomes.

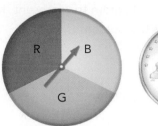

Solution

First, draw branches for each outcome of the first event, the spinner. The end of each branch becomes a node for the second event, flipping a coin.

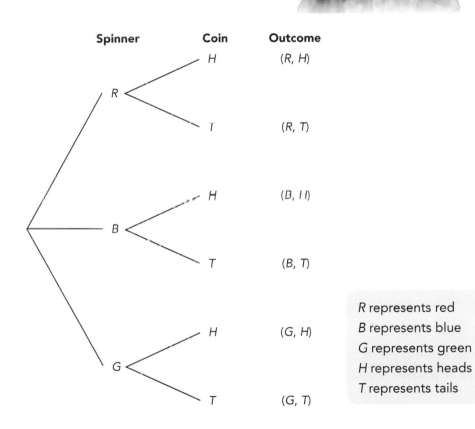

Spinner	Coin	Outcome
R	H	(R, H)
	T	(R, T)
B	H	(B, H)
	T	(B, T)
G	H	(G, H)
	T	(G, T)

R represents red
B represents blue
G represents green
H represents heads
T represents tails

There are 6 possible outcomes in this compound event.

Think Math

How can you draw the tree diagram if the two simple events are switched: first the coin, second the spinner?

Continue on next page

b) Eric has a yellow, a pink, and a green highlighter in his pencil case. He also has 1 red pen and 2 black pens. Eric randomly selects a highlighter and a pen. Draw a tree diagram to represent the possible outcomes. Then tell the number of possible outcomes.

Solution

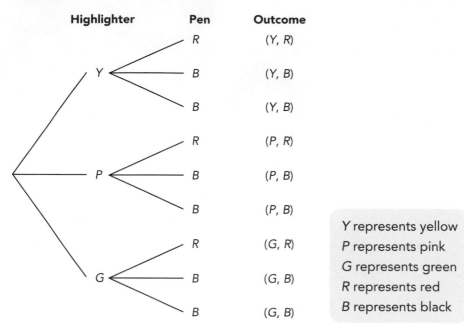

Y represents yellow
P represents pink
G represents green
R represents red
B represents black

There are 9 possible outcomes in this compound event.

Think Math

Are the outcomes shown at the end of the branches equally likely? Explain.

Guided Practice

For each compound event, draw a tree diagram to represent the possible outcomes. Then tell the number of possible outcomes.

8 Joshua has two bags. In the first bag, there are 2 blue beads and 1 green bead. In the second bag, there are 3 lettered cards with the letters P, Q, and R. Joshua randomly takes an item from the first bag, and then from the second bag.

9 A fair coin is tossed then a fair four-sided color die with faces painted yellow, green, blue, and black is rolled. The color facing down is the result recorded.

Practice 11.1

Tell whether each statement is True or False.

1 Selecting letter A from the word PROBABILITY is a compound event.

2 Selecting letter B from the word BASEBALL and ABLE is a simple event.

3 Tossing a fair six-sided number die to get either an even number or a five is a compound event.

4 Umberto has 3 red cards and 4 blue cards. Drawing two red cards in a row, without replacing the first card before drawing the second card, is a compound event.

Tell whether the outcomes described are from a simple or compound event. If it is a compound event, identify the simple events that form the compound event.

5 Getting a 6 when a fair six-sided number die is rolled.

6 Rolling three fair six-sided number dice and obtaining a sum of 18 from the throws.

7 Getting an eighteen when a fair twenty-sided number die is rolled.

8 Susan has 3 red cards and 4 blue cards. She first draws a blue card. Without replacing the first card, she then draws another blue card.

Solve. Show your work.

9 In the top drawer, there are two battery operated flash lights, one red and one yellow. In the second drawer, there are three packages of batteries: small, medium, and large. A flashlight and a package of batteries are randomly selected.

  a) Use a possibility diagram to represent the possible outcomes.

  b) How many possible outcomes are there?

10 Two electronic spinners, A and B, are spun by pressing a button. Spinner A has four sectors labeled 1 to 4, while B has three sectors, labeled 1 to 3. Spinner B, due to technical error, will never land on number 2 if spinner A lands on a 4.

  a) Use a possibility diagram to represent the possible outcomes.

  b) How many possible outcomes are there?

11 Winston has two boxes. The first box has 3 black pens and 1 red pen. The second box has 1 green ball and 1 yellow ball. Use a tree diagram to represent the possible outcomes for randomly drawing a pen and a ball. Then tell the number of possible outcomes.

12 Seraphina first tosses a fair six-sided number die. She then tosses a fair coin. Use a tree diagram to represent the possible outcomes.

13 A game was designed such that a participant needs to accomplish 2 rounds to be considered the overall winner. The first round is to roll a 4 from a fair four-sided number die labeled 1 to 4. The result recorded is the number facing down. The second round is to randomly draw a red ball from a box of 2 differently colored balls.

a) Draw a tree diagram to represent the possible outcomes.

b) How many possible outcomes are there?

c) *Math Journal* If the participant first draws the colored ball and then rolls the four-sided number die, will the number of possible outcomes be the same? Use a diagram to explain your reasoning.

14 Zoe first rolls a fair four-sided number die labeled 1 to 4. Then she rolls another fair four-sided number die labeled 2 to 5. The result recorded is the number facing down.

a) Use a possibility diagram to find the number of favorable outcomes for an odd sum.

b) Use a possibility diagram to find the number of favorable outcomes for a difference greater than 2.

11.2 Probability of Compound Events

Lesson Objective

• Use possibility diagrams to find probability of compound events.

Use Possibility Diagrams to Find Probability of Compound Events.

You have seen how to find all the outcomes in the sample space of a compound event by using a possibility diagram. From a possibility diagram, you are able to count the number of favorable outcomes and the total number of outcomes.

You can then find the probability of a compound event E using the definition of probability:

$$P(E) = \frac{\text{Number of outcome favorable to event } E}{\text{Number of equally likely outcomes}}$$

You have learned how to use a tree diagram to represent the possible outcomes of tossing coins. Consider finding the probability of landing heads, then tails when tossing a coin twice.

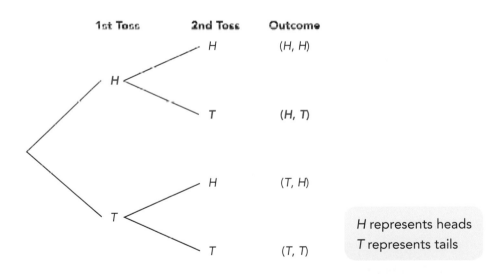

H represents heads
T represents tails

You can see that there are four possible outcomes: (H, H), (H, T), (T, H), and (T, T). However, there is only one favorable outcome, (H, T).

So, $P(H, T) = \dfrac{1}{4}$

> You want to find the probability of landing heads then tails, so the order of events is important. $P(H, T)$ is not the same as $P(T, H)$ here.

Example 4 **Use a possibility diagram to find the probability of a compound event.**

Use a possibility diagram to find each probability.

a)   A fair coin and a fair six-sided number die are tossed together. Find the probability of landing heads and a 5.

Solution

Method 1

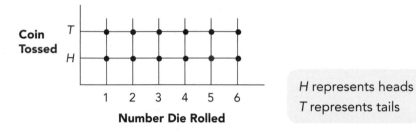

Coin Tossed

Number Die Rolled

H represents heads
T represents tails

$P(H, 5) = \dfrac{1}{12}$

Think Math

Would the probability be different if the possibility diagram were drawn with the axis labels interchanged? Explain your answer.

You can see that there is only one outcome with heads and a 5.

Method 2

Number Die

Coin	1	2	3	4	5	6
H	(1, H)	(2, H)	(3, H)	(4, H)	(5, H)	(6, H)
T	(1, T)	(2, T)	(3, T)	(4, T)	(5, T)	(6, T)

H represents heads
T represents tails

$P(H, 5) = P(5, H)$
$ = \dfrac{1}{12}$

b) Two fair six-sided number dice are rolled. Find the probability that the sum of the two numbers rolled is a prime number.

Solution

1st Number Die

<table>
<tr><td>+</td><td>1</td><td>2</td><td>3</td><td>4</td><td>5</td><td>6</td></tr>
<tr><td>1</td><td>2</td><td>3</td><td>4</td><td>5</td><td>6</td><td>7</td></tr>
<tr><td>2</td><td>3</td><td>4</td><td>5</td><td>6</td><td>7</td><td>8</td></tr>
<tr><td>3</td><td>4</td><td>5</td><td>6</td><td>7</td><td>8</td><td>9</td></tr>
<tr><td>4</td><td>5</td><td>6</td><td>7</td><td>8</td><td>9</td><td>10</td></tr>
<tr><td>5</td><td>6</td><td>7</td><td>8</td><td>9</td><td>10</td><td>11</td></tr>
<tr><td>6</td><td>7</td><td>8</td><td>9</td><td>10</td><td>11</td><td>12</td></tr>
</table>

(2nd Number Die along the vertical axis)

Math Note

Recall that a prime number is a positive number greater than 1 that is divisible by only 1 and itself.

The prime numbers in the possibility diagram are **2**, **3**, **5**, **7**, and **11**. There are 15 prime numbers out of 36 equally likely possible outcomes.

$$P(\text{sum is prime}) = \frac{15}{36}$$
$$= \frac{5}{12}$$

c) Two fair four-sided number dice, one red (*R*) and one blue (*B*), are rolled, and the number on the bottom is recorded. The red number die has numbers 1, 2, 4, and 7. The blue number die has numbers 2, 5, 8, and 9. Find the probability that the number recorded from the blue number die is more than 3 greater than the number recorded from the red number die. That is, find $P(B - R > 3)$.

Solution

Method 1

Red Number Die

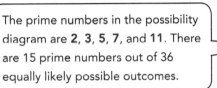

	1	2	4	7
2	(1, 2)	(2, 2)	(4, 2)	(7, 2)
5	(1, 5)	(2, 5)	(4, 5)	(7, 5)
8	(1, 8)	(2, 8)	(4, 8)	(7, 8)
9	(1, 9)	(2, 9)	(4, 9)	(7, 9)

(Blue Number Die along the vertical axis)

$$P(B - R > 3) = \frac{7}{16}$$

Continue on next page

Method 2

Red Number Die

Blue Number Die	−	1	2	4	7
2		1	0	−2	−5
5		④	3	1	−2
8		⑦	⑥	④	1
9		⑧	⑦	⑤	2

You can list the differences instead of the numbers rolled. Then look for differences greater than 3.

$$P(B - R > 3) = \frac{7}{16}$$

d) The two spinners shown are spun. Find the probability that the pointers stop at 1 and blue (*B*).

Spinner 1

Spinner 2

Solution

Spinner 1

Spinner 2	1	1	2	4
B	(1, B)	(1, B)	(2, B)	(4, B)
G	(1, G)	(1, G)	(2, G)	(4, G)
R	(1, R)	(1, R)	(2, R)	(4, R)

$$P(1, B) = \frac{2}{12} = \frac{1}{6}$$

Guided Practice

Use a possibility diagram to find each probability.

1 Two fair four-sided number dice, each numbered 1 to 4 are rolled together. The result recorded is the number facing down. Find the probability that the product of the two numbers is divisible by 2.

2 One colored disc is randomly drawn from each of two bags. Both bags each have 5 colored discs: 1 red, 1 green, 1 blue, 1 yellow, and 1 white. Find the probability of drawing a blue or yellow disc.

3 A box has 1 black, 1 green, 1 red, and 1 yellow marble. Another box has 1 white, 1 green, and 1 red marble. A marble is taken at random from each box. Find the probability that a red marble is not drawn.

Example 5 **Use tree diagrams to find probability of compound events.**

Suppose that it is equally likely to rain or not rain on any given day. Draw a tree diagram and use it to find the probability that it rains in exactly one of two consecutive days.

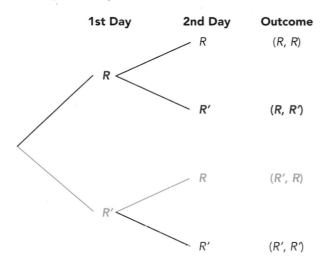

| 1st Day | 2nd Day | Outcome |

R represents rain
R' represents not raining

The favorable outcome is "rain in exactly one of two consecutive days." So, you should look for the outcome that gives **(R, R')** or (*R'*, *R*), meaning either it rains on the first day or rains on the second day.

Solution

$P(\text{rain on exactly one day}) = \dfrac{2}{4}$

$= \dfrac{1}{2}$

So, the probability of (*R*, *R'*) or (*R'*, *R*) is $\dfrac{1}{2}$.

Guided Practice

Solve. Show your work.

4 Three fair coins are tossed together.

a) Draw a tree diagram to represent the possible outcomes.

b) Using your answer in **a)**, find the probability of getting all heads.

c) Using your answer in **a)**, find the probability of getting at least two tails.

Solve. Show your work.

1. A bag contains 2 blue balls and 1 red ball. Winnie randomly draws a ball from the bag and replaces it before she draws a second ball. Use a possibility diagram to find the probability that the balls drawn are different colors.

2. A letter is randomly chosen from the word FOOD, followed by randomly choosing a letter from the word DOG. Draw a tree diagram to find the probability that both letters chosen are the same.

3. Three pebbles are placed in a bag: 1 blue, 1 green, and 1 yellow. First a pebble is randomly drawn from the bag. Then a fair four-sided number die labeled from 1 to 4 is rolled. The result recorded is the number facing down. Use a possibility diagram to find the probability of drawing a yellow pebble and getting a 4.

4. Thomas rolled a fair six-sided number die and a fair four-sided number die labeled 1 to 4 together. Use a possibility diagram to find the probability of rolling the number 3 on both.

5. At a bike shop, there are 3 bikes with 20-speed gears and 2 bikes with 18-speed gears. The bike shop also sells 1 blue helmet and 1 yellow helmet. Use a possibility diagram to find the probability of getting an 18-speed bicycle and a blue helmet if randomly selecting one bike and one helmet from among these.

6 Susan randomly draws a card from three number cards: 1, 3, and 6. After replacing the card, Susan randomly draws another number card. The product of the two numbers drawn is recorded.

a) Use a possibility diagram to represent the possible outcomes.

b) Using your answer in **a)**, what is the probability of forming a number larger than 10 but less than 30?

7 Jane and Jill watch television together for 2 hours. Jane selects the channel for the first hour, and Jill selects the channel for the second hour. Jane's remote control randomly selects from Channels A, B, and C. Jill's remote control randomly selects from Channels C, D, and E.

a) Use a possibility diagram to represent the possible outcomes for the channels they watch on television for 2 hours.

b) Using your answer in **a)**, what is the probability of watching the same channel both hours?

8 A color disc is randomly drawn from a bag that contains the following discs.

After a disc is drawn, a fair coin is tossed. Use a possibility diagram to find the probability of drawing a red disc and landing on heads.

9 Karen tosses a fair coin three times. Draw a tree diagram to find the probability of getting the same result in all three tosses.

10 Mrs. Bridget's recipes require her to put in some fine maize flour in bowl 1, followed by wheat flour in bowl 2, and rice flour in bowl 3. However, the jars of flour are not labeled, so she randomly guesses which flour to put in which bowl.

a) Draw a tree diagram to represent the possible outcomes.

b) Using your answer in **a)**, find the probability of getting the correct flour in the correct order.

11.3 Independent Events

Lesson Objectives

- Understand independent events.
- Use multiplication rule and addition rule of probability to solve problems with independent events.

Vocabulary

independent events

multiplication rule of probability

addition rule of probability

Understand Independent Events.

Suppose you are playing a game. You have a spinner with two congruent sectors and some color cards as shown below. Your goal is to randomly spin a 2 and draw a red card.

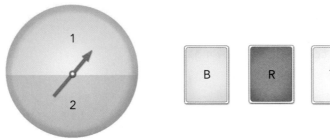

The event of spinning a 2 and the event of drawing a red card are considered independent events. Two events are independent if the occurrence of one event does not affect the probability of the other event. When you spin the spinner, regardless of the result, it will not affect the probability of drawing a blue, yellow or red card.

Caution ///////

Independent events are not the same as mutually exclusive events. Mutually exclusive events cannot occur at the same time. But independent events refer to whether the occurrence of an event affects the probability of the other event.

Use the Multiplication Rule of Probability to Solve Problems with Independent Events.

Consider the spinner and the 3 color cards again. You can draw a tree diagram to represent the independent events that form the compound event and their corresponding probabilities.

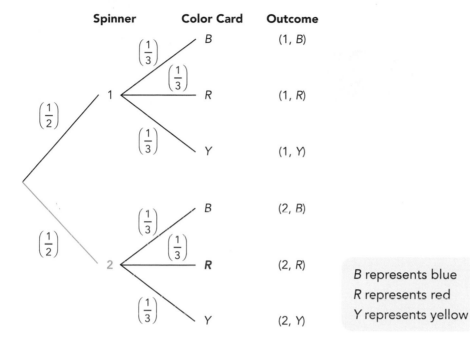

Spinner	**Color Card**	**Outcome**

B represents blue
R represents red
Y represents yellow

Because both events are independent, the outcome on the spinner does not affect the probabilities of outcomes when drawing a card. The area of the spinner is equally divided into 2 portions, so the probability of spinning one of the two numbers is $\frac{1}{2}$.

Because there is an equal chance of drawing each color, the probability of choosing one of the three cards is $\frac{1}{3}$. The probabilities are labeled on the tree diagram branches.

You can see that there are a total of 6 equally likely outcomes, and spinning a 2 and drawing a red card is one of those 6 equally likely outcomes. So, you can write the probability of spinning a 2 and drawing a red card as follows:

$$P(2, R) = \frac{1}{6}$$

You can also use the multiplication rule of probability to find the probability of spinning a 2 and drawing a red card.

$$P(2, R) = P(2) \cdot P(R)$$

$$= \frac{1}{2} \cdot \frac{1}{3} \qquad \text{Multiply } P(2) \text{ and } P(R).$$

$$= \frac{1}{6} \qquad \text{Simplify.}$$

Continue on next page

In general, for two independent events A and B, the multiplication rule of probability states that:
$$P(A \text{ and } B) = P(A) \cdot P(B)$$

Suppose the blue card is replaced by another red card as shown.

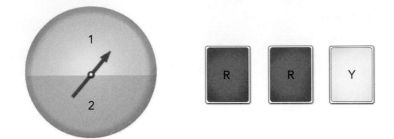

A tree diagram can be drawn to represent the possible outcomes as shown.

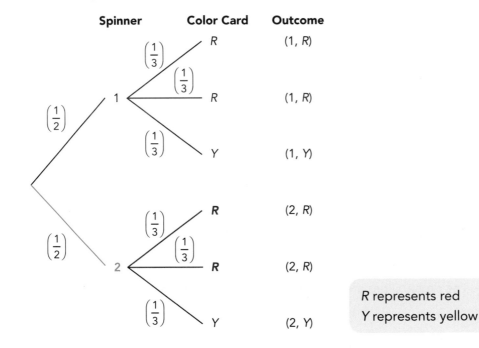

R represents red
Y represents yellow

You can see that there are a total of 6 outcomes. Suppose you want to find the probability of spinning a 2 and drawing a red card, you can see that 2 out of 6 outcomes are favorable. So, you can write the probability of spinning a 2 and drawing a red card as follows:

$$P(2, R) = \frac{2}{6}$$
$$= \frac{1}{3}$$

The tree diagram constructed previously for this compound event with two red cards can be simplified by combining the identical outcomes (2, R) and (2, R) together as shown below.

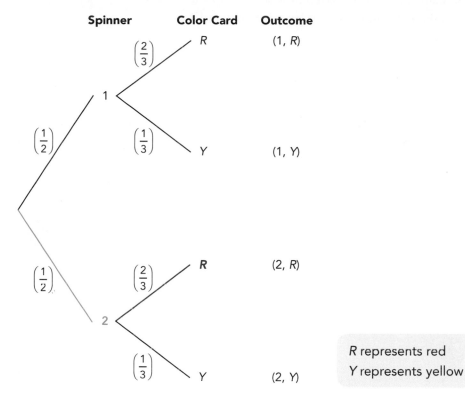

Spinner	Color Card	Outcome

R represents red
Y represents yellow

You can see that the probability of drawing a red card is higher compared to the previous scenario when each color was equally likely. So the simple event of drawing a color card has become a biased event because the probability of drawing a red card is not the same as the probability of drawing a yellow card.

Using the multiplication rule to find the probability of spinning a 2 and drawing a red card:

$P(2, R) = P(2) \cdot P(R)$

$\qquad = \dfrac{1}{2} \cdot \dfrac{2}{3}$ Multiply $P(2)$ and $P(R)$.

$\qquad = \dfrac{1}{3}$ Simplify.

Caution ///////

For compound events involving biased outcomes, the probability of an outcome is not necessarily equal to $\dfrac{1}{\text{Number of different outcomes}}$ because the outcomes are not equally likely.

Example 6 **Solve probability problems involving two independent events.**

A game is played with a fair coin and a fair six-sided number die. To win the game, you need to randomly obtain the outcome of heads on a fair coin and 3 on a fair number die.

a)   Draw the tree diagram to represent this compound event.

Solution

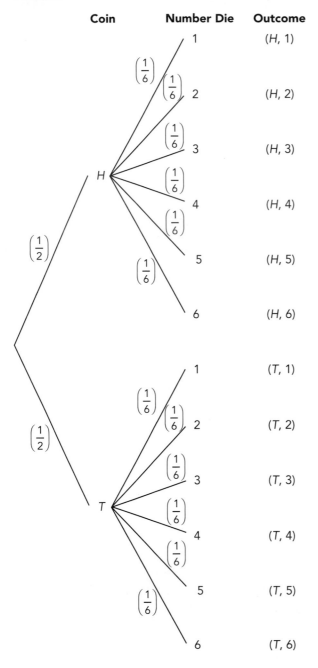

The compound event is independent since throwing a coin and number die do not affect the results of each other.

H represents heads
T represents tails

b) Use the multiplication rule of probability to find the probability of winning the game in one try.

Solution

P(winning the game) = P(H, 3)

$$= P(H) \cdot P(3)$$

$$= \frac{1}{2} \cdot \frac{1}{6}$$

$$= \frac{1}{12}$$

The probability of winning the game is $\frac{1}{12}$.

Think Math

If the coin and number die are biased, could the chance of winning the game be the same? Explain.

Guided Practice

Solve. Show your work.

 A game is played with a bag of 6 color tokens and a bag of 6 letter tiles. The 6 tokens consist of 2 green tokens, 1 yellow token, and 3 red tokens. The 6 letter tiles consist of 4 tiles of letter A and 2 tiles of letter B. To win the game, you need to randomly get a yellow token and a tile of letter B from a random selection in each bag.

a) Copy and complete the tree diagram.

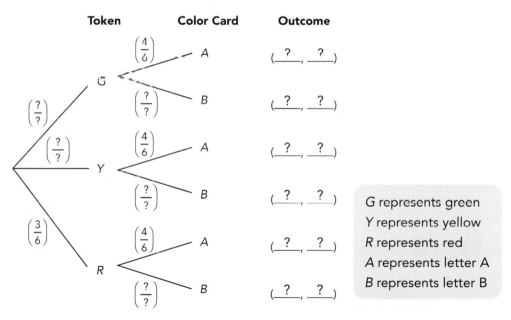

G represents green
Y represents yellow
R represents red
A represents letter A
B represents letter B

b) Use the multiplication rule of probability to find the probability of winning the game in one try.

P(winning the game) = P(Y, B)

$$= P(Y) \cdot P(B)$$

$$= \underline{\;?\;} \cdot \underline{\;?\;}$$

$$= \underline{\;?\;}$$

The probability of winning the game is __?__.

 **Technology Activity**

Materials:
- spreadsheet software

 SIMULATE RANDOMNESS

Work in pairs.

Background

Two fair six-sided number dice are thrown. Using a spreadsheet, data will be generated to investigate how frequently the outcome of doubles (1 and 1, 2 and 2, ... , 6 and 6) occurs.

STEP 1 Label your spreadsheet as shown.

	Sheets	Charts	SmartArt Graphics	WordArt		
◇	**A**	**B**	**C**	**D**	**E**	**F**
1	Number Die A	Number Die B	Difference			
2						
3						
4						
5						

STEP 2 To generate a random integer between 1 and 6, in cell A2, enter the formula = INT(RAND()*6+1) to simulate rolling a die. A random number from 1 to 6 should appear in the cell.

	Sheets	Charts	SmartArt Graphics	WordArt		
◇	**A**	**B**	**C**	**D**	**E**	**F**
1	Number Die A	Number Die B	Difference			
2	=INT(RAND()*6+1)					
3						
4						
5						

STEP 3 To model 100 rolls, select cells A2 to A101 and choose Fill Down from the Edit menu.

STEP 4 Repeat **STEP 2** and **STEP 3** for cells B2 to B101.

	Sheets	Charts	SmartArt Graphics	WordArt		
◇	**A**	**B**	**C**	**D**	**E**	**F**
1	Number Die A	Number Die B	Difference			
2	4	3				
3	6	4				
4	4	5				
5	1	1				

STEP 5 In cell C2, enter the formula = A2 − B2. Select cells C2 to C101 and choose Fill Down from the Edit menu. This column serves as a check to see if the random numbers generated in columns A and B are the same. If the numbers are the same, their difference is 0. A zero difference indicates doubles outcome.

	Sheets	Charts	SmartArt Graphics	WordArt		
◇	A	B	C	D	E	F
1	Number Die A	Number Die B	Difference			
2	4	3	=A2-B2			
3	6	4	2			
4	4	5	-1			
5	1	1	0			

STEP 6 To see how many times the data shows double occurring, in cell E1, enter the formula = COUNTIF(C2:C101,0).

	Sheets	Charts	SmartArt Graphics	WordArt		
◇	A	B	C	D	E	F
1	Number Die A	Number Die B	Difference	=COUNTIF(C2:C101,0)		
2	4	3	1			
3	6	4	2			
4	4	5	-1			
5	1	1	0			

STEP 7 Find the experimental probability of the occurrence of two number dice showing the same number by dividing the number you get in cell E1 by the total, 100 rolls.

Math Journal Find the theoretical probability of rolling doubles with 2 fair number dice. Compare this theoretical probability with the experimental probability you obtained in the spreadsheet simulation. Are these two values the same?

> When you use a greater number of simulations, such as 100 instead of 20, the result is more likely to be closer to the theoretical probability.

A jar contains 8 green marbles and 4 red marbles. One marble is randomly drawn and the color of the marble is noted. The marble is then put back into the jar and a second marble is randomly drawn. The color of the second marble is also noted.

a) Find the probability of first drawing a green marble followed by a red marble.

Solution

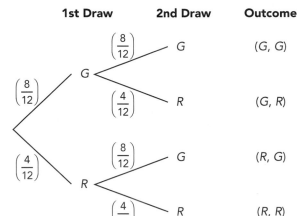

1st Draw	2nd Draw	Outcome

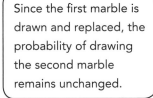
Since the first marble is drawn and replaced, the probability of drawing the second marble remains unchanged.

G represents green
R represents red

$P(G, R) = P(G) \cdot P(R)$
$$= \frac{8}{12} \cdot \frac{4}{12} = \frac{2}{9}$$

The probability of first drawing a green marble followed by a red marble is $\frac{2}{9}$.

b) Find the probability of first drawing a red marble followed by a green marble.

Solution

$P(R, G) = P(R) \cdot P(G)$
$$= \frac{4}{12} \cdot \frac{8}{12} = \frac{2}{9}$$

The probability of first drawing a red marble followed by a green marble is $\frac{2}{9}$.

c) Find the probability of drawing two green marbles.

Solution

$P(G, G) = P(G) \cdot P(G)$
$$= \frac{8}{12} \cdot \frac{8}{12} = \frac{4}{9}$$

The probability of drawing two green marbles is $\frac{4}{9}$.

Guided Practice

Solve. Show your work.

2 In a bag, there are 9 magenta balls and 1 orange ball. Two balls are randomly drawn, one at a time with replacement.

a) Find the probability of drawing two magenta balls.

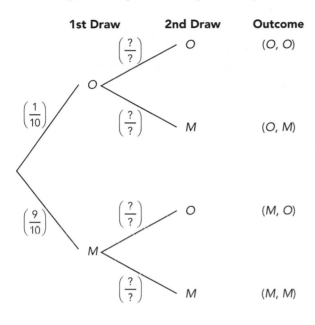

1st Draw	2nd Draw	Outcome

$\left(\dfrac{?}{?}\right)$ — O   (O, O)

$\left(\dfrac{1}{10}\right)$

$\left(\dfrac{?}{?}\right)$ — M   (O, M)

$\left(\dfrac{9}{10}\right)$

$\left(\dfrac{?}{?}\right)$ — O   (M, O)

$\left(\dfrac{?}{?}\right)$ — M   (M, M)

> *O* represents orange
> *M* represents magenta

$P(M, M) = P(M) \cdot P(M)$

$\qquad = \underline{\ ?\ } \cdot \underline{\ ?\ }$

$\qquad = \underline{\ ?\ }$

The probability drawing two magenta balls is $\underline{\ ?\ }$.

b) Find the probability of drawing an orange ball followed by a magenta ball.

$P(O, M) = P(O) \cdot P(M)$

$\qquad = \underline{\ ?\ } \cdot \underline{\ ?\ }$

$\qquad = \underline{\ ?\ }$

The probability drawing an orange ball followed by a magenta ball is $\underline{\ ?\ }$.

c) Find the probability of drawing both orange balls.

$P(O, O) = P(O) \cdot P(O)$

$\qquad = \underline{\ ?\ } \cdot \underline{\ ?\ }$

$\qquad = \underline{\ ?\ }$

The probability drawing both orange balls is $\underline{\ ?\ }$.

Use the **Addition Rule of Probability** to Solve Problems with Independent Events.

You have learned how to use the multiplication rule of probability to find the probability of one favorable outcome in a compound event. Now you will learn to use the addition rule of probability to find the probability of more than one favorable outcome in a compound event.

A jar contains 8 green marbles and 4 red marbles. One marble is randomly drawn and the color of the marble is noted. The marble is then put back into the jar and a second marble is randomly drawn. The color of the second marble is also noted.

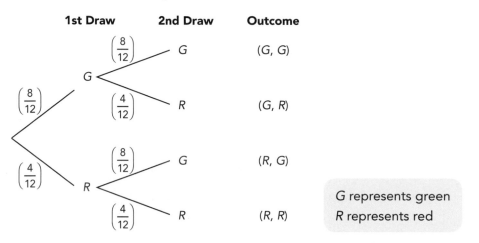

G represents green
R represents red

Suppose you want to find the probability of drawing two marbles of the same color. There are two favorable outcomes, (G, G) and (R, R), and they are mutually exclusive.

$$P(R, R) = \frac{4}{12} \cdot \frac{4}{12}$$
$$= \frac{4}{9}$$

$$P(G, G) = \frac{8}{12} \cdot \frac{8}{12}$$
$$= \frac{1}{9}$$

To find the probability of (R, R) or (G, G), you can find the sum of their probabilities.

Using the addition rule of probability:

$P(\text{same color}) = P(R, R) + P(G, G)$
$$= \frac{1}{9} + \frac{4}{9}$$
$$= \frac{5}{9}$$

Math Note

Because (R, R) and (G, G) are mutually exclusive events, you can add the probabilities to find the probability of (R, R) or (G, G).

In general, for two mutually exclusive events A and B, the addition rule of probability states that:

$$P(A \text{ or } B) = P(A) + P(B)$$

Example 8 **Solve probability problems with independent events involving more than one favorable outcome.**

Alex is taking two tests. The probability of him passing each test is 0.8.

a) Find the probability that Alex passes both tests.

Solution

To make a tree diagram, first find the probability that Alex fails the test.

Let P represent pass and F represent fail.

$$P(F) = 1 - P(P)$$
$$= 1 - 0.8$$
$$= 0.2$$

> **Math Note**
>
> Recall that for two complementary events, their probabilities sum up to 1.

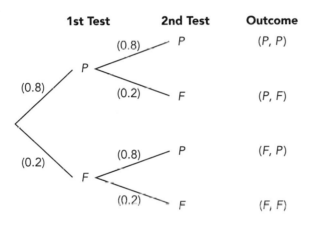

> P represents pass
> F represents fail

$$P(P, P) = P(P) \cdot P(P)$$
$$= 0.8 \cdot 0.8$$
$$= 0.64$$

The probability that Alex passes both tests is 0.64.

b) Find the probability that he passes exactly one of the tests.

Solution

Using the addition rule of probability:

$$P((P, F) \text{ or } (F, P)) = P(P, F) + P(F, P)$$
$$= P(P) \cdot P(F) + P(F) \cdot P(P)$$
$$= 0.8 \cdot 0.2 + 0.2 \cdot 0.8$$
$$= 0.32$$

The probability that he passes exactly one of the tests is 0.32.

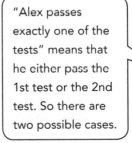

"Alex passes exactly one of the tests" means that he either pass the 1st test or the 2nd test. So there are two possible cases.

> **Think Math**
>
> What is the probability of passing at least one test? Show your reasoning.

Guided Practice

Solve. Show your work.

 On weekends, Carli either jogs (*J*) or plays tennis (*T*) each day, but never both. The probability of her playing tennis is 0.75.

a) Find the probability that Carli jogs on both days.

Because *J* and *T* are complementary,

$P(J) = 1 - P(T)$

$ = 1 - \underline{\quad?\quad}$

$ = \underline{\quad?\quad}$

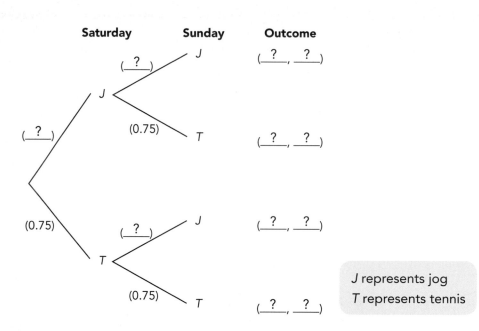

J represents jog
T represents tennis

$P(J, J) = P(J) \cdot P(J)$

$P(J, J) = \underline{\quad?\quad} \cdot \underline{\quad?\quad}$

$ = \underline{\quad?\quad}$

The probability that Carli jogs both days is $\underline{\quad?\quad}$.

b) Find the probability that Carli jogs on exactly one of the days.

Using the addition rule of probability:

$P(J, T) + P(T, J) = P(J) \cdot P(T) + P(T) \cdot P(J)$

$ = \underline{\quad?\quad} \cdot \underline{\quad?\quad} + \underline{\quad?\quad} \cdot \underline{\quad?\quad}$

$ = \underline{\quad?\quad}$

The probability that Carli jogs on exactly one of the days is $\underline{\quad?\quad}$.

Practice 11.3

Draw a tree diagram to represent each compound event.

1 Tossing a fair coin followed by drawing a marble from a bag of 3 marbles:
1 yellow, 1 green, and 1 blue.

2 Drawing two balls randomly with replacement from a bag with 1 green ball and
1 purple ball.

3 Drawing a ball randomly from a bag containing 1 red ball and 1 blue ball, followed
by tossing a fair six-sided number die.

4 Tossing a fair coin twice.

5 Reading or playing on each day of a weekend.

6 On time or tardy for school for two consecutive days.

Solve. Show your work.

7 Mindy is playing a game that uses the spinner shown below and a fair coin. An
outcome of 3 on the spinner and heads on the coin wins the game.

a) Draw a tree diagram to represent the possible outcomes of this game.

b) Find the probability of winning the game in one try.

c) Find the probability of losing the game in one try.

8 There are 2 blue balls and 4 yellow balls in a bag. A ball is randomly drawn from
the bag, and it is replaced before a second ball is randomly drawn.

a) Draw a tree diagram to represent the possible outcomes.

b) Find the probability that a yellow ball is drawn first, followed by another
yellow ball.

c) Find the probability that a yellow ball is drawn after a blue ball is drawn first.

9 Jasmine has 3 blue pens and 2 green pens in her pencil case. She randomly selects a pen from her pencil case, and replaces it before she randomly selects again.

a) Draw a tree diagram to represent the possible outcomes.

b) Find the probability that she selects 2 blue pens.

c) Find the probability that she selects 2 green pens.

d) Find the probability that she selects 2 pens of the same color.

10 Henry has 4 fiction books, 6 non-fiction books, and 1 Spanish book on his bookshelf. He randomly selects two books with replacement.

a) Draw a tree diagram to represent the possible outcomes.

b) Find the probability that he selects a fiction book twice.

c) Find the probability that he first selects a non-fiction book, and then a Spanish book.

d) Find the probability that he first selects a fiction book, and then a non-fiction book.

11 Andy tosses a fair six-sided number die twice. What is the probability of tossing an even number on the first toss and a prime number on the second toss?

12 The probability that Fiona wakes up before 8 A.M. when she does not need to set her alarm is $\frac{4}{10}$. On any two consecutive days that Fiona does not need to set her alarm, what is the probability of her waking up before 8 A.M. for at least one of the days?

13 A globe is spinning on a globe stand. The globe surface is painted with 30% yellow, 10% green, and the rest is painted blue. Two times Danny randomly points to a spot on the globe while it spins. The color he points to each time is recorded.

a) What is the probability that he points to the same color on both spins?

b) What is the probability that he points to yellow at least one time?

14 *Math Journal* Sally thinks that for two independent events, because the occurrence of one event will not have any impact on the probability of the other event, they are also mutually exclusive. Do you agree with her? Explain your reasoning using an example.

15 A game is designed so that a player wins when the game piece lands on letter A. The game piece begins on letter G. A fair six-sided number die is tossed. If the number tossed is odd, the game piece moves one step counterclockwise. If the number tossed is even, the game piece moves one step clockwise.

a) What is the probability that a player will win after tossing the number die once?

b) What is the probability that a player will win after tossing the number die twice?

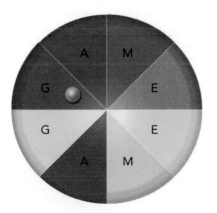

Dependent Events

Lesson Objectives

- Understand dependent events.
- Use the rules of probability to solve problems with dependent events.

Vocabulary

dependent events

Understand Dependent Events.

Suppose there are 3 yellow cards and 2 red cards. They are shuffled and placed in a stack. You are asked to draw two cards randomly, one at a time, from the stack without looking at the cards.

When the first card is drawn, it is not replaced. So when the second card is drawn, there are only 4 cards left in the stack. The probability of drawing a particular color card will change after the first draw because the sample space for the second event changes. In the first draw, there are 5 cards while in the second draw, there are 4 cards left.

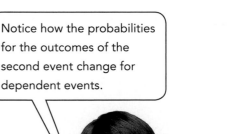

When the occurrence of one event causes the probability of another event to change, the two events are said to be dependent.

You can represent the dependent events described above with a tree diagram, as shown.

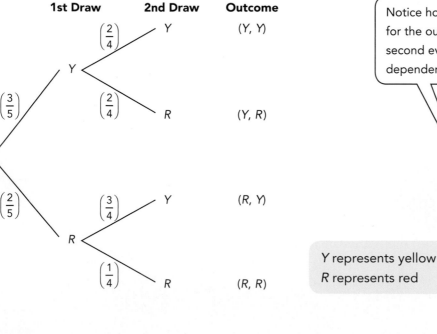

1st Draw	2nd Draw	Outcome
Y $\left(\frac{3}{5}\right)$	Y $\left(\frac{2}{4}\right)$	(Y, Y)
	R $\left(\frac{2}{4}\right)$	(Y, R)
R $\left(\frac{2}{5}\right)$	Y $\left(\frac{3}{4}\right)$	(R, Y)
	R $\left(\frac{1}{4}\right)$	(R, R)

Notice how the probabilities for the outcomes of the second event change for dependent events.

Y represents yellow
R represents red

Use the Multiplication Rule of Probability to Solve Problems with Dependent Events.

Consider the 5-card scenario again. To find the probability of drawing two red cards, first you locate the branches that will give the favorable outcome (R, R). Then you multiply the probabilities along the branches. In other words, you multiply the probability of drawing a red card in the first draw with the probability of drawing a red card in the second draw.

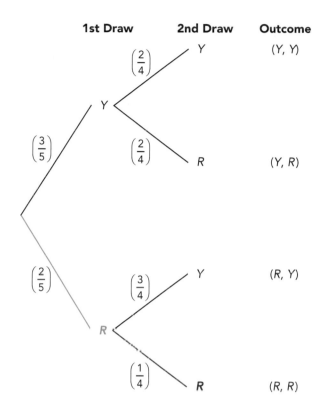

	1st Draw	2nd Draw	Outcome

Y represents yellow
R represents red

$$P(R, R) = P(R) \cdot P(R \text{ after } R)$$
$$= \frac{2}{5} \cdot \frac{1}{4}$$
$$= \frac{1}{10}$$

Math Note

For dependent events, you cannot simply count the outcomes to find the probability of the compound events.

In general, for two dependent events A and B, the multiplication rule of probability states:

$$P(A \text{ and } B) = P(A) \cdot P(B \text{ after } A)$$

Example 9 **Understand dependent events.**

Inside a jar, there are 3 blue marbles and 7 green marbles. Rena randomly draws out two marbles, one after another without replacement. Draw a tree diagram to represent the possible outcomes of this compound event.

Solution

Let *B* represent blue and *G* represent green.

1st draw

$P(B) = \dfrac{3}{10}$

$P(G) = \dfrac{7}{10}$

Math Note

Because the events are dependent, the number of possible outcomes for the second event is reduced by 1 after the first event occurs.

2nd draw

$P(B \text{ after } B) = \dfrac{2}{9}$ There are 2 blue marbles left after 1 blue marble is drawn.

$P(G \text{ after } B) = \dfrac{7}{9}$ There are 7 green marbles left after 1 blue marble is drawn.

$P(B \text{ after } G) = \dfrac{3}{9}$ There are 3 blue marbles left after 1 green marble is drawn.

$P(G \text{ after } G) = \dfrac{6}{9}$ There are 6 green marbles left after 1 green marble is drawn.

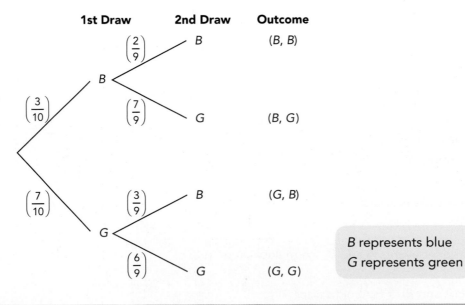

B represents blue
G represents green

Guided Practice

Solve. Show your work.

1. A deck of four cards with the letters D, E, E, D are placed facing down on a table. Two cards are turned at random to show the letter. Draw a tree diagram to represent the possible outcomes in this compound event.

Let *D* represent letter D and *E* represent letter E.

1st draw

$P(D) = \dfrac{2}{4}$

$P(E) = \dfrac{2}{4}$

2nd draw

$P(D \text{ after } D) = \dfrac{?}{?}$ There is __?__ D left after 1 D is drawn.

$P(E \text{ after } D) = \dfrac{?}{?}$ There are __?__ E still after 1 D is drawn.

$P(D \text{ after } E) = \dfrac{?}{?}$ There are __?__ D still after 1 E is drawn.

$P(E \text{ after } E) = \dfrac{?}{?}$ There is __?__ E left after 1 F is drawn.

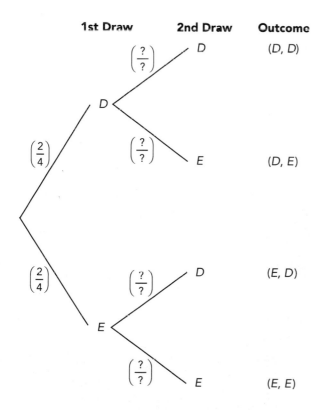

Example 10 **Solve a probability problem involving dependent events without replacement.**

A jar contains 8 green marbles and 4 red marbles. Two marbles are randomly drawn, one at a time without replacement.

a) Find the probability of drawing a green marble followed by a red marble.

Solution

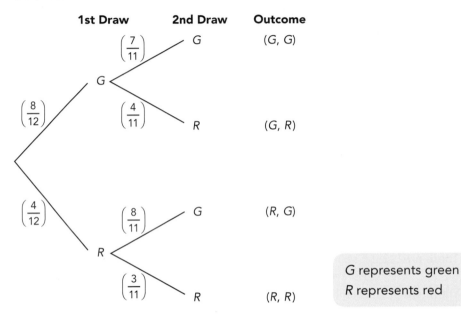

G represents green
R represents red

$P(G, R) = P(G) \cdot P(R \text{ after } G)$

$\qquad = \dfrac{8}{12} \cdot \dfrac{4}{11}$

$\qquad = \dfrac{8}{33}$

The probability of randomly drawing a green marble followed by a red marble is $\dfrac{8}{33}$.

Recall that for two dependent events A and B, $P(A \text{ and } B) = P(A) \cdot P(B \text{ after } A)$

b) Find the probability of randomly drawing a red marble followed by a green marble.

Solution

$P(R, G) = P(R) \cdot P(G \text{ after } R)$

$\qquad = \dfrac{4}{12} \cdot \dfrac{8}{11}$

$\qquad = \dfrac{8}{33}$

The probability of randomly drawing a red marble followed by a green marble is $\dfrac{8}{33}$.

c) Find the probability of randomly drawing two green marbles.

Solution

$P(G, G) = P(G) \cdot P(G \text{ after } G)$

$\qquad = \dfrac{8}{12} \cdot \dfrac{7}{11}$

$\qquad = \dfrac{14}{33}$

The probability of randomly drawing two green marbles is $\dfrac{14}{33}$.

d) Find the probability of randomly drawing two red marbles.

Solution

$P(R, R) = P(R) \cdot P(R \text{ after } R)$

$\qquad = \dfrac{4}{12} \cdot \dfrac{3}{11}$

$\qquad = \dfrac{1}{11}$

The probability of randomly drawing two marbles of the same color is $\dfrac{1}{11}$.

Think Math

If there is just 1 red marble in the jar, what is the probability of drawing two red marbles? Justify your answer.

Guided Practice

Solve. Show your work.

2 There are 16 different color pebbles in a jar. 11 of them are blue and the rest are orange. Two pebbles are randomly selected from the jar, one at a time without replacement.

a) Find the probability of taking an orange pebble followed by a blue pebble.

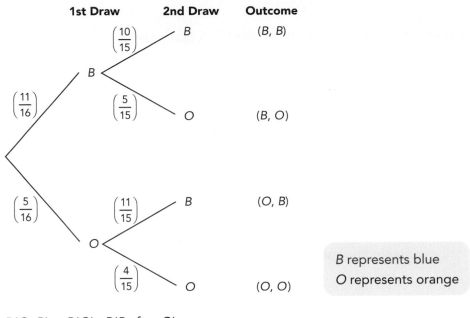

1st Draw   **2nd Draw**   **Outcome**

$\left(\frac{10}{15}\right)$ — B   (B, B)

B

$\left(\frac{11}{16}\right)$ $\left(\frac{5}{15}\right)$ — O   (B, O)

$\left(\frac{5}{16}\right)$ $\left(\frac{11}{15}\right)$ — B   (O, B)

O

$\left(\frac{4}{15}\right)$ — O   (O, O)

B represents blue
O represents orange

$P(O, B) = P(O) \cdot P(B \text{ after } O)$

$= \dfrac{?}{?} \cdot \dfrac{?}{?}$

$= \dfrac{?}{?}$

The probability of randomly taking an orange pebble followed by a blue pebble is __?__.

b) Find the probability of taking two orange pebbles.

$P(O, O) = P(O) \cdot P(O \text{ after } O)$

$= \dfrac{?}{?} \cdot \dfrac{?}{?}$

$= \dfrac{?}{?}$

The probability of randomly taking two orange pebbles is __?__.

c) Find the probability of taking two blue pebbles.

$P(B, B) = P(B) \cdot P(B \text{ after } B)$

$= \dfrac{?}{?} \cdot \dfrac{?}{?}$

$= \dfrac{?}{?}$

The probability of randomly taking two blue pebbles is __?__.

Example 11 **Solve probability problems involving dependent events involving more than one favorable outcome.**

Scott randomly chooses to take to school either bus or bicycle, but not both. The tree diagram below shows that the mode of transportation Scott chooses depends on the weather. The probability of rain on a particular day is denoted by a. Assume that rainy and sunny are mutually exclusive events.

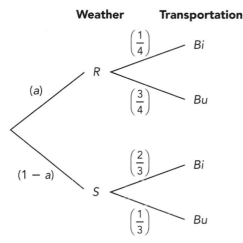

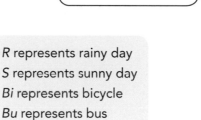

Remember that the probabilities of all branches from a node must have a sum of 1.

R represents rainy day
S represents sunny day
Bi represents bicycle
Bu represents bus

a) If $a = \frac{1}{2}$, find the probability that Scott will take a bus to school on any day.

Solution

You need to find the probability that Scott takes the bus on a rainy day plus the probability that he takes the bus on a sunny day.

$P(R) = \frac{1}{2}$

$P(S) = 1 - \frac{1}{2} = \frac{1}{2}$ Events R and S are complementary.

$P(Bu) = \frac{1}{2} \cdot \frac{3}{4} + \frac{1}{2} \cdot \frac{1}{3}$ Evaluate $P(R, Bu) + P(S, Bu)$.

$\quad\;\; = \frac{13}{24}$

If the probability of rain is $\frac{1}{2}$, then the probability that Scott will take a bus to school is $\frac{13}{24}$.

b) If $a = \frac{5}{8}$, find the probability that Scott will ride a bicycle to school.

Solution

$P(S) = 1 - \frac{5}{8} = \frac{3}{8}$ Events R and S are complementary.

$P(Bi) = \frac{5}{8} \cdot \frac{1}{4} + \frac{3}{8} \cdot \frac{2}{3}$ Evaluate $P(R, Bi) + P(S, Bi)$.

$\quad\;\; = \frac{13}{32}$

If the probability of rain is $\frac{5}{8}$, then the probability that Scott will ride a bicycle is $\frac{13}{32}$.

Guided Practice

Solve. Show your work.

3 The tree diagram below shows how passing an examination depends on whether a student studies (*S*) or does not study (*NS*) for the exam. The probability that a student studies is denoted by *p*. Assume that *S* and *NS* are mutually exclusive events.

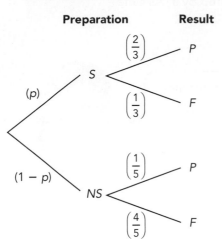

Preparation   **Result**

$\left(\frac{2}{3}\right)$ P

S

(p)

$\left(\frac{1}{3}\right)$ F

$(1 - p)$

$\left(\frac{1}{5}\right)$ P

NS

$\left(\frac{4}{5}\right)$ F

> *S* represents study
> *NS* represents no study
> *P* represents pass
> *F* represents fail

a) If $p = 0.4$, find the probability that a student passes the examination.

$P(S) = \dfrac{?}{?}$ Write the fraction for 0.4.

$P(NS) = 1 - P(S)$ Events *S* and *NS* are complementary.

$\quad = 1 - \dfrac{?}{?}$

$\quad = \dfrac{?}{?}$

$P(P) = \dfrac{?}{?} \cdot \dfrac{?}{?} + \dfrac{?}{?} \cdot \dfrac{?}{?}$ Evaluate $P(S, P) + P(NS, P)$.

$\quad = \dfrac{?}{?}$

If the probability of studying is 0.4, then the probability of passing is __?__.

b) If $p = 0.75$, find the probability that a student fails the examination.

$P(S) = \dfrac{?}{?}$ Write the fraction for 0.75.

$P(NS) = 1 - P(S)$ Events *S* and *NS* are complementary.

$\quad = 1 - \dfrac{?}{?}$

$\quad = \dfrac{?}{?}$

$P(F) = \dfrac{?}{?} \cdot \dfrac{?}{?} + \dfrac{?}{?} \cdot \dfrac{?}{?}$ Evaluate $P(S, F) + P(NS, F)$.

$\quad = \dfrac{?}{?}$

If the probability of studying is 0.75, then the probability of failing is __?__.

Practice 11.4

State whether each event is a dependent or independent event.

1 Drawing 2 red balls randomly, one at a time without replacement, from a bag of six balls.

2 Tossing a coin twice.

3 Reaching school late or on time for two consecutive days.

4 Flooding of roads during rainy or sunny days.

Draw the tree diagram for each compound event.

5 2 balls are drawn at random, one at a time without replacement, from a bag of 3 green balls and 18 red balls.

6 The probability of rain on a particular day is 0.3. If it rains, then the probability that Renee goes shopping is 0.75. If it does not rain, then the probability that she goes jogging is 0.72. Assume that shopping and jogging are mutually exclusive and that rain and no rain are complementary.

Solve. Show your work.

7 Geraldine has a box of 13 colored pens: 3 blue, 4 red, and the rest black. What is the probability of drawing two blue pens randomly, one at a time without replacement?

8 A box contains 8 dimes, 15 quarters, and 27 nickels. A student is to randomly pick two items, one at a time without replacement, from the bag. Find the probability that 2 quarters are picked.

9 There are 9 green, 2 yellow, and 5 blue cards in a deck. Players A and B each randomly pick a card from the deck. Player A picks a card first before player B picks. Find the probability that both players pick the same color cards.

10 The probability diagram below shows the probability of Xavier going to library or park depending if the weather is sunny or rainy. The probability of rain on a particular day is denoted by *a*. Assume that going to the library and going to the park are mutually exclusive and complementary.

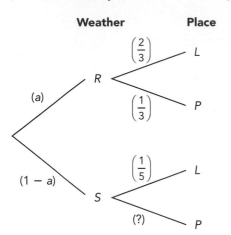

Weather   **Place**

$\left(\frac{2}{3}\right)$ — L

R

(*a*)

$\left(\frac{1}{3}\right)$ — P

$\left(\frac{1}{5}\right)$ — L

(1 − *a*)

S

(?) — P

> *R* represents rainy
> *S* represents sunny
> *L* represents library
> *P* represents park

a) If *a* = 0.3, find the probability that Xavier goes to the park on any day.

b) If *a* = 0.75, find the probability that he goes to the library on any day.

11 There are 15 apples in a fruit basket. 6 of them are red apples and the rest green apples. Two apples are picked randomly, one at a time without replacement.

a) Draw a tree diagram to represent the possible outcomes.

b) Find the probability of picking a green apple and then a red apple.

c) Find the probability of picking two green apples.

d) Find the probability of picking two red apples.

12 There are 8 people in a room: 3 of them have red hair, 2 have blonde hair, and the rest have dark hair. Two people are randomly selected to leave the room, one after another, and they do not re-enter the room.

a) Draw a tree diagram to represent the possible outcomes.

b) What is the probability of a person with dark hair leaving the room first?

c) What is the probability of a person with red hair leaving the room, followed by a person with blonde hair?

d) What is the probability of two people with the same hair color leaving the room?

13 Along a stretch of road there are 2 traffic light intersections. Having red or green light for the first intersection is equally likely. Having a red light at the second intersection is twice as likely as a green light, if the first intersection traffic light was red. What is the probability of having a red light on the first intersection and a green light on the second intersection? Draw a tree diagram to show the possible outcomes.

14 To get to work, Mr. Killiney needs to take a train and then a bus. The probability that the train breaks down is 0.1. When the train breaks down, there is a 0.7 probability that the bus will be overcrowded. When the train is operating normally, there is a 0.2 probability that the bus will be overcrowded. What is the probability of getting a seat in the bus? Draw a tree diagram to show the possible outcomes.

Brain @ Work

1 If there are 12 green and 6 red apples, find the probability of randomly choosing three apples of the same color in a row, without replacement. Show your work.

2 William has five $1 bills, ten $10 bills, and three $20 bills in his wallet. He picks three bills randomly in a row, without replacement. What is the probability of him picking three of the same type of bills? Show your work.

3 Daniel plans to visit Australia. Whether he goes alone or with a companion is equally likely. If he travels with a companion there is a 40% chance of joining a guided tour. If he travels alone, there is an 80% chance of joining a guided tour.

a) What is the probability of traveling with a companion and not joining a guided tour?

b) What is the chance of joining a guided tour?

Chapter Wrap Up

Concept Map

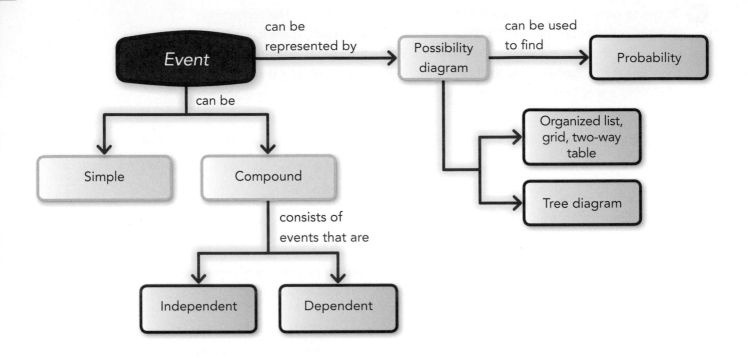

Key Concepts

▶ Compound events are events that are made up of two or more simple events.

▶ Possible outcomes of compound events can be displayed in possibility diagrams: organized list, two-way grid, table with ordered pairs, or tree diagram.

▶ Simple events that make up compound events can be dependent or independent.

▶ When two events A and B are independent, the multiplication rule of probability states: $P(A \text{ and } B) = P(A) \cdot P(B)$

▶ When two events A and B are dependent, the multiplication rule of probability states: $P(A \text{ and } B) = P(A) \cdot P(B \text{ after } A)$

▶ For two mutually exclusive events A and B the addition rule of probability states: $P(A \text{ or } B) = P(A) + P(B)$

Chapter Review/Test

Concepts and Skills

State whether each event is a simple or compound event.

 Drawing 2 yellow marbles in a row from a bag of yellow and green marbles.

 Drawing 1 red pebble and 1 yellow pebble in a row from a bag of red and yellow pebbles.

 Tossing a coin once.

Draw the possibility diagram and state the number of possible outcomes for each compound event.

 From three cards labeled A, B, and C, draw two cards, one at a time with replacement.

 From a pencil case with 1 red pen, 1 green pen, and 1 blue pen, select two pens, one at a time without replacement.

 Toss a fair four-sided number die, labeled 1 to 4, and a coin.

Draw the tree diagram for each compound event.

7 Spinning a spinner divided into 4 equal areas labeled 1 to 4, and tossing a coin.

8 Picking two green apples randomly from a basket of red and green apples.

State whether each compound event consists of independent events or dependent events.

9 From a pencil case, two color pencils are randomly drawn, one at a time without replacement.

10 From two classes of 30 students, one student is selected randomly from each class for a survey.

Problem Solving

Solve. Show your work.

 There are two tables in a room. There are 2 history textbooks and 1 math textbook on the first table. There are 1 history workbook and 1 math workbook on the second table. Use a possibility diagram to find the probability of randomly selecting a history textbook from the first table and a math workbook from the second table.

12 A fair four-sided number die is marked 1, 2, 2, and 3. A spinner equally divided into 3 sectors is marked 3, 4, and 7. Jamie tosses the number die and spins the spinner.

a) Use a possibility diagram to find the probability that the sum of the two resulting numbers is greater than 5.

b) Use a possibility diagram to find the probability that the product of the two resulting numbers is odd.

13 A juggler is giving a performance by juggling a red ball, a yellow ball, and a green ball. All 3 balls have equal chance of dropping. If one ball drops, the juggler will stop and pick up the ball and resume juggling. If another ball drops again, the juggler will stop the performance.

a) Draw a tree diagram to represent the possible outcomes and the corresponding probabilities.

b) Find the probability of dropping the same colored ball twice.

c) Find the probability of dropping one green and one yellow ball.

14 In a marathon, there is a half-marathon and a full-marathon. There are 60 students who participated in the half-marathon and 80 participated in the full-marathon. Half of the students in the half-marathon warm up before the run, while three-quarters of the students in the full-marathon warm up. Assume that warming up and not warming up are mutually exclusive and complementary.

a) Draw a tree diagram to represent the possible outcomes and the corresponding probabilities.

b) What is the probability of randomly picking a marathon participant who warms up before running a full-marathon?

c) What is the probability of randomly picking a marathon participant who does not warm up before running?

15 The probability of Cindy waking up after 8 A.M. on a weekend day is p. Assume the events of Cindy waking up after 8 A.M. and by 8 A.M. are mutually exclusive and complementary.

a) If $p = 0.3$, find the probability that she will wake up after 8 A.M. on two consecutive weekend days.

b) If $p = 0.56$, find the probability that she will wake up by 8 A.M. on two consecutive weekend days.

16 In a jar, there are 2 raisin cookies and 3 oat cookies. Steven takes two cookies one after another without replacement.

a) Draw a tree diagram to represent the possible outcomes and the corresponding probabilities.

b) Find the probability of Steven randomly getting two of the same type of cookie.

c) Find the probability of Steven randomly getting at least one raisin cookie.

17 Out of 100 raffle tickets, 4 are marked with a prize. Matthew randomly selects two tickets from the box.

a) Draw a tree diagram to represent the possible outcomes and the corresponding probabilities.

b) What is the probability that Matthew does not win any prizes?

c) What is the probability that Matthew gets exactly one of the prizes?

18 The tree diagram shows the probability of how Shane spends his day gaming or cycling, depending on the weather. The probability of rain is denoted by a. Assume that gaming and cycling are mutually exclusive.

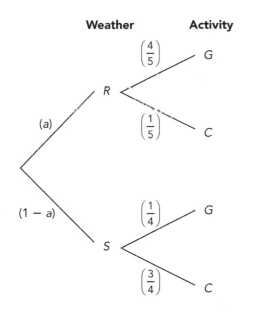

Weather   **Activity**

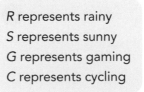

R represents rainy
S represents sunny
G represents gaming
C represents cycling

a) If $a = 0.4$, find the probability that he will spend his day gaming.

b) If $a = 0.75$, find the probability that he will spend his day cycling.

Cumulative Review Chapters 10–11

Concepts and Skills

Construct a scatter plot for each table of bivariate data. Identify any outliers. (Lesson 10.1)

 Use 1 centimeter on the horizontal axis to represent 1 unit and 1 centimeter on the vertical axis to represent 100 units.

x	3	1	6	5	2	2	8	6	3
y	200	20	620	460	100	140	980	600	180

x	5	2	4	8	7	6	4	4	1
y	420	80	320	960	800	660	380	280	0

2 Use 1 centimeter on the horizontal axis to represent 0.2 units for x interval from 36.0 to 38.0 and 1 centimeter on the vertical axis to represent 2 units for y interval from 230 to 252.

x	36.8	37.4	38.0	37.0	36.4	36.2	37.6	37.0	36.8
y	242.4	246.0	250.8	243.2	242.4	237.2	246.8	241.6	244.8

x	36.2	37.0	37.2	37.4	38.0	36.4	36.0	37.0	36.8
y	238.0	243.6	245.2	230.0	248.8	239.6	236.0	244.8	241.6

Describe any association between the bivariate data in each scatter plot. (Lesson 10.1)

3
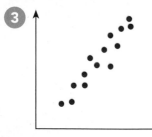

4
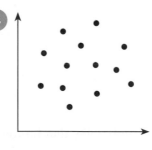

State the line that represents a line of best fit for each scatter plot. (Lesson 10.2)

5
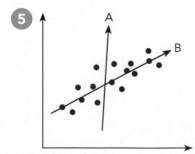

6
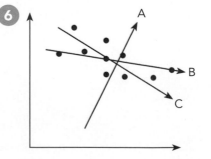

Construct each scatter plot and draw a line of best fit for the given table of bivariate data. (Lesson 10.2)

7 Use 1 centimeter on the horizontal axis to represent 1 unit and 1 centimeter on the vertical axis to represent 2 units.

Population of State (in 1,000,000s)	2.8	2.4	3.7	2.9	4.4	6.5	9.2	4.9	7.7
Corresponding Number of US Representatives for State	4	15	5	4	6	9	13	7	11

Population of State (in 1,000,000s)	2.7	2.6	2.7	1.5	1.7	3.6	2.8	5.2	5.9
Corresponding Number of US Representatives for State	3	3	3	2	3	5	5	8	9

8 Use 1 centimeter to represent 1 unit on both axes.

Age of Car (*t* years)	10	3	7	8	9	1	8	4	6
Market Price (*p* dollars in 1,000s)	4.9	15.4	8.1	6.8	5.8	21.3	8.3	13.1	9.4

Age of Car (*t* years)	5	7	9	3	8	4	5	6	2
Market Price (*p* dollars in 1,000s)	11.1	7.6	5.5	13	6.4	15	12.6	11.1	18.1

Identify whether the given data is qualitative or quantitative. (Lesson 10.3)

9 Number of eggs hatched

10 Ice cream flavors

Copy and fill in the missing information in the two-way table. (Lesson 10.3)

11

<table>
<tr><td></td><td colspan="6" align="center">Ethnicity</td></tr>
<tr><td></td><td></td><td>Caucasian</td><td>Hispanic</td><td>African</td><td>Asian</td><td>Total</td></tr>
<tr><td rowspan="3">Gender</td><td>Male</td><td>100 million</td><td>__?__ million</td><td>21 million</td><td>8 million</td><td>154 million</td></tr>
<tr><td>Female</td><td>96 million</td><td>25 million</td><td>__?__ million</td><td>__?__ million</td><td>__?__ million</td></tr>
<tr><td>Total</td><td>196 million</td><td>__?__ million</td><td>40 million</td><td>14 million</td><td>300 million</td></tr>
</table>

Construct a two-way table using the given data. (Lesson 10.3)

12

Watch Documentary	W	NW	NW	W	W	NW	W	W	NW	NW	W	NW
Science Test	P	P	NP	P	P	P	NP	P	NP	P	P	P

W represents watch the documentary
NW represents did not watch the documentary
P represents passed the science test
NP represents did not pass the science test

Tell whether the outcomes described are from a simple or compound event. If it is a compound event, identify the simple events that form the compound event. (Lesson 11.1)

13 Drawing a blue marble followed by a green marble, without replacing the first marble, from a box containing 2 red, 5 blue, and 3 green marbles.

14 Getting a number between 2 and 5 when rolling a fair six-sided number die.

15 Getting a product of 12 when rolling two fair six-sided number dice.

Solve. Show your work.

16 A fair four-sided number die, labeled 4 to 7, and a letter cube, labeled A, B, C, D, E, and E, are rolled. (Lessons 11.1, 11.2)

   a) Draw a possibility diagram to represent the possible outcomes.

   b) Find the probability of getting the letter E.

17 Two fair six-sided number dice numbered 1 to 6 are rolled. (Lessons 11.1, 11.2)

   a) Draw a possibility diagram to represent the possible outcomes.

   b) Find the probability that the outcomes for both six-sided number dice are even.

   c) Find the probability that the product of the two numbers is a prime number.

18 Spinner P is divided into 5 equal areas and labeled from 5 to 9. The spinner is spun and a coin is tossed. (Lessons 11.1, 11.2)

   a) Draw a possibility diagram to represent the possible outcomes.

   b) Find the probability of getting heads and an even number.

19 There are 4 yellow highlighters, 2 blue highlighters, and 3 purple highlighters in bag A. There are 2 white balls and 4 blue balls in bag B. A highlighter is randomly drawn from bag A, and then a ball is randomly drawn from bag B. (Lesson 11.3)

a) Draw a tree diagram to represent the possible outcomes and their corresponding probabilities.

b) What is the probability of drawing a yellow highlighter and a blue ball?

c) What is the probability of drawing a highlighter and a ball that are the same color?

d) What is the probability of drawing exactly one blue item?

20 A box contains 16 color cards: 5 red, 4 blue, and 7 green. Two cards are picked at random from the box, one after another without replacement. The tree diagram shows the possible outcomes and the corresponding probabilities. (Lesson 11.4)

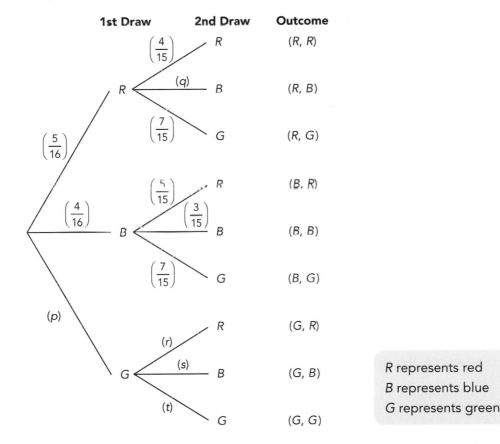

R represents red	
B represents blue	
G represents green	

a) Find the values of p, q, r, s, and t.

b) Find the probability that both cards are green.

c) Find the probability that both cards are the same color.

d) Find the probability that both cards are different colors.

e) Find the probability that both cards are blue or both are green.

Problem Solving

Solve. Show your work.

21 Alan has 3 pencils in a box: 1 blue, 1 red, and 1 orange. He has 1 blue marker and 2 red markers in another box. Alan randomly selects a pencil and a marker. Use a possibility diagram to represent the possible outcomes. Then find the probability of getting the same colors for the pencil and marker. (Chapter 11)

22 Joyce rolled a fair six-sided number die labeled 1 to 6 and a fair four-sided number die labeled 2 to 5. Use a possibility diagram to find the probability that the product of the two resulting numbers is at least 20. (Chapter 11)

Refer to the scenario below to answer questions 23 to 28.

The data below shows the amount of electricity consumption and cost for some households in a particular month. (Chapter 10)

Electricity Consumption (x kilowatt hour)	920	800	980	880	820	840	900	880	920
Cost (y dollars)	99.20	86.40	106.00	93.20	88.00	90.40	97.20	97.60	100.80

Electricity Consumption (x kilowatt hour)	860	840	960	900	820	920	960	840	940
Cost (y dollars)	92.00	89.60	103.60	96.00	89.20	100.00	100.80	91.20	100.00

23 Construct a scatter plot for the given bivariate data. Use 1 centimeter on the horizontal axis to represent 20 kilowatt hour for the x interval from 800 to 1,000 and 1 centimeter on the vertical axis to represent 2 dollars for the y interval from 86 to 108.

24 Describe the association between the electricity consumption and the cost.

25 Draw a line of best fit.

26 Write an equation for the line of best fit. Use points (820, 88) and (900, 97).

27 Using the equation in **26**, predict the cost per month for an electricity consumption of 888 kilowatt hour in that particular month.

28 Using the equation in **26**, predict the cost per month for an electricity consumption of 1,000 kilowatt hour in that particular month.

Solve. Show your work.

29 Bag A contains 25 tomatoes, 4 of which are rotten. Bag B contains 15 tomatoes, 6 of which are rotten. Jamie randomly selects a tomato from bag A followed by another random selection from bag B. (Chapter 11)

    a) Draw a tree diagram to represent the possible outcomes and their corresponding probabilities.

    b) What is the probability that both tomatoes are rotten?

    c) What is the probability that exactly one tomato is rotten?

    d) What is the probability that at least one tomato is not rotten?

30 The probability that Jeremy wakes up late is 0.3. Jeremy can choose to cycle, take a bus, or drive a car to the gym. If he does not wake up late, the probability that he cycles is 0.5, takes a bus is 0.4, and drives a car is 0.1. If he wakes up late, the probability that he cycles is 0.05, takes a bus is 0.2, and drives a car is 0.75. (Chapter 11)

    a) Draw a tree diagram to represent the possible outcomes and their corresponding probabilities.

    b) Find the probability that Jeremy will wake up and cycle to the gym.

    c) Find the probability that Jeremy will not wake up late and will drive a car to the gym.

    d) Find the probability that Jeremy will take a bus to the gym.

Refer to the scenario below to answer questions 31 to 34.

The data below shows the gender and favorite sport of 12 students surveyed. (Chapter 10)

Gender	Male	Female	Female	Female	Male	Female
Favorite Sport	Baseball	Swimming	Basketball	Basketball	Baseball	Swimming

Gender	Male	Female	Female	Male	Female	Male
Favorite Sport	Basketball	Swimming	Baseball	Swimming	Swimming	Baseball

31 Construct a two-way table using the above data.

32 Describe the association between genders and favorite sports based on the given data.

33 Copy and find the relative frequencies (to the nearest hundredth) to compare the distribution of the genders among the different favorite sports (columns).

34 Copy and find the relative frequencies (to the nearest hundredth) to compare the distribution of the favorite sports among the genders (rows).

Selected Answers

CHAPTER 7

Lesson 7.1, Guided Practice (pp. 9−15)

1. 12^2; 81; 144; 225; $\sqrt{225}$; 15; 15 **2.** 2^2; 4; 4; 4; 4; 4; 2.25; $\sqrt{2.25}$; 1.5; 1.5; 2^2; 1.5; 1.5; 2^2; 3^2; 4; 9; 13; $\sqrt{13}$; 3.6; 3.6 **3.** 18^2; 169; 225; 324; 394; ≠; 324; is not

4. 18^2; 9^2; 324; 81; 324; 81; 81; 81; 81; 243; $\sqrt{243}$; 15.6; 15.6 **5.** 15^2; 9^2; 225; 81; 225; 81; 81; 81; 81; 144; $\sqrt{144}$; 12; 12 **6.** 40^2; 32^2; 1,600; 1,024; 1,600; 1,024; 1,024; 1,024; 1,024; 576; $\sqrt{576}$; 24; 24; 2; 48; 48

Lesson 7.1, Practice (pp. 16−19)

1.

3. $x = 15$ **5.** $x = 7.5$ **7.** $x = 3$; $y = 12.6$ **9.** $x = 5.7$; $y = 11.5$ **11.** Triangle B **13.** 71.0 in. **15.** 33.4 ft **17.** 48 in. **19.** $x = 7.1$; $y = 14.3$ **21.** $BC = 35$ m; $AD = 16.8$ m **23a.** 17.3 in. **23b.** 129.9 in. **25.** Yes; It is a right triangular table.

Lesson 7.2, Guided Practice (pp. 22−27)

1. −5; −6 ; 3; (−6); 9 ; 3; (−5); 8; PR^2 ; QR^2 ; 9^2; 8^2; 81; 64; 145; $\sqrt{145}$; 12.0; $\sqrt{145}$; 12.0 **2.** (−2); 6^2; $\sqrt{45}$; $\sqrt{45}$; (−1); $(−5)^2$; $\sqrt{34}$; $\sqrt{34}$; (−1); −1; 6^2; 1^2; $\sqrt{37}$; $\sqrt{37}$; no two sides are of the same length; not an isosceles triangle **3.** 3; $(−7)^2$; $\sqrt{53}$; $\sqrt{53}$; (−4); $(−1)^2$; $\sqrt{17}$; $\sqrt{17}$; −1; 2^2; $\sqrt{40}$; $\sqrt{40}$; no two sides are of the same length; not an isosceles triangle

Lesson 7.2, Practice (pp. 28−30)

1. $\sqrt{98}$ units **3.** Because $RS = RT$, triangle RST is an isosceles triangle. **5.** Zoo and swimming pool **7.** Route passing through Port B is shorter. **9a.** 60 mi **9b.** 1.2 h **11.** Jose's method uses counting, whereas the formula uses the absolute value of the difference of coordinates. The two methods are the same, as the distance formula is derived from the Pythagorean Theorem.

Lesson 7.3, Guided Practice (pp. 32−33)

1. 5^2; 25; 64; Multiply; 25; 25; 64; 25; Subtract 25 from both sides; 39; Simplify; $\sqrt{39}$; 6.2; Round; 6.2

2. XY^2; XZ^2; 7.8^2; 10.5^2; 60.84; 110.25; 171.09; $\sqrt{171.09}$; 13.1; $\sqrt{171.09}$; 13.1

Lesson 7.3, Practice (pp. 34−35)

1. $w = 8$ **3.** $y = 16$ **5.** 480 cm² **7.** 3.9 cm **9.** 4 in. **11.** Yes. The diagonal of the 14.5 cm-by-4 cm base is approximately 15.04 cm long, so you can fit the ruler so that it sits diagonally with the ends of the ruler resting against the edges that are 3.5 centimeters high.

Lesson 7.4, Guided Practice (p. 39)

1. 12^2; 6^2; 144; 36; 144; 36; 36; 36; 108; $\sqrt{108}$; $\frac{1}{3} \cdot 3.14 \cdot 6^2 \cdot \sqrt{108}$; 391.6; $3.14 \cdot 6^2 \cdot 5$; 565.2; 391.6; 565.2; 956.8; 956.8

Lesson 7.4, Practice (pp. 40−43)

1a. 450.0 cm³ **1b.** 98.4 cm³ **3a.** 1.5 m **3b.** 508.7 m³ **5.** 39.8 in³ **7.** 660 ft³ **9.** No. The volume is actually 4 times its original.

Lesson 7.4, Brain@Work (p. 43)

1. 846.5 cm **2.** 111.7 m

Chapter Review/Test (pp. 45−47)

1a. $x = 20$ **1b.** $x = 12$ **1c.** $x = 15$ **3a.** $x = 10$ **3b.** $x = 4.2$ **5a.** 4.5 km **5b.** 6.4 km **5c.** 5.8 km **5d.** 7.8 km **7.** 24 in. **9.** 11.4 in. **11.** 16 in. **13.** 88.9 ft **15.** 10.0 ft

CHAPTER 8

Lesson 8.1, Guided Practice (pp. 53−58)

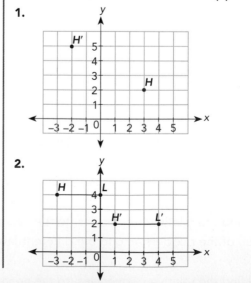

3.

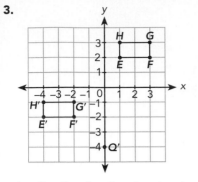

−4; −2; −2; −2; −2; −1; −4; −1;   **4.** 0; 4; 1; 5; −1; 7;
x − 2; y + 3

Lesson 8.1, Practice (pp. 59−60)

1. (−8, 2)   **3.** (−5, 4)

5.

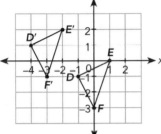

7. 2; −2; 2; −4; 0, −4   **9.** (1, 6)

11. 2 units to the right; (x, y) is mapped onto (x + 2, y).

Lesson 8.2, Guided Practice (pp. 62−69)

1. 6 in.

2a.

2b.

2c.

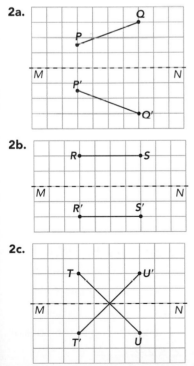

2d.

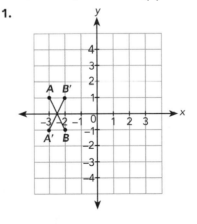

3.

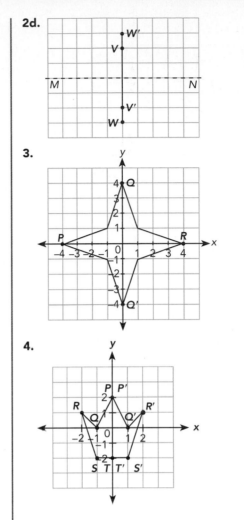

4.

5. opposites; the same;   3; 0;   5; 3;   3; 6;   −1; 3;   −x; y

Lesson 8.2, Practice (pp. 70−72)

1.

3.

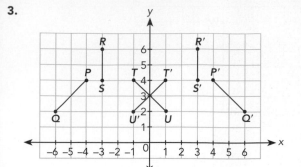

5a. and 5c.

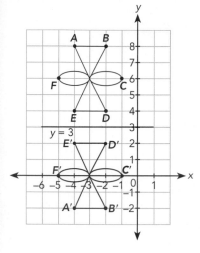

5b. *A'* (−4, −2), *B'* (−2, −2), *C'* (−1, 0), *D'* (−2, 2), *E'* (−4, 2), *F'* (−5, 0) **7.** Construct the perpendicular bisectors of $\overline{AA'}$ **9a.** 6 units **9b.** (−3, −4)

Lesson 8.3, Guided Practice (pp. 75−82)

1a. 90° **1b.** 180°

2.

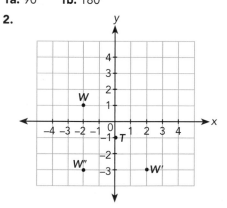

3a. Center of the clock face **3b.** 120° clockwise

4. 3; −2; 1; −2; 1; −3

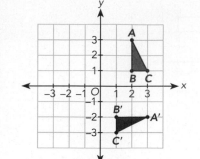

5. −1; −3; −2; −1; −1; 2; 0; −1

6a.

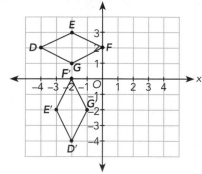

6b. −2; −4; −3; −2; −2; 0; −1; −2

Lesson 8.3, Practice (pp. 83−85)

1a. 90° **1b.** 180°

3.

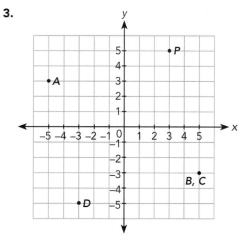

5a. (4, −2) **5b.** (−4, 2) **5c.** (−2, −4)

7. Rotations of 60°, 120°, 180°, 240°, and 300°

Lesson 8.4, Guided Practice (pp. 87−95)

1a. △*STU* and △*PTR*; They have a center of dilation, *T*, and the sides of △*PTR* are twice as long as the sides of △*STU*.

1b. △*PQS* and △*PUT*; They have a center of dilation, *P*, and the sides of △*PUT* are $1\frac{1}{2}$ times as long as the sides of △*PQS*. **2a.** 3; 2 **2b.** 3; 2; 6; 2; 2; 4

2c. 3; $\frac{1}{2}$; $1\frac{1}{2}$; 2; $\frac{1}{2}$; 1   **2d.** Scale factor 2: (10, 2); (6, 2); (6, 8); (10, 8); Scale factor $\frac{1}{2}$: (2.5, 0.5); (1.5, 0.5); (1.5, 2); (2.5, 2)

3.

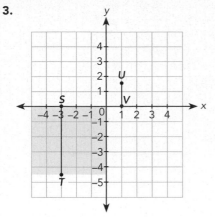

4a. $C(-1, 1)$; Scale factor $= -2$

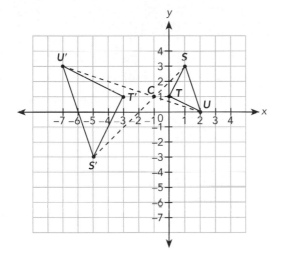

4b. $C(3, 4)$; Scale factor $= 3$

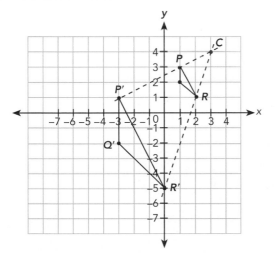

Lesson 8.4, Practice (pp. 96–97)

1. Yes; $\triangle ABC$ and $\triangle ADE$. They have a center of dilation at A, and the sides of $\triangle ADE$ are twice as long as the sides of $\triangle ABC$.   **3a.** 9 in., 6 in.; Enlargement   **3b.** 12 in., 8 in.; Enlargement   **3c.** 1.5 in., 1 in.; Reduction   **3d.** 8.4 in., 5.6 in.; Enlargement

5a.

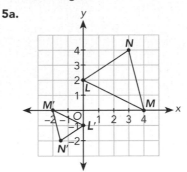

5b.

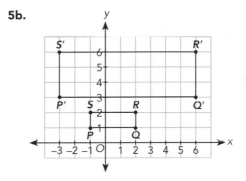

7a. $C(1, 2)$, Scale factor $= -0.5$

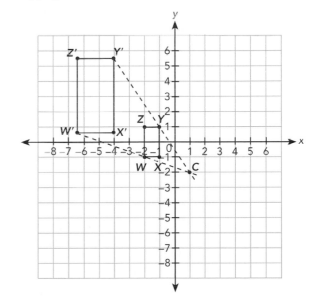

7b. C (1, −2); Scale factor = 2.5

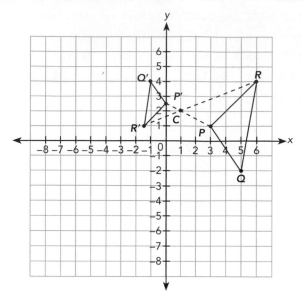

Lesson 8.5, Guided Practice (p. 102)

1a. Translation of 4 units to the right and 2 units up, because the coordinates of each vertex of △ABC increase the x value by 4 and the y value by 2 to get △PQR.

1b. Reflection in the x-axis, because the x-axis is the perpendicular bisector of segments AL, BM, and CN. The x-coordinates of the vertices of △ABC stayed the same but the y-coordinates are opposites in △LMN.

1c. Rotation 90° counterclockwise about the origin, O, because ∠AOX is 90°, and so are ∠BOY and ∠COZ, or the triangle has moved from Quadrant I to Quadrant II and the absolute values of the x- and y-coordinates of △XYZ are interchanged from △ABC.   **1d.** Both the lengths and angle measures of △ABC are preserved in all three transformations.

1a. to 1d.

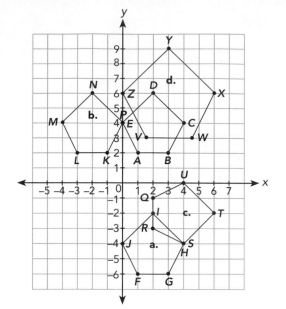

1e. Both the lengths and angle measures of pentagon ABCDE are preserved under transformations a) to c). Transformation d) preserves the shape of the pentagon but the size is increased by 1.5 times.

3a.

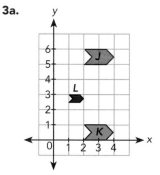

3b. Dilation with center at the origin and scale factor 0.5.

3c. The shape of arrow J is preserved in a) and b). The size of arrow J is preserved in a) but not in b).

5a.

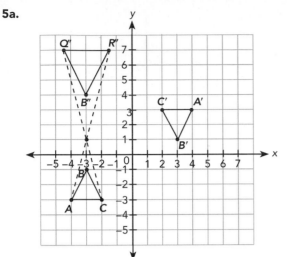

5b. Rotation 180° about O   **5c.** Dilation with center (−3, 1) and scale factor −1.5   **5d.** The shape of △ABC is preserved for both transformations. The size of △ABC remains the same in △A'B'C' but the △A"B"C" is an enlargement of △ABC.

Lesson 8.5, Brain@Work (p. 106)

1. 00, 11, or 88   **2a.** Reflection in the line x = 1 or y = 3
2b. Rotation 90° clockwise about (1, 3)   **3.** (1, −1); All pairs of corresponding points must be the same distance from the center. So I drew the perpendicular bisectors of AX and CZ and found where they intersected to obtain center P.   **4.** 0.9; I found a number such that when squared, the result was $\frac{6.48}{8}$.

Chapter Review/Test (pp. 109−111)

1. Rotation   **3.** Translation   **5.** Translation of 8 units to the left (or right) and 8 units up   **7.** x = 0   **9.** y = 0

11.

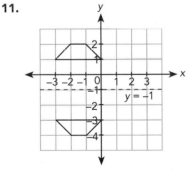

13a.

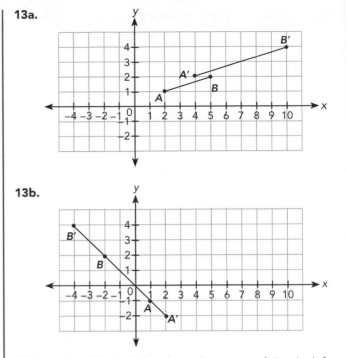

13b.

15. Rotation 30° clockwise about the centre of the clock face
17a. 4   **17b.** y = 0, x = 0, y = x, y = −x   **19.** $\frac{1}{180}$

CHAPTER 9

Lesson 9.1, Guided Practice (pp. 117−125)

1. C and D; Both are regular octagons of the same size. A and F; They have the same size and shape (right triangle).
2. C and D; They have the same size and shape (square).
3. U; V; W; T; UVWT   **4.** LM; MN; NK; KL; 12; GH; y + 2; NK; y + 2 + 5; y + 7; y + 7 − y; 7; z; KL; 12; z; 12; 6; 12; 7; 6; 12; 10; 9; 6; 9; 6; 12; 10 **5a.** XZ; NLM; ZXY; XY; △XYZ
5b. BCD; CBD; BDC; congruent

Lesson 9.1, Practice (pp. 126−128)

1. △BAD is congruent to △DCB. $\overline{AB}$ and $\overline{CD}$; $\overline{BD}$ and $\overline{DB}$; $\overline{AD}$ and $\overline{CB}$; ∠ABD and ∠CDB; ∠BAD and ∠DCB; ∠ADB and ∠CBD   **3a.** WZ = XY, WX = ZY, and WY = WY
3b. Answers vary. Possible answer: WZ = XY, m∠ZWY = m∠XYW, and WY = WY.   **3c.** Answers vary. Possible answer: m∠ZWY = m∠XYW, WY = WY, and m∠ZYW = m∠XWY   **3d.** △WXY and △YZW are right triangles, WY = WY (hypotenuse), and WZ = XY or WX = ZY.
5. x = 3.4; y = 8; z = 23   **7a.** x = 7; y = 49.5; z = 3
7b. p = 10.4; q = −2.8; r = 67   **9a.** SAS; Each triangle has a right angle at R and the pairs of adjacent sides are congruent.   **9b.** 10, because each cable between $\overline{RP}$ and $\overline{SP}$ has a triangle congruent to it on the opposite side of $\overline{PR}$.

Lesson 9.2, Guided Practice (pp. 130–139)

1. C and E; They have the same shape (equilateral triangle) but are not the same size.   **2.** 6; 3; 6; 3; 6; 6; 3; 6; 6; 3.6

3. $\frac{QR}{QT}$; $\frac{48}{12}$; $4 \cdot 8$; $\frac{x}{8}$; 8; 8; 32; 32   **4.** equal; A; 62°; B; 51°; 62°; 51°; 67°   **5.** AX; $\frac{9}{4}$; $\frac{81}{16}$; $\frac{81}{16}$; $\frac{81}{16}$; 12; $\frac{81}{16}$; 12; 12; 60.75; 60.75   **6.** $\frac{12}{4.8}$; 2.5; $\frac{10}{4}$; 2.5; $\frac{8}{3.2}$; 2.5;   **7.** $\frac{5}{10}$; $\frac{1}{2}$; $\frac{3}{5}$; $\frac{1}{2}$; different; is not similar to;   **8.** $\frac{12}{6}$; 2; $\frac{14}{7}$; 2; $\frac{16}{10}$; 2; EDF; same; different; is not similar to;

Lesson 9.2, Practice (pp. 140–143)

1. A and D; They have the same shape (isoceles right triangle) but different sizes.   **3.** 1.5   **5.** $1\frac{1}{3}$

7. $x = 38$; $y = 38$ **9.** $b = 7.8$; $z = 35$ **11.** $x = 3$; $y = 6$; m∠DAE = m∠BAC and m∠ADE = m∠ABC Two pairs of corresponding angles have equal measures. So △ADE ~ △ABC.   **13a.** 45 ft   **13b.** 2 ft   **15.** $x = 6$; $y = 20$ **17.** 2 in.   **19.** Similar figures are not congruent unless the scale factor is 1 or −1; Two triangles are similar when all three pairs of corresponding side lengths have the same ratio. When the ratio or scale factor is 1 or −1, the corresponding side lengths are the same. When all three pairs of corresponding side lengths are the same, the triangles are congruent.

Lesson 9.3, Guided Practice (pp. 145–153)

1. Rotation of △ABC 90° counterclockwise about (−2, 2)

2a. similar; J; 180°; 100°; 100°   **2b.** ×; 3   **3a.** 40°; 110°; 30°; Y; similar   **3b.** VW; 12; $\frac{1}{2}$; dilation; $\frac{1}{2}$ **4.** $y = 2$

5a. y-axis; 180°; a reflection in the x-axis

5b.

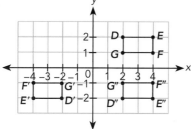

No

6a. △PQR is mapped onto △P'Q'R' by a reflection in the line $y = -1$. △P'Q'R' is mapped onto △P"Q"R" by using a rotation of 90° counterclockwise about the point (−3, −3).

6b.

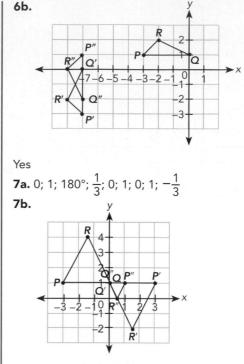

Yes

7a. 0; 1; 180°; $\frac{1}{3}$; 0; 1; 0; 1; $-\frac{1}{3}$

7b.

Lesson 9.3, Practice (pp. 154–157)

1. Congruent   **3.** Similar   **5.** Congruent

7a. A dilation with center (0, 1) and scale factor 0.5 and then a reflection in the y-axis.   **7b.** A translation of 1 unit up and then a rotation of 90° counterclockwise about the origin   **7c.** A reflection in the x-axis and then a reflection in the y-axis.   **9.** A translation of 30 m forward followed by a rotation of 90° clockwise about the center of the square   **11.** $\sqrt{3}$ or about 1.74   **13a.** A dilation with scale factor 3 and then a translation of 8 units to the right and 11 units up.   **13b.** 6 cm

Lesson 9.3, Brain@Work (p. 158)

1.

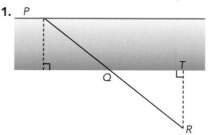

Take the hanging bridge down. Lay the hanging bridge on the ground from Q to R, so that P, Q, and R all lie on a straight line. Measure the distance TR such that $\overline{TR}$ is perpendicular to the river bank. TR is the length of the new bridge because the two right triangles are congruent.

2. 24.3 cm by 15.5 cm by 14.1 cm

Chapter Review/Test (pp. 160–165)

1. $\triangle XZY$ **3.** $\triangle TSR$ **5a.** $x = 2.5$; $y = 10$ **5b.** $w = 5$; $x = 13\frac{1}{3}$; $y = 5$ **7a.** Yes; Two pairs of angles have equal measures. **7b.** No; The included angles have the same measure, but the two pairs of side lengths have different ratios $\left(\frac{5}{6} \neq \frac{8}{9}\right)$. **9.** Translation of $\triangle ABC$ 3 units to the right; Dilation of $\triangle A'B'C'$ with center (0, 0) and scale factor 0.5; Dilation of $\triangle ABC$ with center (3, 0) and scale factor 0.5 **11.** Translation of $\triangle ABC$ 8 units to the right; Reflection of $\triangle A'B'C'$ in the y-axis; Reflection of $\triangle ABC$ in the line $x = -4$. **13a.** 1 : 5 **13b.** 6 ft **15a.** 9 in. **15b.** 8 in. **17.** 252 in^2 **19a.** $\angle UVW$; $\angle SZY$ **19b.** 3 in., 16 in.; 4.5 in. **19c.** 106 in.

Cumulative Review Chapters 7-9 (pp. 166–171)

1. $x = 8$ **3.** Not a right triangle **5.** 8.2 units **7.** $w = 24$ **9.** 69.1 in^3 **11.** (4, 6)

13.

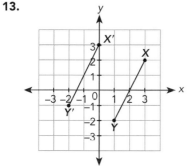

15a. A' (−3, 4); B' (−3, 0)

15b.

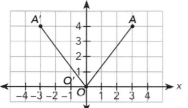

17a. 90° clockwise or 270° counterclockwise
17b. 90° counterclockwise or 270° clockwise
19. $\triangle ACB$ is a dilation of $\triangle ECD$ with center C and the sides of $\triangle ACB$ are $1\frac{1}{2}$ times as long as the sides of $\triangle ECD$.

21a.

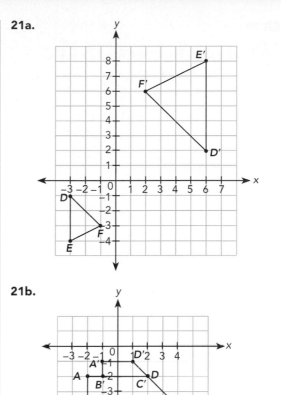

21b.

23a. Translation of 7 units to the left and 1 unit up
23b. 90° counterclockwise rotation about (0, 0) or 270° clockwise rotation about (0, 0). **25.** $x = 7$; $y = 4$
27. AAA; $x = 25.2$ **29.** 11.0 in. **31a.** GHIJF
31b. $w = 4.1$ ft; $x = 1.5$ ft; $y = 0.5$ ft **33a.** 15.75 in.
33b. 2 : 7 **35a.** Similar figures; Possible answer: The corresponding angles of $PQRST$ and $ABCDE$ are congruent. All corresponding side lengths are in the ratio 1: 1.45 because the first transformation is a dilation, and the second transformation is a reflection, which preserves the properties of the dilation. **35b.** 120° **35c.** 42.05 in^2

CHAPTER 10

Lesson 10.1, Guided Practice (p. 177—182)

1.

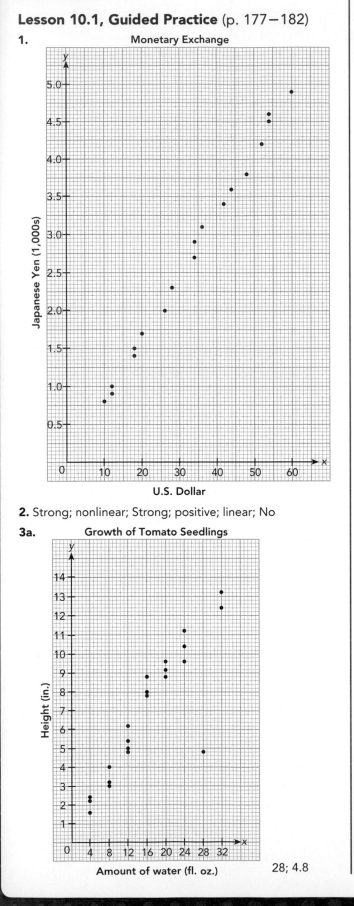

Monetary Exchange

2. Strong; nonlinear; Strong; positive; linear; No

3a.

Growth of Tomato Seedlings

28; 4.8

3b. 28 fluid ounces of water daily; a growth of 4.8 inches

3c. strong; positive; linear; more; 12—13; 4.8; 28

Lesson 10.1, Practice (pp. 183—185)

1.

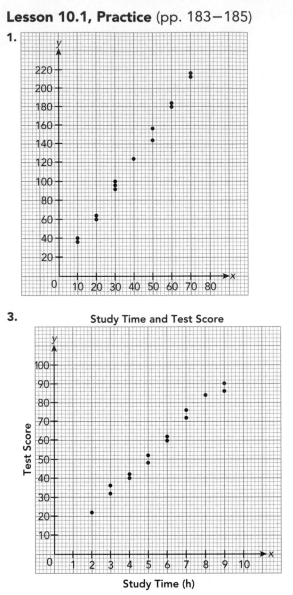

3.

Study Time and Test Score

5. Strong, negative, and linear association   **7.** Strong, negative, and nonlinear association   **9.** (0, 1) and (5, 0.4)

11. (50, 52); There could have been an accident or construction that blocked the access to the store for a long time that day.   **13.** Yes; If the association occurs over a greater range of values, then a narrow range of values may not be enough to recognize the trend in the data.

15. No outliers   **17.** 4 min; By analyzing the association between bivariate data, useful information on the optimum results for a given set of data can be known.

Lesson 10.2, Guided Practice (pp. 189–194)

1a.

Weekly Collection of Litter

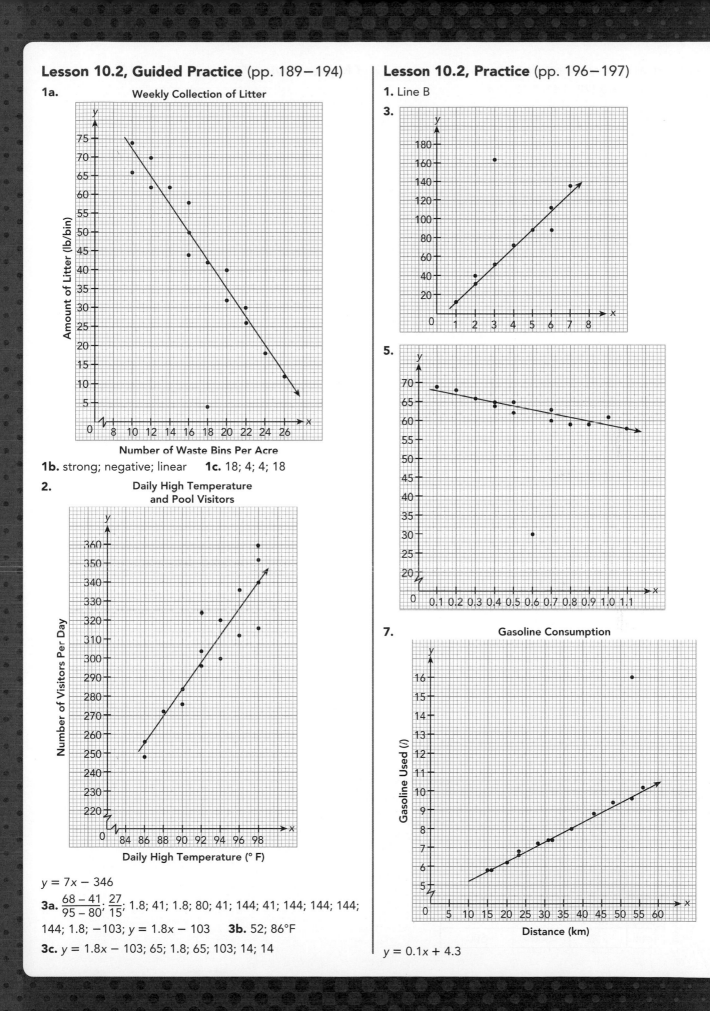

Number of Waste Bins Per Acre

1b. strong; negative; linear   **1c.** 18; 4; 4; 18

2.

Daily High Temperature
and Pool Visitors

$y = 7x - 346$

3a. $\dfrac{68 - 41}{95 - 80}$; $\dfrac{27}{15}$; 1.8; 41; 1.8; 80; 41; 144; 41; 144; 144; 144;

144; 1.8; −103; $y = 1.8x - 103$ **3b.** 52; 86°F

3c. $y = 1.8x - 103$; 65; 1.8; 65; 103; 14; 14

Lesson 10.2, Practice (pp. 196–197)

1. Line B

3.

5.

7.

Gasoline Consumption

Distance (km)

$y = 0.1x + 4.3$

9. Strong, positive, and linear association

11. $y = 0.008x + 0.172$ **13.** 0.10 g/cm³

Lesson 10.3, Guided Practice (pp. 200–206)

1a. 1,000; 481; 519; 519 **1b.** 519; 125; 279; 115; 115

1c. 125; 295; 420; 420

2a.

Cardio Exercises

Read Sport Magazines	Cycling	Running	Swimming	Total
Yes	5	2	3	10
No	1	7	2	10
Total	6	9	5	20

2b. 6; 9; 5; running **2c.** 20; 10; 50%

2d. 5; 2; 3; cyclists; no **3a.** $\frac{125}{420}$; 0.30; $\frac{279}{347}$; 0.80; $\frac{115}{233}$;

0.49; $\frac{295}{420}$; 0.70; $\frac{68}{347}$; 0.20; $\frac{118}{233}$; 0.51 **3b.** female; male;

male; female; almost evenly; female **3c.** $\frac{125}{519}$; 0.24; $\frac{279}{519}$;

0.54; $\frac{115}{519}$; 0.22; $\frac{295}{481}$; 0.61; $\frac{68}{481}$; 0.14; $\frac{118}{481}$; 0.25

3d. weight; both; cardio; weight

Lesson 10.3, Practice (pp. 207–208)

1. Color **3.** Categorical **5.** 225 **7.** 35

9. From the table, it appears that passengers who know the seat belt law tend to obey the seat belt law.

11. Fewer people; There are 13 households who have life insurance and only 12 households who do not.

13.

Sales Target Met

Commission	Yes	No	Total
Yes	0.74	0.26	1
No	0.16	0.84	1

15. Salespersons who are not paid on commission tend to not meet the sales target, while the salespersons who are paid on commission tend to meet the sales target.

Lesson 10.3, Brain@Work (p. 209)

1a. There are missing data points in between and within the interval that has no data points, the data points may not necessary follows a linear trend. **1b.** There are only three data points, and that is an insufficient amount of data to conclude the association between the bivariate data.

2a. 315; 185

2b.

Learn Second Language

Learn Music	Yes	No	Total
Yes	180	135	315
No	20	165	185
Total	200	300	500

Chapter Review/Test (pp. 211–215)

1.

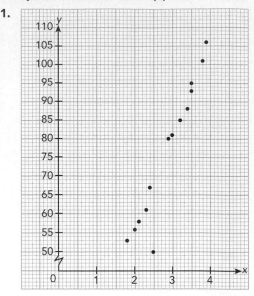

3. Strong, negative, and linear association **5.** Line B

7. (4, 2)

9.

English and Math Test Scores

[Scatter plot with "Score for Math Test" on the y-axis (ranging from 10 to 70) and "Score for English Test" on the x-axis (ranging from 10 to 80), with a line of best fit.]

$y = 0.68x + 13$

11.

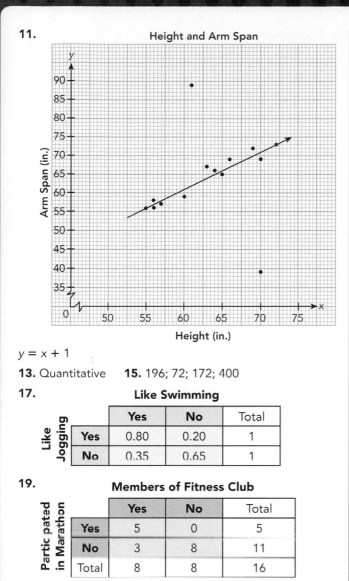

Height and Arm Span

$y = x + 1$

13. Quantitative   **15.** 196; 72; 172; 400

17.

Like Swimming

		Yes	No	Total
Like Jogging	Yes	0.80	0.20	1
	No	0.35	0.65	1

19.

Members of Fitness Club

		Yes	No	Total
Participated in Marathon	Yes	5	0	5
	No	3	8	11
	Total	8	8	16

21. As the number of ATMs increases, the number of teller hours per month decreases.

23.

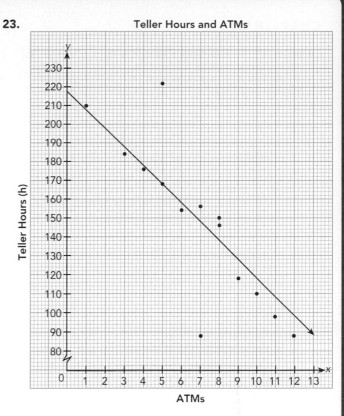

Teller Hours and ATMs

25. 196 h   **27.** The prediction lies too far from the range of the given data sets. When extrapolating the line of best fit, we are making assumption that the linear trend continues outside the range of the given data sets. So, the predicted result is not accurate as it deviates farther from the range.   **29.** Fewer people

31.

Customer Recommend

		Yes	No
Nutritional Information	Yes	0.43	0.33
	No	0.57	0.67
	Total	1	1

CHAPTER 11

Lesson 11.1, Guided Practice (pp. 220–226)

1. Compound event; There are two simple events: each consists of tossing a coin.   **2.** Simple event

3. Simple event   **4.** Compound event; There are two simple events: each consists of rolling a fair number die.

5. 4 outcomes

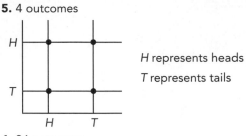

H represents heads
T represents tails

6. 36 outcomes

Number Die 1

×	1	2	3	4	5	6
1	1	2	3	4	5	6
2	2	4	6	8	10	12
3	3	6	9	12	15	18
4	4	8	12	16	20	24
5	5	10	15	20	25	30
6	6	12	18	24	30	36

(left label: Nummber Die 2)

7. 24 outcomes

Number Die 1

	1	2	3	4	5	6
1	(1, 1)	(2, 1)	(3, 1)	(4, 1)	(5, 1)	(6, 1)
2	(1, 2)	(2, 2)	(3, 2)	(4, 2)	(5, 2)	(6, 2)
3	(1, 3)	(2, 3)	(3, 3)	(4, 3)	(5, 3)	(6, 3)
4	(1, 4)	(2, 4)	(3, 4)	(4, 4)	(5, 4)	(6, 3)

(left label: Nummber Die 2)

8. 9 outcomes

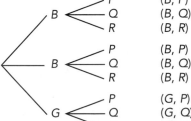

1st Bag	2nd Bag	Outcome

B represents blue
G represents green
P represents letter P
Q represents letter Q
R represents letter R

9. 8 outcomes

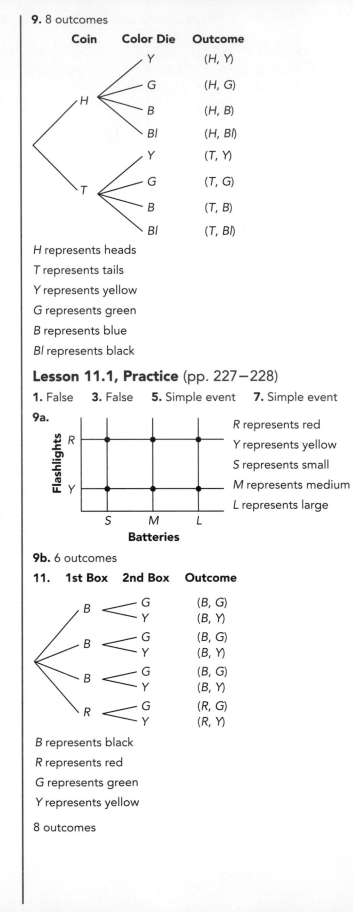

Coin	Color Die	Outcome

H represents heads
T represents tails
Y represents yellow
G represents green
B represents blue
Bl represents black

Lesson 11.1, Practice (pp. 227–228)

1. False   **3.** False   **5.** Simple event   **7.** Simple event

9a.

R represents red
Y represents yellow
S represents small
M represents medium
L represents large

(axis labels: Flashlights — R, Y; Batteries — S, M, L)

9b. 6 outcomes

11.

1st Box	2nd Box	Outcome
B	G	(B, G)
	Y	(B, Y)
B	G	(B, G)
	Y	(B, Y)
B	G	(B, G)
	Y	(B, Y)
R	G	(R, G)
	Y	(R, Y)

B represents black
R represents red
G represents green
Y represents yellow

8 outcomes

13a.

Number Die	Ball	Outcome

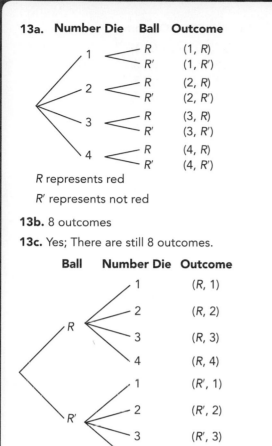

R represents red

R' represents not red

13b. 8 outcomes

13c. Yes; There are still 8 outcomes.

Ball	Number Die	Outcome

R — 1 (R, 1)
— 2 (R, 2)
— 3 (R, 3)
— 4 (R, 4)

R' — 1 (R', 1)
— 2 (R', 2)
— 3 (R', 3)
— 4 (R', 4)

R represents red

R' represents not red

Lesson 11.2, Guided Practice (pp. 232–233)

1.

Number Die 1

×	1	2	3	4
1	1	②	3	④
2	②	④	⑥	⑧
3	3	⑥	9	⑫
4	④	⑧	⑫	⑯

Number Die 2

$\frac{3}{4}$

2.

1st Bag

		R	G	B	Y	W
2nd Bag	**R**	(R, R)	(G, R)	(B, R)	(Y, R)	(W, R)
	G	(R, G)	(G, G)	(B, G)	(Y, G)	(W, G)
	B	(R, B)	(G, B)	(B, B)	(Y, B)	(W, B)
	Y	(R, Y)	(G, Y)	(B, Y)	(Y, Y)	(W, Y)
	W	(R, W)	(G, W)	(B, W)	(Y, W)	(W, W)

R represents red

G represents green

B represents blue

Y represents yellow

W represents white

$\frac{16}{25}$

3.

1st Box

		B	G	R	Y
2nd Box	**W**	(B, W)	(G, W)	(R, W)	(Y, W)
	G	(B, G)	(G, G)	(R, G)	(Y, G)
	R	(B, R)	(G, R)	(R, R)	(Y, R)

B represents black

G represents green

R represents red

Y represents yellow

W represents white

$\frac{1}{2}$

4a.

1st Coin	2nd Coin	3rd Coin	Outcome

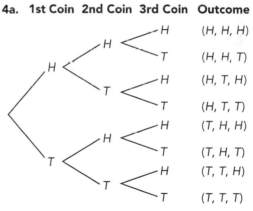

H — H — H (H, H, H)
— T (H, H, T)
— T — H (H, T, H)
— T (H, T, T)
T — H — H (T, H, H)
— T (T, H, T)
— T — H (T, T, H)
— T (T, T, T)

H represents heads

T represents tails

4b. $\frac{1}{8}$ **4c.** $\frac{1}{2}$

Lesson 11.2, Practice (pp. 234–235)

1. $\frac{4}{9}$ **3.** $\frac{1}{12}$ **5.** $\frac{1}{5}$

7a.

Jane

		A	**B**	**C**
Jill	**C**	AC	BC	(CC)
	D	AD	BD	CD
	E	AE	BE	CE

7b. $\frac{1}{9}$

9.

1st Coin	2nd Coin	3rd Coin	Outcome

H represents heads

T represents tails

$\frac{1}{4}$

Lesson 11.3, Guided Practice (pp. 241–248)

1a. G; A; $\frac{2}{6}$; $\frac{2}{6}$; G; B; Y; A; $\frac{1}{6}$; $\frac{2}{6}$; Y; B; R; A; $\frac{2}{6}$; R; B

1b. $\frac{1}{6}$; $\frac{2}{6}$; $\frac{1}{18}$; $\frac{1}{18}$ **2a.** $\frac{1}{10}$; $\frac{9}{10}$; $\frac{1}{10}$; $\frac{9}{10}$; $\frac{9}{10}$; $\frac{9}{10}$; $\frac{81}{100}$; $\frac{81}{100}$

2b. $\frac{1}{10}$; $\frac{9}{10}$; $\frac{9}{100}$; $\frac{9}{100}$ **2c.** $\frac{1}{10}$; $\frac{1}{10}$; $\frac{1}{100}$; $\frac{1}{100}$

3a. 0.75; 0.25; 0.25; J; J; 0.25; J; T; 0.25; T; J; T; T; 0.25; 0.25; 0.125; 0.125   **3b.** 0.25; 0.75; 0.75; 0.25; 0.375; 0.375

Lesson 11.3, Practice (pp. 249–251)

1.

Coin	Marble	Outcome

H represents heads

T represents tails

Y represents yellow

G represents green

B represents blue

Ball	Number Die	Outcome

3.

R represents red

B represents blue

5.

Saturday	Sunday	Outcome

R represents reading

P represents playing

7a.

Spinner	Coin	Outcome

H represents heads

T represents tails

7b. $\frac{1}{6}$ **7c.** $\frac{5}{6}$

9a.

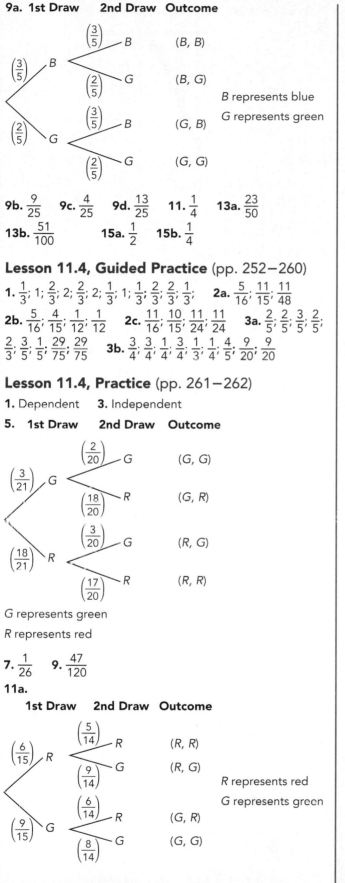

1st Draw	2nd Draw	Outcome

B represents blue
G represents green

9b. $\dfrac{9}{25}$ **9c.** $\dfrac{4}{25}$ **9d.** $\dfrac{13}{25}$ **11.** $\dfrac{1}{4}$ **13a.** $\dfrac{23}{50}$

13b. $\dfrac{51}{100}$ **15a.** $\dfrac{1}{2}$ **15b.** $\dfrac{1}{4}$

Lesson 11.4, Guided Practice (pp. 252–260)

1. $\dfrac{1}{3}$; 1; $\dfrac{2}{3}$; 2; $\dfrac{2}{3}$; 2; $\dfrac{1}{3}$; 1; $\dfrac{1}{3}$; $\dfrac{2}{3}$; $\dfrac{2}{3}$; $\dfrac{1}{3}$;   **2a.** $\dfrac{5}{16}$; $\dfrac{11}{15}$; $\dfrac{11}{48}$

2b. $\dfrac{5}{16}$; $\dfrac{4}{15}$; $\dfrac{1}{12}$; $\dfrac{1}{12}$ **2c.** $\dfrac{11}{16}$; $\dfrac{10}{15}$; $\dfrac{11}{24}$; $\dfrac{11}{24}$ **3a.** $\dfrac{2}{5}$; $\dfrac{2}{5}$; $\dfrac{3}{5}$; $\dfrac{2}{5}$;

$\dfrac{2}{3}$; $\dfrac{3}{5}$; $\dfrac{1}{5}$; $\dfrac{29}{75}$; $\dfrac{29}{75}$ **3b.** $\dfrac{3}{4}$; $\dfrac{3}{4}$; $\dfrac{1}{4}$; $\dfrac{3}{4}$; $\dfrac{1}{3}$; $\dfrac{1}{4}$; $\dfrac{4}{5}$; $\dfrac{9}{20}$; $\dfrac{9}{20}$

Lesson 11.4, Practice (pp. 261–262)

1. Dependent   **3.** Independent

5.

1st Draw	2nd Draw	Outcome

G represents green
R represents red

7. $\dfrac{1}{26}$ **9.** $\dfrac{47}{120}$

11a.

1st Draw	2nd Draw	Outcome

R represents red
G represents green

11b. $\dfrac{9}{35}$ **11c.** $\dfrac{12}{35}$ **11d.** $\dfrac{1}{7}$

13. $\dfrac{1}{6}$

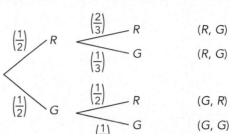

1st Intersection	2nd Intersection	Outcome

R represents red
G represents green

Lesson 11.4, Brain@Work (p. 263)

1. $\dfrac{12}{18} \cdot \dfrac{11}{17} \cdot \dfrac{10}{16} + \dfrac{6}{18} \cdot \dfrac{5}{17} \cdot \dfrac{4}{16} = \dfrac{5}{17}$

2. $\dfrac{5}{18} \cdot \dfrac{4}{17} \cdot \dfrac{3}{16} + \dfrac{10}{18} \cdot \dfrac{9}{17} \cdot \dfrac{8}{16} + \dfrac{3}{18} \cdot \dfrac{2}{17} \cdot \dfrac{1}{16} = \dfrac{131}{816}$

3a. 0.3 or $\dfrac{3}{10}$ **3b.** 0.6 or $\dfrac{3}{5}$

Chapter Review/Test (pp. 264–267)

1. Compound event   **3.** Simple event

5.

First	Second	Outcome

R represents red
G represents green
B represents blue

7.

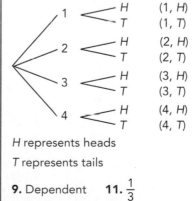

Spinner	Coin	Outcome

H represents heads
T represents tails

9. Dependent   **11.** $\dfrac{1}{3}$

13a. 1st Drop   2nd Drop

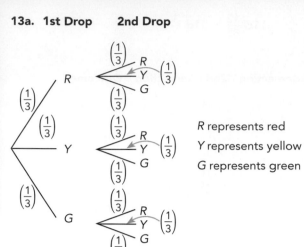

R represents red
Y represents yellow
G represents green

13b. $\frac{1}{3}$ **13c.** $\frac{2}{9}$ **15a.** 0.09   **15b.** 0.1936

17a.   1st Draw   2nd Draw

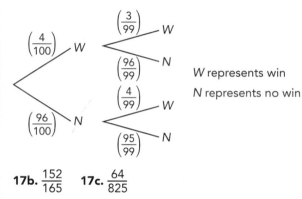

W represents win
N represents no win

17b. $\frac{152}{165}$ **17c.** $\frac{64}{825}$

Cumulative Review Chapters 10-11
(pp. 268–273)

1. No apparent outliers

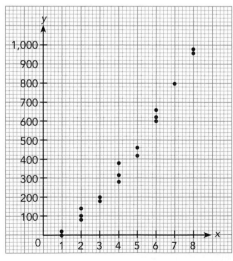

3. Strong, positive, linear association   **5.** Line B

7.

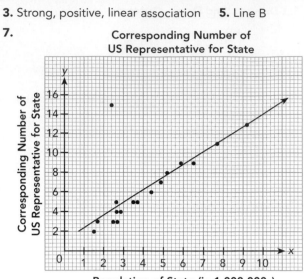

Corresponding Number of US Representative for State

9. Quantitative   **11.** 25; 19; 6; 146; 50

13. Compound event; There are two simple events: drawing the first marble and drawing the second marble.   **15.** Compound event; There are two events: rolling a number die and rolling another number die.

17a.

Number Die 1

	1	**2**	**3**	**4**	**5**	**6**
1	(1, 1)	(2, 1)	(3, 1)	(4, 1)	(5, 1)	(6, 1)
2	(1, 2)	(2, 2)	(3, 2)	(4, 2)	(5, 2)	(6, 2)
3	(1, 3)	(2, 3)	(3, 3)	(4, 3)	(5, 3)	(6, 3)
4	(1, 4)	(2, 4)	(3, 4)	(4, 4)	(5, 4)	(6, 4)
5	(1, 5)	(2, 5)	(3, 5)	(4, 5)	(5, 5)	(6, 5)
6	(1, 6)	(2, 6)	(3, 6)	(4, 6)	(5, 6)	(6, 6)

Number Die 2

17b. $\frac{1}{4}$ **17c.** $\frac{1}{6}$

19a.

Highlighter	Ball	Outcome

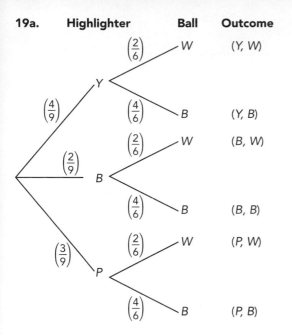

Y represents yellow

B represents blue

P represents purple

W represents white

19b. $\frac{8}{27}$ **19c.** $\frac{4}{27}$ **19d.** $\frac{16}{27}$ **21.** $\frac{1}{3}$

23. and 25.

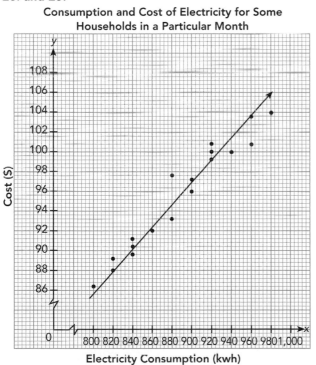

Consumption and Cost of Electricity for Some Households in a Particular Month

27. About $96.45

29a.

Bag A	Bag B	Outcome

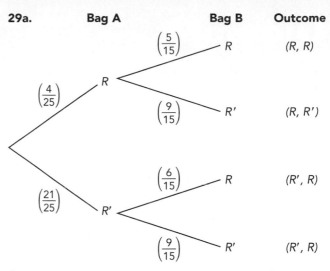

R represents rotten tomatoes

R' represents not rotten tomatoes

29b. $\frac{8}{125}$ **29c.** $\frac{54}{125}$ **29d.** $\frac{117}{125}$

31.

Favorite Sport

Gender	Baseball	Swimming	Basketball	Total
Male	3	1	1	5
Female	1	4	2	7
Total	4	5	3	12

33.

Favorite Sport

Gender	Baseball	Swimming	Basketball
Male	0.75	0.2	0.33
Female	0.25	0.8	0.67
Total	1	1	1

Glossary

A

addition rule of probability

For two mutually exclusive events *A* and *B*, the addition rule of probability states that P(*A* or *B*) = P(*A*) + P(*B*).

angle bisector

A ray that divides an angle into two angles with equal measures.

angle of rotation

The angle through which a point is rotated under a rotation

association

The relationship between two variables that are statistically dependent

Example:

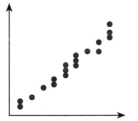

The scatterplot shows strong association between two variables.

B

bivariate data

Data that involve two variables

C

categorical data

Data that involve variables that cannot be measured numerically

center of dilation

The point about which a figure is dilated under a dilation.

center of rotation

The angle through which a point is rotated under a rotation.

clockwise

In the direction that a clock hand moves.

clustering

Data values occurring closely together

compound event

Two or more events occurring together or one after another.

congruence

The property of two figures that can be mapped onto one another using an isometry or a series of isometries.

Example:

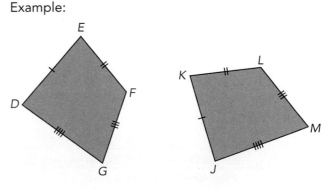

Figure *DEFG* is congruent to *JKLM*.

corresponding angles

A pair of matching angles in two congruent or similar polygons under a given correspondence.

Example: If triangle *ABC* is congruent to triangle *DEF*, then ∠*A* corresponds to ∠*D*, ∠*B* corresponds to ∠*E*, and ∠*C* corresponds to ∠*F*.

corresponding sides

A pair of matching sides in two congruent or similar polygons under a given correspondence.

Example: If triangle *KLM* is similar to triangle *PQR*, then $\overline{KL}$ corresponds to $\overline{PQ}$, $\overline{LM}$ corresponds to $\overline{QR}$, and $\overline{KM}$ corresponds to $\overline{PR}$.

counterclockwise

In the opposite of the direction that a clock hand moves.

D

dependent events

When the occurrence of one event causes the probability of another event to change, the two events are dependent.

dilation

A transformation that assigns to each point *A* of the plane a point *A'* such that from a given point *O*, *OA* = *kOA'* and *A*, *O*, and *A'* lie on the same line.

E

extrapolate

To estimate data values outside a known data set

H

half turn

A 180° rotation.

Example:

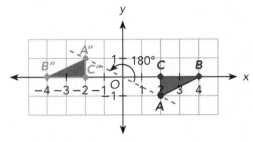

Triangle *ABC* is mapped onto triangle *A'B'C'* by a half turn about the origin.

hypotenuse

The longest side of a right triangle, and the side that is directly opposite the right angle of the right triangle.

I

independent events

Two events are independent if the occurrence of one event does not affect the probability of the other event.

image

The resulting figure after a transformation.

interpolate

To estimate data values within a known data set

invariant

A point that remains unchanged, or a point that is mapped onto itself, under a transformation.

isometry

A transformation that preserves lengths and angle measures.

L

leg

Either of the two shorter sides of a right triangle that are adjacent to the right angle.

line of best fit

A line that seems to best fit the general trend of data values from a given set of bivariate data

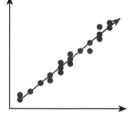

line of reflection

The given line of a reflection that is the perpendicular bisector of all segments formed by a point and its image.

M

map

To assign to each point in a plane its image under a transformation.

multiplication rule of probability

For two independent events A and B, the multiplication rule of probability states that $P(A \text{ and } B) = P(A) \cdot P(B)$. For two dependent events A and B, the multiplication rule of probability states that $P(A \text{ and } B) = P(A) \cdot P(B \text{ after } A)$.

P

possibility diagram

A diagram, such as a two-way grid or table that provides a list of all the possible outcomes of a simple or compound event.

Example:

	R	**B**	**G**
H	(R, H)	(B, H)	(G, H)
T	(R, T)	(B, T)	(G, T)

There are 6 possible outcomes.

Pythagorean Theorem

The square of the length of the hypotenuse of a right triangle is equal to the sum of the squares of the lengths of the two legs. For the triangle shown, you can write this equation: $a^2 + b^2 = c^2$.

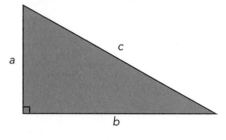

Q

qualitative data

Data that involve variables that cannot be measured numerically

Example: Answers to yes/no or true/false questions

quantitative data

Data that involves variables that can be measured numerically

Examples: Height, number of cars on a street

R

reflection

A transformation that maps each point A in a plane to a point A' such that a given line is the perpendicular bisector of $\overline{AA'}$. It may also be called a flip.

Example:

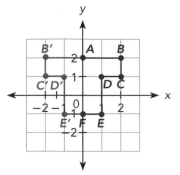

ABCEDF is mapped onto *A'B'C'E'D'F'* by a reflection in the *y*-axis.

rotation

A transformation that maps each point *A* of a plane a point *A'* such that, given a center *O*, m∠*AOA'* is a given angle measure. It may also be called a turn.

Example:

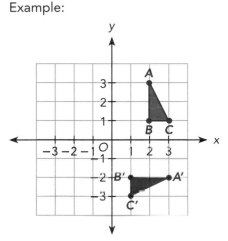

Triangle *ABC* is mapped onto triangle *A'B'C'* by a 90° clockwise rotation about the origin.

S

scale factor

The ratio of a length $\overline{A'B'}$ of a figure's image to the length *AB* of the original figure under a dilation.

scatter plot

A display of two corresponding sets of data plotted on a coordinate plane.

Example:

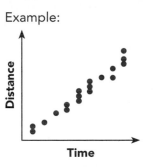

Each dot on the scatter plot represents how long it took to travel the corresponding distance.

statement of congruence

Statement that relates the names for two congruent figures using the symbol ≅, such as ∠*A* ≅ ∠*B*. For two polygons, the statement also indicates which correspondence of the vertices produces congruent angles and congruent sides.

Example: The statement Figure *ABCD* ≅ Figure *EFGH* implies that ∠*A* ≅ ∠*E*, and ∠*B* ≅ ∠*F*, and so on. Also that $\overline{AB}$ ≅ $\overline{EF}$, $\overline{BC}$ ≅ $\overline{FG}$, and so on.

similarity

The property of two figures that can be mapped onto one another using a dilation that may or may not include one or more isometries. The figures have the same shape, but not necessarily the same size.

Example:

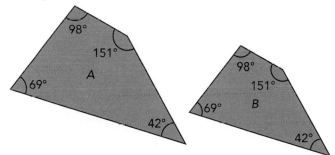

Figure *A* is an enlargement of Figure *B*, so the two figures are similar.

simple event

An event that has one outcome.

T

transformation

A function that maps every point on the plane to another point on the plane.

translation

A transformation that maps each point *A* of a plane to a point *A'* such that $\overline{AA'}$ is the same length and has the same direction for all points of the plane. It may also be called a slide.

Example:

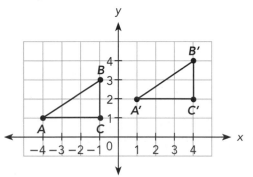

Triangle *ABC* is mapped onto triangle *A'B'C'* by a translation 5 units to the right and 1 unit up.

tree diagram

A type of possibility diagram that may also include the corresponding probabilities along the branches.

Example:

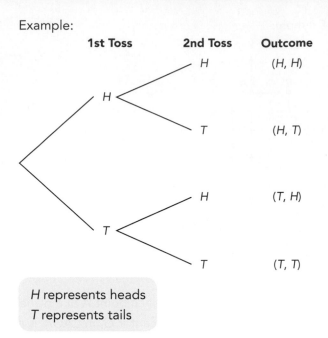

H represents heads

T represents tails

There are 4 possible outcomes.

two-way table

A table that shows frequencies for two corresponding sets of categorical or qualitative data

Example:

		Glasses		
		Yes	**No**	Total
Gender	**Boy**	8	7	15
	Girl	9	16	25
	Total	17	23	40

Table of Measures, Formulas, and Symbols

METRIC / CUSTOMARY

Length

METRIC	CUSTOMARY
1 kilometer (km) = 1,000 meters (m)	1 mile (mi) = 1,760 yards (yd)
1 meter = 10 decimeters (dm)	1 mile = 5,280 feet (ft)
1 meter = 100 centimeters (cm)	1 yard = 3 feet
1 meter = 1,000 millimeters (mm)	1 yard = 36 inches (in.)
1 centimeter = 10 millimeters	1 foot = 12 inches

Capacity

METRIC	CUSTOMARY
1 liter (L) = 1,000 milliliters (mL)	1 gallon (gal) = 4 quarts (qt)
	1 gallon = 16 cups (c)
	1 gallon = 128 fluid ounces (fl oz)
	1 quart = 2 pints (pt)
	1 quart = 4 cups
	1 pint = 2 cups
	1 cup = 8 fluid ounces

Mass and Weight

METRIC	CUSTOMARY
1 kilogram (kg) = 1,000 grams (g)	1 ton (T) = 2,000 pounds (lb)
1 gram = 1,000 milligrams (mg)	1 pound = 16 ounces (oz)

TIME

1 year (yr) = 365 days	1 week = 7 days
1 year = 12 months (mo)	1 day = 24 hours (h)
1 year = 52 weeks (wk)	1 hour = 60 minutes (min)
leap year = 366 days	1 minute = 60 seconds (s)

Centimeters

0 1 2 3 4 5 6 7 8 9 10 11 12 13 14 15 16 17 18 19 20

CONVERTING MEASUREMENTS

You can use the information below to convert measurements from one unit to another.

To convert from a smaller unit to a larger unit, divide.	To convert from a larger unit to a smaller unit, multiply.
Example: 48 in. = __?__ ft	Example: 0.3 m = __?__ cm

Recall: 12 in. = 1 ft
48 ÷ 12 = 4
48 in. = 4 ft

Recall: 1 m = 100 cm
0.3 · 100 = 30
0.3 m = 30 cm

PERIMETER, CIRCUMFERENCE, AND AREA

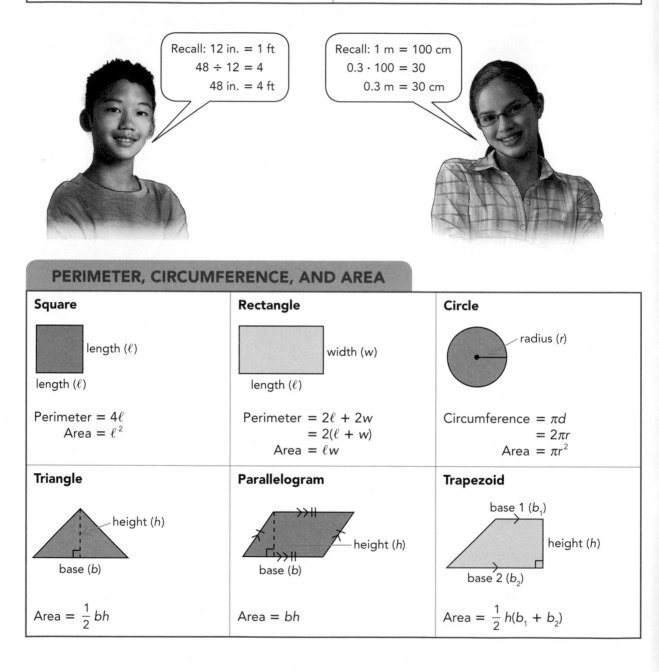

Square

length (ℓ)
length (ℓ)

Perimeter = 4ℓ
Area = ℓ^2

Rectangle

width (w)
length (ℓ)

Perimeter = $2\ell + 2w$
= $2(\ell + w)$
Area = ℓw

Circle

radius (r)

Circumference = πd
= $2\pi r$
Area = πr^2

Triangle

height (h)
base (b)

Area = $\frac{1}{2} bh$

Parallelogram

height (h)
base (b)

Area = bh

Trapezoid

base 1 (b_1)
height (h)
base 2 (b_2)

Area = $\frac{1}{2} h(b_1 + b_2)$

0   Inches

SURFACE AREA AND VOLUME

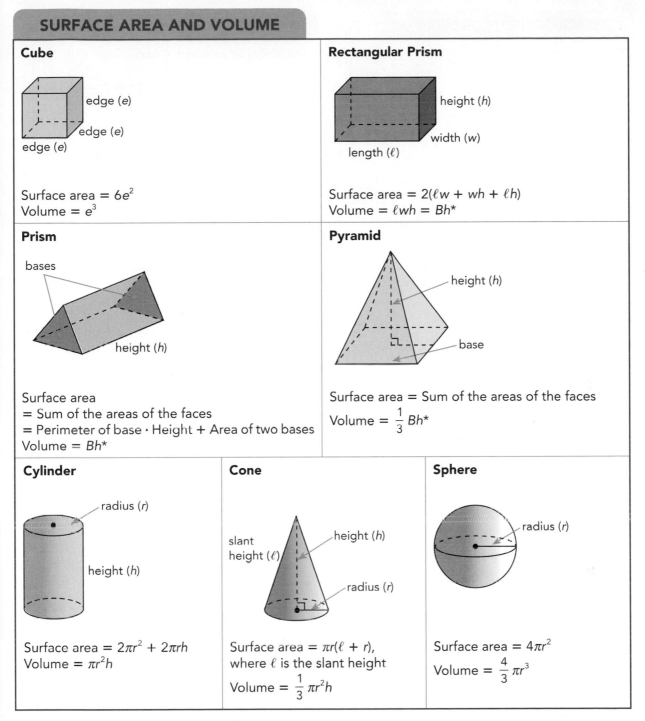

Cube

edge (*e*)
edge (*e*)
edge (*e*)

Surface area = $6e^2$
Volume = e^3

Rectangular Prism

height (*h*)
width (*w*)
length (*ℓ*)

Surface area = $2(\ell w + wh + \ell h)$
Volume = $\ell wh = Bh*$

Prism

bases
height (*h*)

Surface area
= Sum of the areas of the faces
= Perimeter of base · Height + Area of two bases
Volume = $Bh*$

Pyramid

height (*h*)
base

Surface area = Sum of the areas of the faces
Volume = $\frac{1}{3} Bh*$

Cylinder

radius (*r*)
height (*h*)

Surface area = $2\pi r^2 + 2\pi rh$
Volume = $\pi r^2 h$

Cone

slant height (*ℓ*)
height (*h*)
radius (*r*)

Surface area = $\pi r(\ell + r)$,
where ℓ is the slant height
Volume = $\frac{1}{3} \pi r^2 h$

Sphere

radius (*r*)

Surface area = $4\pi r^2$
Volume = $\frac{4}{3} \pi r^3$

*B represents the area of the base of a solid figure.

PYTHAGOREAN THEOREM

Right Triangle

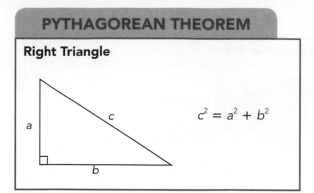

$$c^2 = a^2 + b^2$$

PROBABILITY

Probability of an event A occurring:

$$P(A) = \frac{\text{Number of favorable outcomes}}{\text{Number of equally likely outcomes}}$$

Probability of an event A not occurring:
$$P(A') = 1 - P(A)$$

LINEAR GRAPHS

The slope, m, of a line segment joining points $P(x_1, y_1)$ and $Q(x_2, y_2)$ is given by

$$m = \frac{y_2 - y_1}{x_2 - x_1} \text{ or } m = \frac{y_1 - y_2}{x_1 - x_2}.$$

Given the slope, m, the equation of a line intercepting the y-axis at $(0, b)$ is given by $y = mx + b$.

The distance, d, between two points $P(x_1, y_1)$ and $Q(x_2, y_2)$ is given by

$$d = \sqrt{(x_2 - x_1)^2 + (y_2 - y_1)^2} \text{ or } d = \sqrt{(x_1 - x_2)^2 + (y_1 - y_2)^2}.$$

RATE

Distance = Speed · Time

$$\text{Average speed} = \frac{\text{Total distance traveled}}{\text{Total time}}$$

Interest = Principal · Rate · Time

TEMPERATURE

Celsius (°C)	$C = \frac{5}{9} \cdot (F - 32)$
Fahrenheit (°F)	$F = \left(\frac{5}{9} \cdot C\right) + 32$

Symbol	Meaning	Symbol	Meaning
<	is less than	$\|a\|$	absolute value of the number a
>	is greater than	(x, y)	ordered pair
≤	is less than or equal to	1 : 2	ratio of 1 to 2
≥	is greater than or equal to	/	per
≠	is not equal to	%	percent
≈	is approximately equal to	⊥	is perpendicular to
≅	is congruent to	||	is parallel to
~	is similar to	$\overleftrightarrow{AB}$	line AB
10^2	ten squared	$\overrightarrow{AB}$	ray AB
10^3	ten cubed	$\overline{AB}$	line segment AB
2^6	two to the sixth power	$\angle ABC$	angle ABC
$2.\overline{6}$	repeating decimal 2.66666...	$m\angle A$	measure of angle A
7	positive 7	$\triangle ABC$	triangle ABC
−7	negative 7	°	degree
$\sqrt{a}$	positive square root of the number a	π	pi; $\pi \approx 3.14$ or $\pi \approx \dfrac{22}{7}$
$\sqrt[3]{a}$	cube root of the number a	$P(A)$	the probability of the event A happening

Graphing Calculator Guide

A graphing calculator has different sets of function keys you can use for mathematical calculations and graphing. The screen supports both text and graphic displays.

Four Operations

Enter expressions into the Home Screen. Then press **ENTER** to evaluate.

Keys	Example
Use ⬤ to enter decimals.	To evaluate 2 + 3.5 · 4, press **2** **+** **3** **.** **5** **×** **4** **ENTER**. Notice that graphing calculators use the order of operations. They do not do evaluation from left to right. If they did, you would get an answer of 22. `2+3.5*4` `16`

Use **(-)** to enter negative numbers.
 	
 Use **2ND** **∧** to enter π.
	To evaluate −10 ÷ 2 − 7, press **(-)** **1** **0** **÷** **2** **−** **7** **ENTER**.
	
	 To evaluate 2 · π · 7, press **2** **×** **2ND** **∧** **×** **7** **ENTER**.
	
	 `-10/2-7` `-12`
	 `2*π*7` `43.98229715`

Use **(** **)** to enclose parts of an expression that must be calculated first.	To evaluate (3 + 4) · (2 − 9), press **(** **3** **+** **4** **)** **×** **(** **2** **−** **9** **)** **ENTER**. `(3+4)*(2-9)` `-49`

Fractions

Use **MATH** to enter and convert fractions.

Keys	Example	
Use **MATH** to access Frac to enter fractions.	To enter $\frac{2}{5}$, press **2** **÷** **5** **MATH** then select 1: Frac and press **ENTER** To enter $\frac{5}{2}$, press **5** **÷** **2** **MATH** then select 1: Frac and press **ENTER**	2/5▶Frac $\frac{2}{5}$ 5/2▶Frac $\frac{5}{2}$ ■
Use **MATH** to access Frac and Dec to swap between fractions and decimals.	To convert 0.25 to a fraction, press **.** **2** **5** **MATH** then select 1: Frac and press **ENTER** To convert the fraction back to a decimal, press **MATH** then select 2: Dec and press **ENTER**	.25▶Frac $\frac{1}{4}$ Ans▶Dec .25 ■

Squares and Cubes of Numbers

Use **∧** to enter squares and cubes.

Keys	Example	
Use x^2 to find the square of numbers. Use **∧** to find the cube of numbers.	To evaluate 3^2, press **3** x^2 **ENTER** To evaluate 5^3, press **5** **∧** **3** **ENTER**	3^2 9 5^3 125
Use **2ND** x^2 to find the square root of numbers. Use **MATH** to find the cube root of numbers.	To evaluate $\sqrt{25}$, press **2ND** x^2 **2** **5** **ENTER** To evaluate $\sqrt[3]{27}$, press **MATH** then select 4: $\sqrt[3]{\ (}$ and press **2** **7** **ENTER**	$\sqrt{25}$ 5 $\sqrt[3]{27}$ 3 ■

Exponents

Use 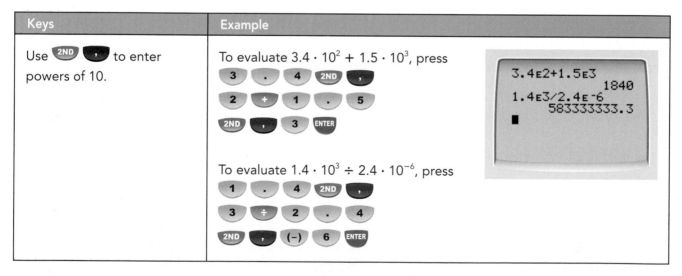 to enter numbers in exponential notation.

Keys	Example	
Use ⌃ to enter positive exponents.	To evaluate $2^2 \cdot 5^0$, press 2 ⌃ 2) × 5 ⌃ 0 ENTER To evaluate $(4^2)^3$, press (4 ⌃ 2)) ⌃ 3 ENTER	$2^2 * 5^0$ <div align="right">4</div>$(4^2)^3$ <div align="right">4096</div>
Use ⌃ and (−) to enter negative exponents.	To evaluate $2^{-2} \cdot 10$, press 2 ⌃ (−) 2) × 1 0 ENTER	$2^{-2} * 10$ <div align="right">2.5</div>

Scientific Notation

Use 2ND , to enter numbers in scientific notation.

Keys	Example	
Use 2ND , to enter powers of 10.	To evaluate $3.4 \cdot 10^2 + 1.5 \cdot 10^3$, press 3 . 4 2ND , 2 + 1 . 5 2ND , 3 ENTER To evaluate $1.4 \cdot 10^3 \div 2.4 \cdot 10^{-6}$, press 1 . 4 2ND , 3 ÷ 2 . 4 2ND , (−) 6 ENTER	3.4ᴇ2+1.5ᴇ3 <div align="right">1840</div>1.4ᴇ3/2.4ᴇ⁻6 <div align="right">583333333.3</div>■

Probability

Use **MATH** to generate random numbers.

Keys	Example

Use **MATH** to access randInt(under PRB to simulate tossing a fair coin multiple times.	To simulate the tossing of a fair coin 20 times and store the outcomes, press **MATH** then select 5: randInt(under PRB and press **0** **,** **1** **,** **2** **0** **)** **ENTER**
	
	`randInt(0,1,20)`
	`{1 0 1 0 0 0 0 ▸`
	`Ans→L₁`
	`{1 0 1 0 0 0 0 ▸`
	
	Here 0 indicates a tail, 1 indicates a head, and 20 indicates the number of times the coin is tossed.

Use **STO›** to store values.	To store the results in a list L1, continue to press **STO›** **2ND** **1** **ENTER**
Use **STAT** to access Edit to enter data.	To view the list in a table, press **STAT** then select 1: Edit <table><tr><td>L1</td><td>L2</td><td>L3</td><td>1</td></tr><tr><td>1 0 1 0 0 0 0</td><td>------</td><td>------</td><td></td></tr><tr><td colspan="4">L1(1) = 1</td></tr></table> To get back to the Home Screen, press **2ND** **MODE**

Use **MATH** to access randInt(under PRB to simulate rolling a fair number cube multiple times.	To simulate the rolling of a fair number cube 10 times and store the outcomes in a list L2, press **MATH** then select 5: randInt(under PRB and press **1** **,** **6** **,** **1** **0** **)** **STO›** **2ND** **2** **ENTER**
	
	`randInt(1,6,10)▸`
	`{4 4 6 3 2 2 5 ▸`
	
	Here 1 and 6 indicate the least and greatest possible results, 10 indicates the number of times the number cube is rolled.

Use **MATH** to access randBin(under PRB to simulate tossing a biased coin multiple times.	To simulate the tossing of a biased coin 20 times and store the outcomes in a list L3, press **MATH** then select 7: randBin(under PRB and press **1** **,** **.** **7** **,** **2** **0** **)** **STO›** **2ND** **3** **ENTER**
	
	`randBin(1,.7,20▸`
	`{1 0 1 0 1 1 1 ▸`
	`■`
	
	Here 1 indicates heads, .7 indicates the probability of landing on heads, 20 indicates the number of times the coin is tossed.

Credits

Pages listed in black type refer to Book A.
Pages listed in blue type refer to Book B.
Pages in **boldface** type show where a term is introduced.

Index

A

Absolute value
  adding integers using, 4
  finding distance between two points using, 4
  of scale factor, 90
  subtracting integers using, 4

Activities
  Hands-On Activity, 26, 40, 43, 131–132, 275; 7–8, 10, 130, 136, 186–187
  Technology Activity, 111, 149, 195, 218; 55, 63, 77, 90, 98–99, 122, 150, 194–195, 242–243

Addition
  of equations, 198
  integers, 4
  measures in different forms, 77–78
  multiplication is distributive over, 68
  in scientific notation, 68–80
    different powers of 10, 73–76
    same power of 10, 68–72
  very large numbers, 74–75
  very small numbers, 71–72, 76

Addition rule of probability, 246–248

Algebra. *See also* Algebraic expressions, Equations, Linear equations, Systems of linear equations and bar models, 99, 197, 200, 203
  equations
    consistent, **105**
    direct proportion, 93, 129; 50
    distributive property, 94, 97
    equivalent, **93**
    of the form $x^2 = p$ and $x^3 = p$, 50–51; 3
    inconsistent, **104**
    linear. see Linear equations
    real-world problem solving using, 192
    representing functions using, 283
    solving, 94
    systems of, 197–209
  functions, **240**
    comparing, 278–288
    decreasing, 273–274
    graphing, 251–254
    identifying, 249–254
    increasing, 273–274
    linear, **260**, 267–273
    nonlinear, **268**
    representing, 259–266
    understanding, 246–250

Algebraic expressions
  bar models, 99, 197, 200, 203
  division of, 19, 36
  evaluating, 32, 241
  multiplying, 34
  power of a product property, 32, 34
  power of a quotient property, 36
  representing unknown quantities using, 241
  simplifying, 21–22
    power of a quotient property, 35
    product of powers property, 15–16
    quotient of powers property, 19–20
  writing, 241

Algebraic reasoning, 192

Algebraic solution methods for systems, 197–209

Alternate exterior angles, 115

Alternate interior angles, 115

Angle bisector, 124

Angle of rotation, **73**

Angle-angle-side (AAS or ASA) test, 123

Angles
  alternate exterior, 115
  alternate interior, 115
  congruent, 118
  corresponding, 115, **118**, 131, 134–135
  exterior, 115
  images of after transformations, 98–99
  interior, 115
  measures of, 115, 130
    in similar figures, 134–135

Applications
  animals, 77
  animation, 48, 82
  architecture, 43, 128, 146
  art, 50; 61, 72
  astronomy, 60, 78, 80, 83, 85
  automotive, 84
  banking, 54, 178–179, 180, 217, 235
  biology, 66
  business, 117, 123, 124, 175–176, 177; 184, 204–205
  chemistry, 217
  construction, 84, 224; 56
  consumer math, 99, 111, 117, 146, 174, 180, 181, 215, 216, 234
  cooking, 269, 89, 235
  demographics, 69–70, 80

distance problems, 117, 130, 134, 147, 179, 180, 182, 222, 224, 263, 266, 278–279; 29, 30, 43
education, 209
engineering, 128, 135, 149, 158
entertainment, 215
games, 241, 251
geometry, 50, 51, 81–82, 85–86, 93, 112, 118, 123, 212, 216
height problems, 112, 143
hobbies, 85, 217; 129
life science, 79; 193, 194
manufacturing, 80, 101, 288
measurement, 71, 72, 74, 75, 79, 100, 101, 108, 212; 13–14, 15, 18–19
medical, 133
models, 113
money, 182, 215, 266, 284
physical science, 67
reasoning, 214, 215, 216, 234
recreation, 92, 172–173, 190
school, 198
science, 65, 86, 181
speed problems, 102, 124, 134, 138, 179, 217
sports, 65, 247, 256; 2, 172, 185, 197, 199, 205
surveys, 199–200, 206
temperature, 146, 222, 224; 191, 197
travel, 123, 179, 196, 217; 148, 157

Approximate irrational numbers by rational numbers, 3; 5

Area
finding, using scale drawing, 114
of a square, 50–51
surface, 81–82

Art, 50, 61, 72

Assessment
Chapter Review/Test, 56–57, 88–89, 126–128, 184–185, 238–239, 291–293; 45–47, 109–111, 160–165, 211–215, 265–267
Cumulative Review, 90–91, 186–189, 294–297; 166–171, 268–273

Association, **175**
identifying patterns of, 177–179, 204–206
linear, 178, 179, 188–189
negative, 178
nonlinear, 178
positive, 178
strong, 177–178
weak, 178

B

Bar models and algebraic expressions, 197, 200, 203

Bar notation, 95

Base, **5**

Best fit, line of, 172, 187–197

Bisectors
angle, 124
perpendicular, 50

Bivariate data, **172**
association of, **175**
identifying patterns of association of, 177–179
line of best fit for, 187–189
scatter plots of, 174–185

Braces {}, 220

Brain @ Work, 54, 86, 124, 182, 235, 289; 43, 106, 158, 209, 261

C

Calculators, graphing
Guide, 322–325; 302–305
line of best fit on, 194–195
linear equations on, 111
scientific notation on, 82, 83
slope-intercept form, 149
systems of linear equations on, 195, 218
table of values on, 111
zero power on, 40

Categorical data, **198**, 207

Celsius, conversion to Fahrenheit, 119

Center of dilation, **86**, 93–95
find in the coordinate plane, 93–95
origin as, 91

Center of rotation, **73**

Chapter Review/Test. *See* Assessment

Chapter Wrap Up, 55, 87, 125, 183, 236, 290; 44, 107, 159, 210, 264

Circles
diameter, 52, 83
radius, 51, 52

Clockwise, **73**

Clustering, **177**

Coefficients, **61**

Coin toss, 220–221, 224, 225

Common terms, **198**

Commutative movement, 51

Compare
geometric transformations, 98–105
graphs, 175–177
irrational numbers, using rational approximations, 3
linear functions, 278–288
numbers in scientific notation, 63–65
proportional relationships using multiple representations, 175–177
unit rates using slopes, 133–134, 138–139

Composite number, prime factorization of, 8

Composite solids, 36–43

Compound events, 216, 219–228
addition rule of probability for, 246–248
identifying, 219–220
possibility diagrams for, **221,** 223–226
probability of, 229–235
representing, 220–226
tree diagrams of, 223–226, 233

Compound interest, 11

Concept Maps, 55, 87, 125, 183, 236, 290; 44, 107, 159, 210, 264

Concepts. *See* Key Concepts

Cones
and Pythagorean Theorem, 32, 35
volume of, 5, 39

Congruence, 116
statement of, **118,** 119

Congruent angles, 118

Congruent figures, 112, **116**
finding unknown measures in, 120–121
identifying, 117
naming, 119
relating to geometric transformations, 144–145, 150–151
tests for, 122–125

Congruent triangles, 118, 120, 122
relating to geometric transformations, 145
tests for, **122–125**

Consistent equations, 105

Constant of proportionality, 129, 130
identifying, 113
in similar figures, 131

Consumer math, 99, 111, 118, 145, 174, 180, 181, 215, 216, 234

Converse of Pythagorean Theorem, 10–11

Cooking, 269, 89, 235

Coordinate plane. *See also* Graphs/Graphing
compare geometric transformations, 98–102
constructing scatter plot on, 175
dilations, 90–95
distance between points on, 20–27
distance from *x*-axis and *y*-axis, 49
graphing points on, 4, 20–22
lengths of horizontal and vertical line segments, 4
ordered pairs on, 251, 260
reflections, 49, 52, 63–69
rotations, 74–82
symmetric point on, 49
systems of linear equations on, 219
translations, 53–58

Coordinates
finding, of points
after dilations, 94–95
after reflections, 68–69
after rotations, 80–82
symmetric points, 49
after translations, 57–58

Corresponding angles, 115, **118,** 131, 134–135

Corresponding sides, 86, 121, 131

Counterclockwise, 73

Cube roots (evaluating), 48–50, 86, **3**

Cubes
finding side lengths, 33
of numbers, 3
of variables
equations involving, 49–50; 3
real-world problems, 50-52

Cumulative Review, 90–91, 186–189, 294–297; 166–171, 268–273

Curves, graphs of, 254

Cylinders
and Pythagorean Theorem, 35
volume of, 5, 38, 39

D

Data
associations between, 177–179, 186–194
bivariate, **172,** 175–179, 176–177, 187–189
categorical, **198,** 207
clustering, **177**
estimating, 192–193
line of best fit for, 172, 187–197
outliers, **180–**182, 189

qualitative, **198**, 207
quantitative, **174**, 177–179
relative frequencies of, 173, 198, 204–206
scatter plots, **174**–185
two-way tables, **198**–208

Decimals
converting to fractions, 95, 98
dividing by powers of 10, 59
expansion of numbers, 3
multiplying by powers of 10, 59
rational numbers as, 3
repeating, 3, 95, 98
terminating, 3

Decreasing functions, 273–274

Dependent events, **252**, 254–255
multiplication rule of probability with, 253
probability problems involving, 256–260

Dependent systems of equations, **230**–233

Dependent variables, 172, 242

Diagonals, 37

Diagrams
identifying constant of proportionality in, 113
mapping, **243**–245, 249–250, 251
possibility, **221**, 223–226, 229–232
scale factor, 86–89, 92
tree, 223–226, 233
Venn, 217, 218

Diameter, 52, 83

Dilations, **86**–97, 99
center of dilation, **86**, 93–95
dimensions of figures after, 88–89
draw images after, 90–92
geometry software for, 90
images of line segment and rectangle, 90
length not preserved under, 99
scale factor, **86**, 90, 93, 94, 99
and similar figures, 146–147, 150

Dimensions of geometric figures after dilations,
88–89

Direct proportions, 93, **129**, 130
recognizing in a table and equation, 50

Distance,
absolute value and, 4
between two points, 20–22
from x-axis and y-axis in the coordinate plane, 49

Distance formula, 23–27
Pythagorean theorem and, 20–22

Distance problems, 117, 130, 134, 147, 179, 180,
182, 222, 224, 263, 266, 278–279; 29, 30, 43

Distributive property, solving equations using, 94, 97

Divisibility rules, 8

Division
of algebraic expressions, 19, 36
in exponential notation, 21–22
of exponents, **17**–20
of integers, 4
by powers of 10, 59
in scientific notation, 81, 83–84

Drawing images
after dilations, 90–92
after reflections, 64–68
after rotations, 77–79
after a sequence of transformations, 148–153
after translations, 55–57

Drawings. *See also* Diagrams
scale, 114

Elimination method, **197**–202, 207–208, 218

Equality, substitution property of, 198

Equations
adding and subtracting, 198
consistent, **105**
direct proportion, 93, 129; 50
equivalent, **93**
of the form $x^2 = p$ and $x^3 = p$, 50–51
functions represented as, 261, 264, 265, 283
inconsistent, **104**
linear, 92
expressing relationships with, 93
graphing, 165–170, 191–192
with infinite solutions, 105–106
for a line of best fit, 190–191, 192–194
with no solution, 104–105
with one variable, 96–103
parallel lines, 157, 160–162
point-slope form, 191
point-slope form of, 158–159
real-world problem solving, 99–101, 171–181
slope-intercept form, 147–153, 154–156
solving, 96–103, 113–115, 118–123, 197–209
systems of. *see* Systems of linear equations
with two variables, 109–117, 118–123
writing, 154–164; 191–194
real-world problem solving using, 192
solving, 94
with squares and cubes, 49–51
of x-axis and y-axis, 49

Equidistant points, 50

Equivalent equations, **93**

Estimation
  mental, 99
  using line of best fit, 192–193

Evaluating algebraic expressions, 32, 241
  with exponents, 25, 32

Evaluating cube roots, **48**–50, 86; 3

Evaluating numerical expressions with exponents, 7, 25, 32, 35

Evaluating square roots, **47**–48, 120; 3

Events
  compound, **216**, **219**–228
    addition rule of probability for, 246–248
    probability of, 229–235
    representing, 220–226
  dependent, **252**–262
  independent, **236**–251
    multiplication rule of probability for, 237–241
  mutually exclusive, 218, 236
  outcome of, 217
  sample space, 217
  simple, 216, **219**
    probability of, 217–218

Exponential expressions, 5–12

Exponential notation, **5**–12
  division of expressions in, 21–22
  multiplication of expressions in, 21–22
  power of a power, **25**–31
  prime factorization, 8–10
  real-world problem solving using, 10–11, 23
  squares and cubes, 47–54

Exponents, **5**
  division of powers, **17**–20
  exponential notation, **5**–12
  multiplication of powers, **13**–16
  negative, **43**–45, 71–72
  positive, 44
  prime factorization, 8–10
  properties of, 28–29, 37–38
  scientific notation, 61
  zero, **40**–42

Expressions
  algebraic
    division of, 19, 36
    evaluating, 32, 241
    multiplying, 34
    simplifying, 15–16, 21–22, 35
    writing, 241
  exponential, 5–12

  numerical, 14, 18–19
    simplifying, 21–22, 33, 36
  simplifying, 27
    numerical, 21–22, 33, 36
    properties of exponents, 28–29, 37–38

Exterior angles
  alternate, 115
  measures of, 115

Extrapolate, **192**

Factoring, prime factorization, 8–10

Fahrenheit, conversion to Celsius, 119

Figures
  congruent, 112, **116**
    finding unknown measures in, 120–121
    identifying, 117
    naming, 119
    relating to geometric transformations, 144–145, 150–151
    tests for, 122–125
  corresponding sides of, 86
  dimensions of, after dilations, 88–89
  sequence of transformations, 148–152
  similar, 112, 129–143
    concept of, 131–132
    finding unknown lengths in, 132–136
    identifying, 129–130
    relating to geometric transformations, 146–147, 150–151
    relating using sequence of transformations, 153

Five, divisibility by, 8

Fold line of a reflection
  as a perpendicular bisector, 61

Formula(s). *See also* Geometry

Formulas
  distance, 23–27
  probability of event, 217, 229
  Table of, 318–320; 298–300
  slope, 142–144
  volume, 5
    of cone, 39
    of cylinder, 38, 39
    of prism, 37, 38
    of pyramid, 36, 37

Fractions, as repeating decimals, 95, 98

Functions, **240**
   comparing, 278–288
   decreasing, 273–274
   describing qualitatively, 273–274
   identifying
      using graphs, 251–254, 270–273
      using mapping diagrams, 249–250
   increasing, 273–274
   inputs, **242**–243
   linear, **260**
      comparing, 278–288
      identifying, 267–273, 276–277
      sketching, 275
   nonlinear, **268**
   outputs, **242**–243
   rate of change, **267**–268, 279
   real-world problems involving, 246–248
   representing, 259–266
      as equations, 261, 264, 265, 283
      as graphs, 261, 263, 266, 273–274
      as tables, 248, 261, 266
   translating verbal descriptions into, 259–260, 265
   understanding, 246–250
   vertical line test, **251**–252, 254

G

Geometric transformations, 48, **52**
   angle measure, 99
   comparing, 98–105
   dilations, **86**–97
   geometry software for, 98–99, 150
   invariant point, **52**, 65
   isometries, **99**
   reflections, **61**–72
   relating congruent figures using, 144–145, 150–151
   relating similar figures using, 146–147, 150–151
   rotations, **73**–85
   sequence of, 148–153
   translations, **51**–60

Geometry. *See also* Geometric transformations
   angles, 115
   applications, 50, 51, 81–82, 85–86, 93, 112, 118, 123, 212, 216
   circles, 51–52, 83
   congruent figures, 116–128, 144–145
   lines. *see* Lines
   perimeter, 93, 118, 120–121, 122
   polygons, 56, 63, 131
   prisms, 5, 34, 37, 38
   pyramids, 5, 31, 36, 37
   Pythagorean Theorem, 2, 6–19, 20–22
   radius, 51, 52, 86
   similar figures, 129–143

   solids, 31–35
      composite, 36–43
   spheres, 51, 52, 83, 86; 5
   surface area, 81–82
   triangles. *see* Triangles
   volume, 52, 86; 5

Geometry software, 55, 63, 77, 90, 122, 150

Giga, 77

Graphical method, **218**, 219–224, 226

Graphing calculator
   EE function, 82, 83
   Guide, 322–325; 302–305
   line of best fit on, 194–195
   linear equations on, 111
   scientific notation on, 82, 83
   slope-intercept form on, 149
   systems of linear equations on, 195, 218
   table of values on, 111
   zero power on, 40

Graphs/graphing
   of curves, 254
   direct proportion, 93, 129, 130
   of functions, 251–254, 261, 263, 266, 270–274
   of linear equations, 165–170, 276–277
      using slope and one point, 169
      using slope and *y*-intercept, 166–168, 192
      using table of values, 165, 191
      using two or more points, 166
   of linear functions, 270–273
   of linear relationships, 171–172, 175–176; 191–194
   lines, 128, 135–137, 156
      parallel lines, 157
      x-intercept, **148**
      y-intercept, **147**
   ordered pairs, 251, 260
   origin, 129
   of points on coordinate plane, 4, 20–22
   scatter plots, **174**–185
   systems of linear equations, 218–224, 226

H

Half turn, **75**

Hands-On Activity
   linear functions, 275
   negative exponents, 43
   power of a power property, 26
   Pythagorean Theorem, 7–8
   Pythagorean triples, 10
   scatter plots, 186–187
   similar figures, 130
   similar triangles, 136

slope, 131–132
  zero exponent, 40

Height problems, 112, 143

Hobbies, 85, 217, 129

Horizontal lines, slope of, 139–141

Horizontal translation, 51

Hypotenuse, **7**–8
  finding length of, 8–9

Hypotenuse-leg (HL) test, 123

Identify
  congruent figures, 117
  constant of proportionality, 113
  events as simple of compound, 219–220
  functions, 249–254, 267–273, 276–277
  outliers, 180–182
  similar figures, 129–130
  similar triangles, 137–138

Identity, **105**–106

Images, drawing, **52**
  after dilations, 90–92
  after reflections, 64–68
  after rotations, 77–79
  after translations, 55–57

Inconsistent equations, **104**

Inconsistent systems of equations, **225**–230

Increasing functions, 273–274

Independent events, **236**
  addition rule of probability for, 246–248
  involving replacement, 244–245
  multiplication rule of probability for, 237–241

Independent variables, 172, 242

Indirect measurement, 13

Input, **242**–243
  representing on mapping diagrams, **243**–245

Integer exponents, 14–23
  negative, **43**–45, 71–72
  positive, 44
  prime factorization, 8–10
  properties of, 28–29, 37–38

Integers, 3
  adding, 4
  dividing, 4
  multiplying, 4
  subtracting, 4

Interest, 54
  compound, 11

Interior angles
  alternate, 115
  measures of, 115

Interpolate, **192**

Intersecting lines, 221

Invariant point, **52**, 65

Irrational numbers, **3**

Isometries, **99**

Isosceles triangles, 24–25, 28

Key Concepts, 55, 87, 125, 183, 237, 290; 44, 107–108, 159, 210, 264

Kilo, 77

Legs of triangle, **7**–9

Length
  finding unknown
    in similar figures, 132–136
    using Pythagorean Theorem, 31–35
    using scale drawing, 114
  of hypotenuse, 8–9
  of legs of right triangle, 9
  of line segment, 4, 20–22
  not preserved under dilations, 99

Line of best fit, **172**, 187
  on graphing calculator, 194–195
  for scatter plot, 187–197
  using equation for, 192–194
  writing linear equation for, 190–191

Line of reflection, **62**, 69

Line of symmetry, **62**,

Line segments
  image under a dilation, 90
  lengths of, 4, 20–22
  perpendicular bisectors, 50
  reflection, 63–66
  rotation of, 76
  translation, 54–55

Pages listed in black type refer to Book A.
Pages listed in blue type refer to Book B.
Pages in **boldface** type show where a term is introduced.

Linear correlations, 186–197
  line of best fit, 187–197

Linear equations, 92
  expressing relationships with, 93
  graphing, 165–170, 191–192; 191–194
  with infinite solutions, 105–106
  for line of best fit, 190–191, 192–194
  with no solution, 104–105
  number of solutions to, 104–108
  parallel lines, 157, 160–162
  point-slope form, 191
  point-slope form of, 158–159
  real-world problem solving using, 99–101, 171–181; 191–194
  slope-intercept form, **147**–153, 154–156; 191–194
  solving, 113–115
    choosing method for, 207–208
    with common terms, 197–199
    with one variable, 96–103
    with table of values, 111–112, 114–115
    with two variables, 118–123
    using algebraic methods, 197–209
    using elimination method, 197–202
    using substitution method, 203–206
  systems of, 190
    common terms, **198**
    dependent, **230**–233
    graphing, 218–224
    inconsistent, **225**–230
    introduction to, **193**–196
    real-world problem solving using, 210–217
    solving, 194–196, 197–208, 218–224, 226
    unique solution to, **193**
    without common terms, 200–202
  with two variables, 109–117
    graphing, 128
    solving for a variable, 118–123
  writing, 154–164
    for parallel lines, 157, 160–161
    using slope and one point, 158–160
    using slope and y-intercept, 154–156; 191–194
    using two points, 162–163
  writing repeating decimals as fractions using, 98

Linear functions, **260**
  comparing, 278–288
    in different forms, 283–285
    with same initial value, 280–281
  identifying
    from graphs, 270–273, 276–277
    from table, 267–269, 276
  sketching, 275

Linear relationships, **171**
  comparing, 175–176, 178–179
  graphs of, 171–172, 175–176

Lines. *See also* Line segments; Linear equations
  graphs of, 135–137, 156, 157
  horizontal, 139–141
  intersecting, 221
  parallel, 157, 160–162, 227; 115
  reflection of, 64–66
  slope of, 128, 130–146
  slope-intercept form, **147**–156
  straight, 270
  translation of, 54
  transversal, 115
  vertical, 140
  x-intercept, **148**
  y-intercept, **147**, 154–158

M

Many-to-many relations, **244**, 247

Many-to-one relations, **244**, 256

Map, **52**

Mapping diagrams, **243**–245, 249–251

Math Journal, *Throughout text. Some examples are* 26, 39, 43, 80, 103, 287; 7, 85, 130, 250

Math Note, *Throughout text. Some examples are* 5, 41, 96, 130, 270; 24, 224, 253

Measurement
  applications, 71, 72, 74, 75, 79, 100, 101, 108, 212; 13–15, 18–19
  indirect, 13
  and the prefix system, 71–78
  Table of Measures, 317–318; 297–298

Mega, 77

Micro, 77

Milli, 77

Models, 113
  bar, 197, 200, 203
  of linear associations, 186–197

Multiplication
  algebraic expressions, 34
  in exponential notation
    algebraic expressions, 15–16, 21–21
    numerical expressions, 14–16
  integers, 4
  powers, **13**–16
  by powers of 10, 59
  scientific notation, 81–82

Multiplication rule of probability, **237**–241, 253

Mutually exclusive events, 218, 236

N

Nano, 77

Negative association, 178

Negative exponents, **43**–45, 71–72

Nonlinear association, 178

Nonlinear functions, **268**

Notation
  exponential, 5–12, 21–31, 47–54
  scientific, **58**, 60–84

Number cubes, 220–221, 222, 230–232, 242–243

Number line
  adding integers on, 4
  real numbers on, 3
  subtracting integers on, 4

Numbers
  comparing
    irrational, 3
    using scientific notation, 64
  decimal expansions, 3
  different powers of 10, 73–76
  divisibility rules, 8
  factored form, 43
  irrational, **3**
  raised to the zero power, 41
  rational, **3**
  real, **3**
  same power of 10, 68–72
  very large numbers, 68–70, 74–75
  very small numbers, 71–72, 74–76
  writing
    in scientific notation, 61–64
    in standard form 62–63

Numerical expressions
  evaluating, 7
  expanding, 7
  in exponential notation, 5–7
  multiplying and dividing, 14–18
  simplifying, 21–22
    power of a product property, 33
    power of a quotient property, 36
    product of powers property, 14
    quotient of powers property, 18–19
  writing, 5–6
    with a single exponent, 27–29, 33, 36–38

O

One-to-many relations, **243**, 248, 256

One-to-one relations, **243**, 256

Ordered pairs, 242–243, 249, 251, 260

Origin, 129
  as a center of dilation, 91
  draw images of geometric shapes about the, 78–79

Outcomes
  of compound events, 220–226, 229–232
  of dependent events, 253, 259
  of event, 217
  more than one favorable, 247, 259
  in possibility diagram, **221**

Outliers, **180**–182, 189

Outputs, **242**–243
  representing on mapping diagrams, **243**–245

P

Parallel lines, 157, 160–162, 227
  angles formed by, 115

Parentheses, in linear equations, 120–121

Perimeter, 93, 118, 120–121, 122

Perfect cubes, cube roots of, 3

Perfect squares, square roots of, 3

Perpendicular bisectors, 50
  reflections and, 61–62

Pi, approximations of, 5

Pico, 77

Plane figures, compare transformations of, 100–102

Point of intersection, **218**, 219, 221

Points
  on coordinate plane, 4, 20–22, 49
  distance between, 23–27
  finding coordinates of
    after reflections, 68–69
    after rotations, 80–82
    after translations, 57–58
  finding distance between, 4, 20–22
  graphing, 4, 20–22
  invariant, **52**, 65
  reflection of, 62
  rotation of, 74–75
  symmetric, 49
  translation of, 53

Point-slope form, 191

Polygons
corresponding angles of, 131
reflection of, 63
translation of, 56

Positive association, 178

Positive exponents, 44

Positive real numbers,
square roots 47–48
cube roots, 48

Possibility diagrams, **221**, 223–226, 229–232

Power, **5**
of 10, 59, 69, 73–76
power of, **25**–31
of product, **32**–34, 37–38
product of, **13**–16, 21–22
of quotient, 35–38
quotient of, **17**–20, 21–22
zero, 40–42

Predictions, using line of best fit, 192–193

Prefix system, **77**

Prime factorization, **8**–10

Prime numbers, 231

Prisms
and Pythagorean Theorem, 34
volume of, 5, 37, 38

Probability, 216
addition rule of, 246–248
of compound events, 229–235
using tree diagrams, 233
of dependent events, **252**–262
of independent events, 236–251
multiplication rule of, 237–241, 253
of simple event, 217–218

Problem solving. *See also* Real-world problem solving
algebraic reasoning, 192
elimination method, 197–202, 207–208, 218
graphical method, 218–224, 226
for probability of independent events, 240, 244–245, 247
with scale drawings, 114
substitution method, 203–208, 218

Product, power of a, **32**–34, **37–38**

Product of powers property, **13**–16, 21–22

Properties
of exponential notation, 14–23
of exponents, 28–30
of negative exponents, 43–45
order of operations, 25, 28–29, 32
power of a product, **32**–34, 37–38

power of a quotient, 35–38
product of powers, **13**–16, 21–22
quotient of powers, **17**–22
substitution property of equality, 198
of zero exponents, 41–42

Proportions, 171
direct, 93, **129**, 130, 50
similar figures, 132–133

Pyramids
and Pythagorean Theorem, 31, 35
slant height of, 31
volume of, 5, 36, 37

Pythagorean Theorem, **2**, 6
converse of, 10–11
finding distance between two points, 20–22, 23–27
finding length of hypotenuse, 8–9
finding length of leg of right triangle, 9
finding side lengths, 32–33
proving, 7–8
real-world problem solving using, 12–14
and solids, 31–35
for volume of composite solids, 36–43

Pythagorean triples, 10

Quadrants, **49**

Qualitative data, **198**, 207

Quantitative data, **174**
identifying patterns of association of, 177–179

Quantities, directly proportional, 50

Quotient, power of a, 35–38

Quotient of powers property, **17**–22

Radius, 51, 52, 86, 5

Randomness, simulation of, 242–243

Rate of change, **267**–268, 270, 279

Rational numbers, **3**

Ratios
of corresponding sides, 131, 132–133
rational numbers as, 3

Real numbers, **3**

Real-world problem solving. *See also* Applications
algebraic equations for, 192
exponential notation for, 10–11, 23

functions for, 246–248
interpreting slopes and y-intercept, 138–139,
    171–174, 264, 270–272, 274; 191–194
with linear equations, 99–101, 171–181; 191–194
Pythagorean Theorem for, 12–14
squares and cubes for, 47–54
systems of linear equations for, 210–217

Reasoning, 214, 215, 216, 234

Recall Prior Knowledge, 3–4, 59, 93–95, 191–192,
241; 3–5, 49–50, 113–115, 173, 217–218

Rectangles
    image under a dilation, 00
    rotate in the coordinate plane, 77
    similar, 131, 132

Rectangular prisms, and Pythagorean Theorem, 34

Reflections, **61**–72, 99
    of an angle, 98–99
    and congruent figures, 144–145, 150
    draw images after, 63–64
    finding coordinates of points after, 68–69
    geometry software for, 63
    line of reflection, **62**, 69
    of lines, 64–66
    of line segments, 63–66
    of points, 49, 62
    of polygons, 63
    of shapes, 63, 66–68

Relations, **242**–243. *See also* Functions
    identifying as functions, 249–254
    inputs and outputs, 242–243
    many-to-many, **244**, 247
    many-to-one, **244**, 256
    one-to-many, **243**, 248, 256
    one-to-one, **243**, 256
    representing, using mapping diagrams, **243**–245,
        249–251

Relative frequencies, 173, 198, 204–206

Repeating decimals, 3, 95, 98

Representing
    compound events, 220–226
    expressions, using bar models, 99, 197, 200, 203
    functions in different forms
        algebraic forms, 259–264
        using equations, 281, 283
        graphical forms, 259–264
        using graphs, 272–274, 278
        using tables, 266–269, 279–280, 282
        verbal descriptions, 259–264
    proportional relationship between two variables,
        using an equation, 93, 109–111, 129, 178–179
        using a graph, 93, 129, 165–169, 175–177
        using a table of values, 112–115, 129

relations, using a mapping diagram, 243–245

Review
    Chapter Review/Test, 56–57, 88–89, 126–128,
        184–185, 238–239, 291–293; 45–47, 109–111,
        160–165, 211–215, 265–267
    Chapter Wrap Up, 55, 87, 125, 183, 236, 290; 44,
        107, 159, 210, 264
    Cumulative Review, 90–91, 186–189, 294–297;
        166–171, 268–273
    Key Concepts, 55, 87, 125, 183, 237, 290; 44,
        107–108, 159, 210, 264
    Recall Prior Knowledge, 3–4, 59, 93–95, 129, 191–
        192, 241; 3–5, 49–50, 113–115, 173, 217–218

Right triangles, **7**–8
    finding unknown side lengths, 7–12
    determining, 12
    hypotenuse, 8–9
    identifying, 12
    legs of, 9
    Pythagorean Theorem, 6
    relationship between sides, 7–8

Rise, **130**–131

Roots
    cube, 48–50, **3**
    square, 47–48, **3**

Rotations, **73**–85, 99
    of an angle, 99
    angle of rotation, **73**
    center of rotation, **73**
    clockwise, **73**, 81
    and congruent figures, 144–145, 150
    counterclockwise, **73**, 81
    draw images after, 77–79
    finding coordinates of points after, 80–82
    geometry software for, 77
    half turn as, **75**
    of line segments, 76–77
    of points, 74–75

Rules
    for congruent triangles, 122–125
    divisibility, 8
    Run, **130**–131

S

Sample space, 217

Scale drawings, 114

Scale factor, **86**, 90, 93, 94, 99, 113, 131

Scatter plots, **174**–185, 198
    drawing, 176–177
    identifying patterns of association on, 177–179,
        191–194
    line of best fit, 187–197
    with linear association, 179, 187–194
    outliers on, **180**–182, 189

Scientific notation, **58**, 60–67
    adding, 68–80
    on calculator, 82
    comparing numbers in, 63–65
    converting to standard form, 63
    with different powers of 10, 73–76
    dividing in, 81, 83–84
    multiplying in, 81–82
    representing numbers in, 63
    small numbers in, 71–72, 76
    subtracting, 68–80
    uses of, 60
    writing numbers in, 61–62

Sequence of transformations, 148–152, 153

Seven, divisibility by, 8

Shapes, reflection of, 66–68

Side-angle-side (SAS) test, 123, 125

Side-side-side (SSS) test, 123

Side lengths, finding unknown, 8–10, 31–33

Sides of a right triangle, 7–8

Signs, multiplying and dividing integers, 4

Similar figures, 112
    concept of, 131–132
    finding unknown lengths in, 132–136
    identifying, 129–130
    relating to geometric transformations, 146–147,
        150–151
    relating using sequence of transformations, 153
    scale factor, 131
    triangles, 135–139

Similarity, **129**, 131–132

Simple events, 216, **219**
    identifying, 219–220
    probability of, 217–218

Simplify
    algebraic expressions, 15–16, 19–22, 35
    exponential expressions, 27–30, 32,41
    negative exponents, 43–45
    numbers raised to the zero power, 41–42,
    numerical expressions, 14, 18, 21–22, 28–30, 33,
        36–38
    using order of operations, 28–29, 32

Simulations, of randomness, 242–243

Slant height, of pyramid, 31

Slide. *See* Translations

Slope, 128
    comparing, 138–139
    comparing unit rates using, 133–134
    finding, **130**–132, 135–137, 142–144, 154
    formula for, 142–144
    graphing using, 166–169, 192
    of horizontal line, 139–141
    of linear function, 264, 267, 270–272, 274
    negative, 135
    and parallel lines, 157, 160–162
    and point-slope form, 158–159
    positive, 135
    rate of change, **267**–268, 270
    real-world problem solving using, 138–139,
        171–174, 264, 270–272, 274; 191–194
    represented by *m*, 148
    rise, **130**–131
    run, **130**–131
    triangles, 131–132
    undefined, 140
    of vertical line, 140
    zero, 139–141

Slope-intercept form, **147**–153, 154–156
    and functions, 264
    and line of best fir, 191–194
    graphing using, 166–168

Solids
    composite, 36–43
    and Pythagorean Theorem, 31–35
    volume of, 5, 36–43

Speed problems, 102, 124, 134, 138, 179, 217; **172**,
    174

Sphere
    diameter of, 83
    radius of, 51, 86
    volume of, 52

Spheres, volume of, 5

Spreadsheet software, 242–243

Square, of number, 3

Square roots, **47**–48, 120; 3

Squares of variables,
    equations involving, 49
    real-world problems, 50–52

Standard form, **63**, 64–65

Statement of congruence, **118**, 119

Statistics
    line of best fit, 187–197
    sample space, 217
    scatter plots, **174**–185
    two-way tables, **198**–208

Straight lines, 270

Substitution method, **203**–208, 218

Substitution property of equality, 198

Subtraction
    equations, 198
    integers, 4
    multiplication is distributive over, 68
    in scientific notation, 68–80
        with different powers of 10, 71, 74–77
        with the same powers of 10, 68–70
    very large numbers, 74–75
    very small numbers 71–72, 76–77

Surface area, 81–82

Surveys, 199–200, 206

Symbols, Table of, 321; 301

Symmetric points, 49

Symmetry line of, and reflections, 62

Systems of linear equations
    common terms, **198**
    dependent, **230**–233
    inconsistent, **225**–230
    introduction to, **193**–196
    point of intersection, 219, 221
    real-world problem solving, 210–217
    solving
        choosing method for, 207–208
        with common terms, 197–199
        with table of values, 194–196
        using algebraic methods, 197–209
        using elimination method, 197–202, 207–208, 218
        using graphical method, 218–224, 226
        using graphing calculator, 195
        using substitution method, 203–208, 218
        without common terms, 200–202
    unique solution to, **193**

Table of Measures, Formulas, and Symbols, 317–321; 297–301

Table of values
    directly proportional quantities, 50
    on graphing calculator, 195
    graphing using, 165, 191, 220
    for linear equations with two variables, 111–112, 114–115, 121, 165
    representing function as, 259–264, 266
    solving systems of linear equations using, 194–196
    translating into graph, 263

Tables
    of bivariate data, 176–177
    identifying linear functions from, 267–269, 276
    to represent functions, 248, 261
    two-way, **198**–208
        constructing, 201–203
        interpreting, 201–203, 207–208
        reading data from, 198–200
        relative frequencies in, 204–206

Technology Activity, 111, 149, 195, 218; 55, 63, 77, 90, 98–99, 122, 150, 194–195, 242–243

Temperature
    applications, 146, 222, 224, 191, 197
    conversion, 119

Tera, 77

Terminating decimals, 3

Test triangle congruence, 122–125

Think Math, *Throughout text. Some examples are* 14, 41, 109, 168, 204, 284; 9, 90, 225, 257

Three, divisibility by, 8

Transformation, **52**

Transformations. *See* Geometric transformations

Translations, **51**–60, 99
    as a commutative movement, 51
    and congruent figures, 144–145, 150
    draw images after, 55–57
    finding coordinates of points after, 57–58
    geometry software for, 55
    horizontal, vertical, or combination, **51**
    image, **52**
    of lines, 54–55
    map, **52**
    of points, 53, 55
    of polygons, 56
    verify experimentally, 55

Transversal, 115

Tree diagrams
    finding probability of compound events using, 233
    representing compound events using, 223–226

Triangles
　angle measures of, 115, 130
　congruent, 118, 120, 122
　　minimum conditions for, 122
　　relating to geometric transformations, 145
　　tests for, 122–125
　hypotenuse, **7–9**
　isosceles, 24–25, 28
　legs of, **7–9**
　right, 6, **7–9**, 12
　and slope, 131–132
　similar, 130, 135–139

Turns. *See* Rotations

Two, divisibility by, 8

Two-way tables, **198**
　constructing, 201–203
　interpreting, 201–203, 207–208
　reading data from, 198–200
　relative frequencies in, 204–206

Unique solution, **193**

Unit rate, 130, 133–134

　use slopes to compare, 177

Variable expressions. *See* Algebraic expressions

Variables
　dependent, 172, 242
　independent, 172, 242
　squared and cubed, 49–51
　in two-way table, 198

Venn diagrams, 217, 218

Verbal descriptions
　comparing functions using, 279, 285
　translating into functions, 259–260, 265

Vertical line test, **251**–252, 254

Vertical lines, slope of, 140

Vertical translation, 51

Volume
　of composite solids, 36–43
　of cone, 39
　of cylinder, 38, 39
　of prism, 37, 38
　of pyramid, 86, 36, 37
　of rectangular prism, 86
　of solids, 5
　of sphere, 52

Weak association, 178

x-axis, 49
　equation of, 49
　as a line of reflection, 63
　reflection of shape in, 66–67

x-intercept, **148**

y-axis, 49
　equation of, 49
　as a line of reflection, 63
　reflection of shape in, 68

y-intercept, **147**, 154–158
　graphing using, 166–168, 192
　real-world problem solving using, 171–174,
　　264, 270–272; 191–194

Z

Zero
　exponent of, **40**–42
　slope of, 139–141